Joseph Francis Thrupp

The Song of Songs

Joseph Francis Thrupp

The Song of Songs

ISBN/EAN: 9783337181116

Printed in Europe, USA, Canada, Australia, Japan

Cover: Foto ©ninafisch / pixelio.de

More available books at **www.hansebooks.com**

THE SONG OF SONGS.

THE SONG OF SONGS

A REVISED TRANSLATION

WITH

INTRODUCTION AND COMMENTARY.

BY

JOSEPH FRANCIS THRUPP, M.A.

VICAR OF BARRINGTON, LATE FELLOW OF TRINITY COLLEGE, CAMBRIDGE,
AUTHOR OF "AN INTRODUCTION TO THE STUDY
AND USE OF THE PSALMS" &c.

MACMILLAN AND CO.
Cambridge and London.
1862.

Cambridge:
PRINTED BY C. J. CLAY, M.A.
AT THE UNIVERSITY PRESS.

PREFACE.

THE object of this volume is to unfold the meaning of one of the least appreciated portions of Holy Scripture. It is hoped that neither the necessary references to the original Hebrew, nor the discussion, which can be passed over at pleasure, of the principal counter-theories of interpretation, will render it less acceptable to the majority of readers. It seemed undesirable, in the interest of the truth, to leave room for suspicion that the traditional interpretation of the Song, howsoever it might have ministered to the edification of nearly fifty generations of Christians, would not be borne out by the results of the investigations of modern scholarship. I have therefore sought throughout to build on the surest attainable foundation. That I have written to the best of my own judgment, not defending received opinions simply because they were received, the opening section of the Introduction will shew. But as it is in reference to the manner in which the Song should be interpreted that the authority of the general consent of the Christian Church will carry most weight, so also am I firmly persuaded that the conclusions of sober criticism will here be found to accord with the traditions of Christian teaching; and that the more closely the Song be examined, the less compatible will its language and structure prove with any other theme than that of the mutual love of the Incarnate Son of God and his redeemed Church.

The use made by me of the labours of others, of whatever critical school, will sufficiently appear in the course of the work itself; which I now humbly commend to Almighty God in the hope that it may in some measure serve to the promotion of his glory.

BARRINGTON VICARAGE, ROYSTON,
November 1862.

CONTENTS.

INTRODUCTION.

SECT.		PAGE
1.	Title, Date, and Authorship	1
2.	History of the Interpretation	16
3.	Refutation of the theory which identifies the Bride with the Virgin Mary	36
4.	Refutation of the typical and hebdomadal-nuptial theories	38
5.	Refutation of the modern dramatic theory	41
6.	Evidence for the allegorical interpretation	49
7.	Is the Beloved God or the Messiah?	61
8.	Is the Bride the Church or the Jewish nation?	64
9.	How far is the Song historico-prophetical?	67
10.	How far may it be interpreted of the individual soul?	71
11.	Form and Divisions of the Song	73
12.	The Prophetical character and announcements of the Song, viewed in reference to the age at which it was written	76
13.	Use of the Song in the Christian Church	82

THE SONG OF SONGS.

	PAGE
The Anticipation, I. 2—II. 7 .	89
The Awaiting, II. 8—III. 5 .	121
The Espousal and its Results, III. 6—V. 1 .	139
The Absence, V. 2—8	191
The Presence, V. 9—VIII. 4 .	209
Love's Triumph, VIII. 5—12 .	261
The Conclusion, VIII. 13, 14 . .	282

THE SONG OF SONGS.

INTRODUCTION.

§ 1.

The Hebrew title of this Book is שיר השירים אשר לשלמה *Shir hash-shirim asher li-Shelomoh*, E. V. "The Song of Songs, which is Solomon's."

The authenticity of this title has been by many called in question on the ground that it contains the relative אשר in its full and usual form, instead of the provincialism, archaism, vulgarism, or abbreviation, ש, which is uniformly employed throughout the Song itself. But it can hardly be deemed unnatural that the idiom of the title should here not conform to that of the Song. And the argument to the prejudice of the title derived from this circumstance is more than counterbalanced by the argument for its authenticity furnished by the homœophony of the words אשר and שיר (*asher* and *shir*), homœophony of a kind of which we have throughout the Song many examples (see on I. 3).

The earlier part of the title denotes "the best or most excellent of songs."

The latter part has been almost universally understood as ascribing the authorship of the Song to Solomon; and it must be admitted, from a comparison of the superscriptions of the psalms, &c. that this is the obvious and *primâ facie* interpretation of its meaning.

The internal evidence of the Song itself does not, however, when fairly weighed, confirm us in the conclusion that Solomon should be viewed as the author.

We know, in the first place, that it has generally pleased God to set apart the fittest human instruments for the different branches of his earthly work. In most books of Scripture there is an evident native harmony between the prophet and the message which he was commissioned to deliver, between the writer and the theme which he was selected to illustrate. Does it then appear from all that can be gathered of the character of Solomon, that he was the man to whom the execution of the Song of Songs was likely to be divinely entrusted?

Some qualifications for the task may indeed be fairly conceded to him. Such were his taste for the beauties of nature, and his scientific acquaintance with those natural objects, animate and inanimate, whence many of the images of the Song are drawn. Such also were his taste for all kinds of artificial magnificence, and the familiarity with such magnificence which he was enabled to acquire by reason of the wealth at his command. On these points the upholders of the Solomonic authorship of the Song have with justice enlarged. Moreover the mention of his thousand and five songs attests his cultivated love of poetry, and especially of poetry allied to the Song of Songs by outward form.

But it is otherwise when we pass from the outward form and imagery of the Song to its innermost essence. That essence is love: love in all its perfectness and purity. Such love there is no evidence that Solomon had been fitted by any training to appreciate. He was voluptuous, perhaps sensual; but there is nought in his history to shew that he ever loved chastely, or tenderly, or self-denyingly, or consistently, or even deeply. His principal marriage, that with Pharaoh's daughter, makes some figure in Scripture; but only so far as it there illustrates his splendour. As to its morality, it was certainly contracted in public violation of the Law of Moses; and that it was otherwise more commendable we have no warrant for assuming, no indication being given that it either originated in love, or terminated in happiness. Of his other love-relations, or quasi-love-relations, we are only informed in general terms, that he "loved many strange women" of the surrounding nations; that, despite the Lord's commandment, he "clave unto them in love;" that he "had seven hundred wives, princesses, and three hundred concubines," and that they "turned away his heart;" and that he made provision for their various idolatries (1 Kings XI. 1—8). Doubtless we must not judge his multitude of wives from a Christian point of view. Polygamy prevailed more or less in ancient times, and there are not wanting in the Old Testament examples, such as Abraham, of polygamists who gave proof of genuine conjugal attachment. Yet polygamy was always a dark cloud on the love-relation, a deep hindrance to love's unalloyed purity. It terribly overshadowed the mutuality of the relations of the bridegroom and the bride, the " I am my beloved's and my beloved is mine," which the Song of Songs brings so emphatically before our gaze (II. 16; VI. 3, &c.). This being so, the allowance which we are bound to make for those who practised it cannot be fairly extended in all its fulness to those who first brought it into vogue; and for the like reason we can hardly acquit of personal hardness of heart the man who with unbridled excess increased his harem far beyond the limits generally observed by even Oriental princes.

If critics had only refrained from surrounding Solomon's Egyptian marriage with a halo of bright fancies for which there is no scriptural warrant, and from connecting, against all reason, with the person of the peaceful Solomon the prophetical Psalm XLV, in which the Messiah appears not only as a bridegroom but also as a warrior, they would have seen how little foundation really exists for the hypothesis of that monarch's ability to depict the pure delights of holy bridal love. It is certainly not easily to be imagined that he in whom culminated the ancient disregard of the true and original position of woman as man's help meet and partner, should have been specially selected by the Holy Spirit of God to delineate, in all its delicacy and sacredness, that purest communion of love between Christ and his

Church, of which natural love in its primeval innocency is the type. When moreover we find Solomon's experiences in connexion with earthly love pleaded as fitting him for the composition of the Song which we possess, one cannot help remarking how different his experiences from those of some of the foremost commentators on the Book, such, for instance, as Origen and Bernard!

But it will be asked, Why then should the Beloved of the Song be designated, as all allegorical interpreters admit to be the case, by Solomon's name? Can it be denied that King Solomon was the type whom the poet, in singing of the Beloved of the Church, had in view; that he haunted him as the shadow of that heavenly Bridegroom flitting beforehand across the stage of history? To a certain extent, no doubt, the person of the historical Solomon was present to the poet's gaze. There were points of view from which Solomon had been a true and important type of Christ; more especially in respect of the peacefulness, the glory, and the wide dominion of his rule. It is to his royal splendour, to the peace with which his reign opened, to his appreciation of all that was outwardly attractive, and to the association of his name with some of the chief beauties of the land of Israel, that the poet has had regard in constituting him the typical figure around which all his conceptions of the future Redeemer should cluster. But this did not prevent him from introducing into his picture of that Redeemer elements which never in any wise belonged to Solomon. Accordingly the name

Solomon is, after all, used but sparingly throughout the Song. It is in fact peculiar to the two passages, III. 6—11, VIII. 11, 12, in which special prominence is given to those features of the Redeemer's person and kingdom which had in Solomon been typified. Into the more direct love-passages of the Song Solomon's name enters not; for indeed not only a greater than Solomon, but a purer than Solomon, is there.

Let it not be deemed that aught that has been here advanced is intended to disparage the spiritual gifts which Solomon really possessed. It was for wisdom that he asked; and wisdom from on high doubtless God bestowed upon him in an eminent degree; wisdom such as that which shines in the inspired Proverbs, with their goodly stores of wholesome instruction. But in earlier equally as in later days men's gifts differed according to the grace that was given them; and there is no evidence in the Book of Proverbs that its author possessed all the qualifications demanded for the accomplishment of a very different work.

There are moreover other circumstances connected with the Song which militate against the current view of its authorship. It is certainly against it, so far as negative evidence may fairly carry weight, that notwithstanding sundry references to Jerusalem, together with one mention of the "daughters of Zion," there should be an entire absence of any allusion to Solomon's greatest and noblest architectural work, the Jewish temple. Reasons for this might possibly be found, and the argument should not be pressed too far; but on the hypothesis of Solomon's authorship, the omission is at least remarkable.

We need have less hesitation in relying on the argument furnished by the way in which the mention of Jerusalem is coupled with that of Tirzah, VI. 4. However beautiful its position, the only known importance which Tirzah possessed was that of being the residence, after the schism, of the earlier sovereigns of the kingdom of Israel. So long as it was a merely private city there would have been an obvious impropriety in putting it, even in imagery, on a level with Jerusalem. The Song cannot well be earlier in date than the period when Tirzah became a royal abode. We cannot however fix the latest date for the composition of the Song at the exact period when the kings of Israel removed their residence from Tirzah to Samaria. The associations of a capital city might hang for a time around it after its authoritative dignity had been transferred to a younger rival: it would not, for example, be derogatory to the array of modern capitals to place such a city as Moscow by their side. And we know from 2 Kings XV. 14 that what importance Tirzah possessed did not, after the removal of the capital to Samaria, altogether disappear.

There are certain special passages of the Song, to be more fully considered in the commentary, which tend to throw light on the date at which it was really written. Particularly important here is the passage I. 5, from which it may be gathered that Jerusalem was no longer the religious metropolis of the whole Israelitish nation. Some evidence, however subordinate, of a date posterior to Solomon may be supplied by what will be observed on IV. 4. To the same effect runs the evidence of II. 15: in the full tide of prosperity in Solomon's reign men troubled themselves but little with thinking of the foxes by whom the vineyard of Israel was ere long to be ravaged. Then again there is a melancholy tone about some parts of the Song, e. g. III. 1—5, which ill accords with the universal joyousness of the days of Solomon.

These various considerations all point to the same general inference. The Song was written after the division of the kingdoms; and most probably by a subject of the northern realm. It cannot be doubted by those who adhere to the church interpretation of the Song that the author was one, who, in spite of the political schism, preserved in its integrity his allegiance to the church of his forefathers, and of Solomon, and of David. But the circumstances of the times might well render unadvisable any allusion to the temple to which the Israelites no longer repaired; nor indeed do we find any allusion ever made to it by the prophets Elijah and Elisha. The former observes the time of the evening sacrifice (1 Kings XVIII. 36); but makes no mention of the place of it[1].

---

[1] It is a blot on Mendelssohn's great oratorio that the name Zion should appear in some of the passages of which the libretto is compacted; a blot the more to be regretted because of the great influence which that immortal work must, like the poetry of Milton, exert on men's views of the sacred themes of which it treats. The mission of Elijah was exclusively to the people of the ten tribes.

It is also probable from the typical use which is made of the figure of Solomon, and of the evident respect which his memory commands, that the Song was not written in the first generations after his death, while his oppressions were still resented with bitterness. Some remarks are made by Renan on this subject, which are intended by him to support a very different conclusion: "Les mécontentements passagers qui résultent des dépenses royales s'oublient vite; bientôt on ne voit plus que les monuments qui en restent, sans que l'on demande ce qu'ils ont coûté. Le souvenir des souffrances qui rendirent odieux au peuple le règne de Louis XIV. et firent insulter ses funérailles fut bientôt effacé par l'impression générale de grandeur que laissa son siècle et par les formules admiratives que les rhéteurs mirent à la mode en parlant de lui. Il en fut de même pour Salomon. Au moment de sa mort, on voit la haine contre son administration produire une révolution violente; plus tard, on ne trouve plus que légende et fascination." This comparison between the posthumous reputations of the two monarchs is no doubt interesting; but it must be remembered that the interval of time requisite for an entire change of public opinion would be considerably greater in ancient Israel than in modern France. Add to this that the evil memories of Solomon would be strengthened and perpetuated by the Israelites' successful renunciation of the authority of his descendants, and by the subsequent labours of their new rulers, from motives of policy, to keep up and widen the estrangement. We may well doubt whether under such circumstances the feeling against Solomon could have subsided in less than a century.

Another indication of the date of the Song is to be found in the relation in which it stands to Psalm XLV. It is obvious that the two have much in common; and it will be generally allowed that the shorter piece is the original, and that the Song is therefore younger than the Psalm. Now the psalm probably dates from the reign of Jehoshaphat (see my Introd. to the Psalms, I. pp. 261, 2); above which therefore the date of the Song must not be allowed to ascend.

We are now in a position to enquire from what quarter the Song of Songs probably proceeded. If it be not the work of Solomon, it is plainly anonymous: that is to say, we have no warrant for ascribing it to any prophet or other sacred writer known to us by name. Whence then its reception into the Canon of Scripture? In all likelihood, because it proceeded from a member of some recognized sacred body. Such a body we have, in the kingdom of Israel, in the "sons of the prophets" so often mentioned in connexion with the history of Elisha (see on I. 6). As the reception of the psalms "of Asaph" and of "of the sons of Korah" depended on their having been produced by members of the Levitical choirs, so may the original reception of the Song of Songs have been grounded on its being a production of a member of one of the prophetical schools.

Such schools existed at Bethel, at Jericho, and at Gilgal. The position of Jericho, in the valley of the

Jordan, is well known. Bethel lay on the hills, twelve miles to the W.N.W.: Gilgal, most probably, higher up in the hills, six miles N.N.W. of Bethel. The scenery described in the Song of Songs is, upon the whole, that with which the inhabitants of Jericho, Bethel, and Gilgal rather than those of Jerusalem would be familiar. It is true that Jerusalem itself is mentioned—it could hardly well be omitted: it is true also that in the description of the garden (IV. 12) there may be an allusion to the gardens of Solomon near Bethlehem. But of aught else in the south-west of the land of Israel,—of the scenery of the territory of Dan and of the greater part of that of Judah,—we find no trace. The word "sharon"—"meadow"—in II. 1 is not a proper name. On the other hand, how natural many of the pictures of the Song to one who, dwelling in the Jordan-valley, thence let the gaze of his imagination roam over those beauties of the land which at one time or another he had actually beheld! He looks southward over the Dead Sea, and amid the barrier-mountains of that sea rise before him the cliffs of Engedi (I. 14); or he looks eastward to the hills that hold up the plateau of Heshbon (VII. 4), and to the mountains of Bether (II. 17) and the slopes of Gilead (IV. 1, VI. 5); in the extreme north he summons before him the gorgeous heights of Lebanon and Amana, of Shenir and Hermon (IV. 8, 15) with the tower "which looketh toward Damascus" (VII. 4); while in the more central portions of the land Tirzah (VI. 4), and probably Baalhamon (VIII. 11), are not so far distant but that he easily pictures them within his range; and these in their turn connect themselves with the luxuriant ridge of Carmel (VII. 5), on which moreover the notice of Elisha's journey thither (2 Kings II. 25) makes it probable that there existed a fourth prophetical school, which the author of the Song may have officially visited, and to which, "for his brethren and companions' sakes," his thoughts may have often turned.

But we pass to the language of the Song, and to the expressions and turns of thought which it embodies. Here first we have to notice the uniform use of the relative שׁ for אשׁר, as marking the idiom of a provincial author. Doubtless the use of it is studied: the author might have abandoned the provincialism had he so preferred. But it is difficult to understand on what grounds it should ever have been deliberately adopted by Solomon; for though it appear as an archaism in Gen. VI. 3, and as an archaism or provincialism in the Song of Deborah, Jud. V. 7, also in Jud. VI. 17, VII. 12, VIII. 26, and though it be once admitted into the Book of Job (XIX. 29), and frequently into the Lamentations, and the later psalms, and Ecclesiastes, yet it was unquestionably eschewed by the polished form of the language in its best period.

We are next arrested by the remarkable phrase "the chariots," i.e. "the strength," "of my people" (VI. 12); which finds its parallel in the words used, first of Elijah, and afterwards of Elisha (2 Kings II. 12; XIII. 14). It is probable that the phrase belonged to the particular period at which the Song was written:

certainly both in earlier and later times we fail to trace it. It must be remembered that the age of Elijah and Elisha was the age of the Syrian wars, and that chariots formed the main strength of the Syrian armies.

Those who defend the view that Solomon was the author of the Song of Songs have naturally sought to draw out its points of contact with the Book of Proverbs. "Common to both," says Hengstenberg, "is the predilection for imagery and enigma, and peculiarly so that for detailed personifications and allegorical descriptions, such as those which we have in the Proverbs where the personifications of Wisdom and Folly come before us. Besides this we have a whole series of separate, and in some instances highly characteristic, resemblances. Compare especially Prov. I. 9 with Cant. IV. 9; Prov. I. 28 with Cant. V. 6; Prov. V. 15—18 with Cant. IV. 12; Prov. V. 18, 19 with Cant. IV. 5; Prov. VI. 30, 31 with Cant. VIII. 7; Prov. IX. 5 with Cant. VII. 2; Prov. XVI. 24 with Cant. IV. 11; Prov. XX. 13 with Cant. V. 2; Prov. XXIII. 31 with Cant. VII. 9; Prov. XXV. 11 with Cant. I. 11; Prov. XXV. 12 with Cant. VII. 1." Are then these resemblances of such a kind as to shew that the Proverbs and the Song proceeded from the same person? Do they not rather agree yet better with the supposition that the author of the Song of Songs had the Proverbs before him; that they formed the latest book of Scripture in existence in his day; that he thus took up, as it were, the sacred thread which Solomon had last dropped; and that he was consequently led to adopt, to a certain extent, the language, imagery, and style which Solomon had bequeathed to him?

For in fact we must not here pursue a onesided course: if we trace the resemblances between the Proverbs and the Song of Songs, we are no less bound to trace those between the Song of Songs and the prophecy of Hosea. We shall then find that the dependence of the Song on the Proverbs is paralleled by the dependence of Hosea on the Song. It is emphatically the imagery of the Song that prepared the way for the symbolical acts of Hosea's ministry, Hos. I. III. The details of the imagery are indeed different: in the Song the spiritual marriage is still in prospect; in Hosea, it is viewed as long accomplished, and since disgracefully broken: in the Song the bridegroom is the Messiah, in Hosea the LORD God of Israel himself. Still the main idea of the marriage is common to both, and in both is carried out with a determinate fulness of which there is no other previous example. Then besides this we have particular connexions between the Song and Hosea in respect of details of imagery or of language. Among these are some in which the images belonging in the Song to the prospective union with the Messiah are adapted by Hosea to the past union with God himself: some in which the gifts, which the Song represents the Bride as receiving from the Bridegroom, are turned in Hosea into the allurements of strange lovers after which Israel is represented as wandering. Compare with Cant. I. 4, Hos. XI. 4; with Cant. I. 10, 11, Hos. II, 8; with Cant. I. 16, 17, Hos. XIV. 8; with Cant. II. 1, Hos. XIV. 5; with Cant.

II. 3, Hos. XIV. 7, 8; with Cant. II. 5, Hos. VII. 5; with Cant. II. 13, Hos. II. 12; with Cant. II. 14, Hos. VII. 11; with Cant. III. 2, Hos. II. 7; with Cant. III. 6, Hos. II. 3; with Cant. IV. 11, Hos. XIV. 6; with Cant. IV. 15, 16, Hos. XIII. 15; with Cant. V. 6, Hos. II. 7; with Cant. V. 15, Hos. XIV. 5, with Cant. VI. 11, Hos. XIV. 7; with Cant. VIII. 5, Hos. II. 3, 14, XIII. 5. Probably also in Hos. XII. 10, "I have ... used similitudes by the ministry of the prophets," the Song of Songs is specially intended.

The conclusion which thus from internal evidence commends itself to us respecting the authorship of the Song of Songs, is that it was probably composed, about a century or more after the death of Solomon, by a member of one of the prophetical schools in the kingdom of the ten tribes; and that it was anterior to the earliest of what we ordinarily designate the prophetical writings.

If this be so, we must hold the "Solomon" of the title to be identical with the "Solomon" of the Song itself, i.e. with the Messiah; and must regard the ל of the title as parallel, not with the ל of authorship in the superscriptions of the psalms, from which indeed, in point of form, the title of the Song differs, but with the ל in the למלך of Psalm XLV. 1 (2), as pointing to the person whose glories are celebrated. The meaning of the title will thus be, "The most excellent of songs, pertaining to him who shall be to us a Solomon indeed." Even Hengstenberg, who contends, on the strength of the title, for the Solomonic authorship, writes in another place (Abhandlung I.) that "in the very title Solomon [i.e. the heavenly Solomon] is set before us as the centre of the whole poem." Now it cannot be proved that the title was meant to indicate both the author and the subject of the Song: if then the latter reference be admitted, the assumption of the former becomes unnecessary. Possibly moreover the LXX. have intended to mark Solomon as the subject rather than as the author of the Song, by rendering the title (according to the Vatican text) Ἄσμα ἀσμάτων, ὅ ἐστι Σαλωμών. Yet one would not lay too much stress on a Greek title of which the reading is somewhat doubtful.

§ 2.

A GENERAL sketch of the history of the interpretation of any book of Scripture can never be without its value. Our aim will here be rather to trace the rise and progress of the different schools of interpretation of the Song of Songs, than to present any full and complete list of the commentators upon it. For notices of their separate works, the reader who desires it will be able to consult the historical analyses of the literature of the Song contained in the recent volumes of Ginsburg (1857) and A. M. Stuart (2nd edit. 1860); of which however the former must be used with some caution, in consequence of the colouring which the author's opposition to the allegorical interpretation has imparted to it.

We shall not enter here, for obvious reasons, upon the manner in which the Song of Songs was understood by our Lord and his apostles. The references made to it in the New Testament will come better under consideration hereafter.

The earliest and oldest commentary therefore, alike of Jew and Christian, with which we have here to deal, is that of Origen, the father of Christian exegetical literature. Only portions of it have come down to us; but these sufficiently attest the way in which the book was by him interpreted. He views it as a nuptial song of a dramatic form, and as purely and exclusively allegorical. The Bridegroom is the Word of God: the Bride is either the soul of man, created after his image, or the Church. In practice it is rather to the mutual loves of Christ and the Church, than to those of Christ and the soul, that the expositions of Origen relate. Of the same spiritual kind was the general interpretation of the Christian Fathers; of Athanasius, of Eusebius, of Basil, of Gregory of Nazianzus, of Gregory of Nyssa, of even (as we learn from his scholar Theodoret) the literal interpreter Diodore of Tarsus, of Theodoret himself, of Chrysostom, of Cyril of Alexandria, of Cyprian, of Ambrose, of Augustine, of Jerome. Especially interesting to us here, less from its own intrinsic value than as shewing the style of the prevalent interpretation, is the extant commentary of Philo, bishop of Carpasia in Cyprus (cir. A.D. 400). It is evidently a breviary, or short expository compendium, mainly derived by the author from the writings of others: occasionally, as on

iii. 6—8, containing a double exposition of the same passage. It is entirely and thoroughly Christian, exhibiting, like the commentary of Origen, nothing that is likely to have come from any Jewish source: in it Christ is the Bridegroom, the Church the Bride. Of the two alternative interpretations of Origen, this was in fact the one generally adopted: the other, which identified the Bride with the human soul, is peculiar, as an exclusive interpretation, to the homilies of Gregory of Nyssa. Respecting the person of the Bridegroom all are agreed. The same Gregory fully defines him as that Solomon "who was born of the seed of David according to the flesh, whose name is Peace, who is the true king of Israel, the builder of the temple of God, who comprehends the knowledge of all things, whose is infinite wisdom, yea who is himself essential wisdom and truth, to whom belongs every name of God, and every intelligible conception that we can form of him." Of all the patristic comments however on the Song those of Theodoret are the most valuable. They are executed with judgment, and with a careful but discriminating regard to the labours of earlier writers; are sufficiently full without being prolix; and have come down to us complete. In them, it is almost needless to say, Christ is the Bridegroom: the Bride is the Church, more especially as the company of those who have been perfected in all virtues; those who have not yet reached the full degree of perfection being represented, according to Theodoret, as the Bride's companions.

It is mainly from Theodoret that we learn of the

early existence of views opposed to the general interpretation placed by the Church upon the Song. He tells us that there were those who calumniated it, and denied its spiritual character, venturing to assert that Solomon had composed it in reference to himself and Pharaoh's daughter; that there were others of the same class who framed a similar theory, substituting only for Pharaoh's daughter Abishag the Shunamitess; while others again spoke of it with somewhat more respect as a royal discourse, the people being the bride, the king the bridegroom. The first of these views was that of Theodore of Mopsuestia, as we see by the extracts from his writings exhibited at the Second Council of Constantinople. Utterly denying to the Song all prophetical character, he formed the theory that it was written by Solomon as a sort of vindication, after the event, of his Egyptian marriage, with the design of allaying the disapproval which that proceeding had excited, and of commending himself, in spite of the reclamations of his countrymen, to his wife's affections. This theory may have been thrown out in haste; and as it is not known to have gained any supporters, so we may not unreasonably suppose that Theodore himself would have attached but little importance to it. The interpretation however of the Song which was generally received in the Church, he, no doubt, determinately rejected. The strong terms in which his remarks on the book were reprobated at the Second Council of Constantinople shew how little acceptable they were to the Church at large.

As we pass from the patristic writings to those of

later Latin authors, we find the expositions of the Song still following in the track already marked out, though on the whole less interesting and less valuable than those of the Fathers. Such is the commentary of Justus Orgelitanus, contemporary with Justinian. Such again, and indeed well worthy of note, is the commentary of Cassiodorus, or at least that which passes under his name; and of which it may be observed that its value will not be diminished, though its style and its references to Gregory the Great should determine it to a later date. The exposition attributed, whether rightly or wrongly, to Gregory himself is not so good. But we may speak well again of the commentary of Aponius, of unknown date[1]. Aponius had a knowledge of Hebrew; and a sentence near the opening of his commentary has apparently induced Ginsburg to hazard the assertion that he follows the Chaldee in viewing the Song as of a historico-prophetical character. An inspection of the commentary will shew that it contains no trace of the influence of the Chaldee, and that it is not more historico-prophetical than the commentaries of the earlier Christians. Aponius finds, in VIII. 1, 13, an indication of the ultimate conversion of the Jews after much suffering; but the germ of a corresponding interpretation of other passages may be traced also in Cassiodorus. How entirely Christian, and un-Jewish, even to excess, is the commentary of Aponius, may be seen by

---

[1] The reference to Aponius and Julian in Bede, Lib. v., reads to me so like a later insertion, that I would not rely upon it as evidence of the time at which the former lived.

the fact that he views the Lord Jesus, the Word of the Father, as the husband in even Ezek. XVI. and Hos. II. Another commentary of the same general period is that of Bede. It consists of five Books (II—VI.), in which he "has followed the footsteps of the Fathers, leaving the works of Gregory intact:" another book (VII.) comprises a series of extracts from all parts of Gregory's writings, bearing upon the Song. To this work Bede prefixed also a controversial preface (Lib. I.) of his own, warning his readers against the commentary of Julian of Eclanum, which that writer had made a vehicle for his Pelagian doctrines. It is observable that in this preface Bede bases no argument of his own on any passage of the Song; and that even in his commentary his remarks upon divine grace are most unobtrusive, such as no practical expositor, in unfolding such a passage as I. 4, could well with justice omit. It could hardly have been foreseen that his work would be perverted by Ginsburg into a foundation for the sneer, that the Song has been made to "contain a treatise upon the doctrine of free grace against Pelagianism[1]."

The primitive churchly interpretation of the Song was further illustrated in the middle ages by the much-prized sermons of Bernard upon the first two chapters; continued, for the next two chapters, by his disciple Gillebert of Hoyland. The real value however of these

[1] Ginsburg, p. 102. With a more illustrious author Ginsburg deals in a manner worthy of more serious blame. He exhibits, as a specimen of Augustine's treatment of the Song, a Donatist interpretation of I. 7, which that Father repeatedly brings forward for the purpose of refuting it.

sermons consists rather in the treasures of thought which they contain, and in the beauty of their language, than in the help which they afford to a student of the Song.

It was during the life-time of Bernard that the first great Christian perversion of the meaning of the Song was made by those who took the Bride as representing the Virgin Mary. It is easy to see that this wresting of Scripture sprang out of the prevalent false doctrine and false practice. The first germs of the improper introduction of Mary into the Song may be traced in the metrical paraphrase of the Greek physician Michael Constantine Psellus († cir. 1105), who views the passage VI. 8, 9, as setting forth her blessedness above that of all other saints. A similar view is taken of that passage in Western literature by the Abbot Lucas, the epitomizer of Aponius. But it is by the Western commentator Rupert of Deutz († 1135) that we first find the Song expounded generally as relating to her. He is followed in part by Richard of St Victor († 1173), and, at a later period, by the Spanish prelate James Perez of Valentia (1507). It became, in fact, the practice in the Romish Church to attribute to the Song a three-fold allegorical sense, the Bride representing alike the Church, the soul, and the Virgin Mary; and on this principle it was expounded in the ponderous tomes of Michael Ghislerius (1613) and Cornelius a Lapide († 1637), each successive verse being compelled by these prolix commentators to submit to the three separate meanings which they imposed upon it.

But meanwhile, in the 14th century, another very different influence was for the first time to make itself felt in the Christian treatment of the Song. Side by side with the interpretation of the Song hitherto received in the Christian Church, there had grown up a conflicting interpretation among the Jewish rejecters of Christianity[1]. The rudiments of it are found in the Talmud. It was fully developed in the Targum, or Chaldee paraphrase, a post-talmudic production, which has been referred to the sixth century, and which must, from its freedom and copiousness, be regarded less in the light of a paraphrase than of an exposition, based, to a large extent, upon the principles of cabbalistic exegesis. The same interpretation may be traced also in the commentary of Saadia († 942), in the Jewish liturgical hymns, and in the commentaries of the great Western Rabbies, Jarchi († 1105), Rashbam († cir. 1155), and Aben Ezra († 1167); in or after whose time a new Jewish philosophical interpretation, with which we are not now concerned, arose to dispute the field with it. The fundamental principles of the older Jewish interpretation were that the Beloved of the Song was the Lord God, and the Bride the congregation of Israel; and that the Song itself was a consecutive allegory of the history of Israel from the earliest times, through all the vicissitudes narrated in the Old Testament, onward to the period when their expectations should be consummated and their sufferings ended. In the details of the parallel between

---

[1] For details, see Ginsburg, pp. 24—46.

the allegory and the history, the Jewish writers differed much from one another; though perhaps not more than might be fairly expected.

This interpretation the converted Jew Nicolaus de Lyra († 1341), uniting in himself the stores of Jewish and Christian learning, was now to introduce, in part, into the Christian Church. With respect to the Bride of the Song, he well pointed out that both Christians and Jews could afford to borrow somewhat of the others' views: the former, in identifying her with the Christian Church, had too much overlooked the career of God's earlier people: the latter, in identifying her with the congregation of Israel, had ignored the Church's real catholicity. He held therefore that the Bride represented the Church in her state under both dispensations; that as there had been but one faith of both the earlier and later believers, although differing in aspect according to the degree in which it had been unfolded, so also there had been but one Church, although differing in aspect according to the degree of the nearness of its conjunction to God; that conjunction being closer since the time of the New Testament. The Bridegroom, he maintained with the Jews, was God himself. Chaps. I—VI. depicted the history of Israel from the days of the Exodus to those of Nehemiah: Chaps. VII, VIII, the history of the Christian Church from its origin to the days of Constantine.

It is evident that De Lyra introduced into the interpretation of the Song a systematic arrangement which, with earlier Christian expositors, it had lacked.

It is no less evident that so far as the particular arrangement adopted was wrong, so far it would only serve to lead the interpreter astray; and De Lyra's own exposition was undoubtedly a failure. The detailed parallelism which he traces between the allegory and the history, and the excessive chronological character which he thus imparts to the Song, are not less forced and less prosaic in his commentary than in the Targum. The true key to the arrangement of the Song had yet to be found.

Although succeeding expositors adhered with as little exactness to the scheme of De Lyra as Jewish expositors had adhered to that of the Targum, the style of interpretation which he had introduced into the Church became widely prevalent. It would be an endless task to unfold the details of the various discrepant schemes to which it gave rise; but we must not omit mention of the remarkable manner in which it was elaborated by those who instead of dividing the Song into Old Testament and New Testament portions, viewed it as setting forth, throughout, primarily the different phases of Old Testament history, and then also, under the figure of these, and simultaneously with them, the mysteries of redemption. Such a treatment of the Song we have in the work of Perez (1507), already mentioned. It resembles one of those double sets of tableaux with which we meet in stained church-windows, where under each subject from the history of the Old Testament is set a corresponding subject from that of the New. He divides the Song into ten separate canticles, commencing respectively I. 2; I. 12; II. 8; III. 6; IV. 1; IV. 16; V. 8; VI. 1; VII. 13, "Return, return, &c.;" VIII. 5. These severally delineate the promises to the Patriarchs; the construction of the tabernacle; the speaking of God from the tabernacle; the carrying of the ark through the wilderness, with attendant miracles; Moses' ascent of Pisgah; the death of Moses; the entrance into Canaan; the conquest and partition of Canaan; the conflicts and victories under the Judges; and the prosperity and peace under Solomon. The corresponding events typified by them are the general expectations of the Old Testament saints; the incarnation of Christ; his teaching; his earthly career and miracles; his going up to Jerusalem; his death; the gathering into the Church of the first Jewish converts; the mission of the Apostles to the Gentiles; the conflicts and victories of the martyr-church; and the prosperity and peace under Constantine.

Was it perhaps such expositions as those of Percz,—rendered all the less welcome, be it remembered, by the place that the Virgin held in them,—from which Luther so strongly recoiled, characterizing them as "intempestivæ et prodigiosæ interpretationes"? His own view, in which he was followed by the Suabian reformer Brentius, has certainly the merit of being more simple: whether in other respects it will compare favourably with them may reasonably be doubted. Reverting to the Jewish doctrine that the Bridegroom and Bride represented God and the people of Israel, he treated the Song as a thanksgiving of Solomon for the divine establishment of his own kingdom. He seems thus in effect to have revived the principle of one of the anonymous interpretations mentioned and condemned by Theodoret. He regarded however the latter half of the Song as prophetical of the subsequent trials of the people and of the kingdom of Christ.

The historicizing interpretations held their ground for some time in the Romish Church. In proof of this we may refer to the Partitiones Theologicæ of Eder, rector of the University of Vienna (1582): he divided the Song into ten dramas, on the same principle, apparently, as Perez. The learned Jesuit Cornelius a Lapide divided it better into five parts, commencing at I. 2; II. 8; III. 6; V. 2; VI. 4: the themes of these parts were respectively the infancy of the Christian Church, its conflicts with the heathen power, its establishment under Constantine, its sufferings from heresy, and its renovation under the later Fathers.

The corresponding interpretations which shot forth in the Reformed Church were, it must be confessed, considerably more extravagant. After that acquaintance with the Targum had become general, they were easily multiplied; and other causes, such as a desire to assimilate the interpretation of the Song to that of the Apocalypse, probably nursed the passion for them. They naturally differed much from each other. By the English interpreters, Brightman († 1607) and Cotton (1650), the Song was referred partly to the history of the Legal, partly to that of the Evangelical Church; and so far it was well; nor amid the many crudities which Brightman's commentary contains are there wanting explanations well worthy of attention. Thus he well recognizes in III. 4 the period of Christ's advent: IV. 6 he justly interprets of his death, and IV. 7 he so far understands as to refer it to the beauty which the Church then received. But the extraordinary minuteness of the details of outward Church-history which he finds foreshewn in the Song deprive his interpretation as a whole of all probability. The foreign expositors, Cocceius (†1669) and Heunisch (1688), viewed the Song as referring exclusively to the history of the Church under the gospel dispensation, and thus erred more hopelessly than Brightman. Without entering into details, we may repeat generally that while this whole school of commentators were so far theoretically in advance of the Fathers that they recognized the principle of orderly arrangement to which the Song must conform, they yet distorted the meaning of isolated passages, which the Fathers had successfully explained, in order to make the interpretation of them square with the particular historical scheme which they adopted. Nor could it be other than a deep loss to the interpretation of the Song when the passage III. 6—11 was, from whatever cause, no longer viewed as setting forth the Saviour's death.

This failure to penetrate into the deep Christian meaning of passages which had once been understood was, it must be owned, common to most interpreters of the age following the Reformation. Still among the more soberminded there were preserved the general outlines of an interpretation which contrasted favourably with the ultra-historical. In proof of this we may point to the headings of the chapters in our English Bible, which have the merit of being sound, though they do not descend much into particulars. Nor must we omit mention of the valuable annotations of the Brownist divine, Ainsworth († 1622), which have been translated into Dutch and German, and which embody a large amount of admirable scriptural illustration. Honourable mention may also be made of the explanations of Bp. Hall († 1656), especially as exemplifying the way in which the Song was probably in practice viewed by the greater number of those who gave their attention to it.

We must now recount the history of a theory which though at length it serves but "to point a moral and adorn a tale," was in its day sanctioned by the authority of high names, and long fascinated the various writers upon the Song. It will be remembered that in the fifth century Theodore of Mopsuestia had ventured on asserting that the Bride of the Song of Songs was none other than the Egyptian princess whom Solomon espoused. Whether or no any relics of the interpretation had been traditionally preserved in the East, we find the Jacobite primate Abul-Faraj († 1286) allowing, in his Arabic history, the Song to be, outwardly, a dialogue between Solomon and Pharaoh's daughter. Otherwise the name of Pharaoh's daughter has not been traced in connexion with the Song till the occurrence of a reference to her, though even then "merely in passing," in some of the first printed English Bibles in the sixteenth century[1]. It was ordered however that the exegetical literature of the succeeding century should open out for her a new career of fame. For this the celebrated Grotius was chiefly responsible. In his commentary on the Bible, mainly written during his Swedish embassy at the court of France (1635-45), he maintained, with much coarseness, that the Song of Songs depicted the intercourse of Solomon with his Egyptian bride; though he did not withal deny therein an undercurrent of allegorical meaning. Later in the century (1690) Bossuet, a learned and accomplished scholar, but one whose writings bear unmistakeable marks of the age in which he lived[2], not only treated the Song as an epithalamium in which Solomon and Pharaoh's daughter appeared as types of Christ and the Church, but also introduced the view that it depicted a nuptial festivity extending, according to Hebrew custom, over seven days, those days being marked by the natural divisions of the

---

[1] See A. M. Stuart. The assertion of Davidson and after him, Ginsburg, that she makes her appearance in Origen, is most improbable; and after a careful search I feel assured that it is incorrect. I may add that Perez unjustly charges the ancient Jews with asserting that the Song was written in praise of her.

[2] Compare the following, from his Præfatio in Cant. Cant., with the landscapes of Claude and G. Poussin: "Cæterum hæc Salomonis cantio tota scatet deliciis; ubique flores, fructus, pulcherrimarumque plantarum copia, veris amœnitas, agrorum ubertas, horti vernantes, irrigui; aquæ, putei, fontes; odoramenta, sive arte confecta, sive quæ sponte sua humus parturit; ad hæc columbæ, turturum voces, mella, lac, vina liquentia; postremo in utroque sexu formæ honestas ac venustas, casta oscula, amplexus, amores tam pudici quam blandi; si quid horrescit, ut rupes, ferique montes, ac leonum cubilia, totum ad voluptatem, ac velut pulcherrimæ tabulæ ornatum varietatemque compositum."

poem. Forthwith these views become classical. They were adopted in France, in whole or in part, by Calmet (1726), and in France, perhaps, their influence was longest felt. In England they were highly commended by the elegant scholar Bp. Lowth (1753); and they may be traced through the subsequent works of Bp. Percy, the editor of the *Reliques of English Poetry* (1764), of Durell (1772), of Hodgson (1786), and of Williams (1801). The general tendency of the school was on the whole to slight the allegorical interpretation, and to lay stress on the natural beauties of the imagery. In fact the former could not but suffer from the contact of the more literal interpretation that was associated with it. Still it was not generally denied; nay, was to some extent even vindicated; and it should also be acknowledged that Bossuet's notes were far better than his theory.

An interpretation of the Song on truer principles was meanwhile preserved in France by Hamon, the physician of Port Royal, and continuator of the expositions of Bernard († 1687); and in England, though, no doubt, with different degrees of judgment, by Patrick (1700), Henry (1710), Durham (1723), and Wesley (1765). The reference to Solomon and Pharaoh's daughter was by the last-named commentator expressly disallowed: the book spoke of the spiritual love and marriage between Christ and his Church. With these expositors we may associate in Germany J. H. Michaelis (1720) and Roos (1773).

In Germany indeed the theory of Bossuet seems

never to have taken root. It was made known only to be condemned by J. D. Michaelis in his animadversions upon Lowth (1758). On its ruins walked a line of literalist critics, commencing with Herder (1778), who viewed the Song as a series of separate idyls. So Kleuker, Hufnagel, Paulus, Gaab, Döderlein, Augusti, Eichhorn, De Wette. The same was in England the view of Sir W. Jones, and of Dr Mason Good (1801). The work of the latter, considerable as is the learning which it displays, and the esteem in which it has been held, cannot on the whole be commended; and it affords a warning of the little good likely to be accomplished by one who, while allowing the allegorical interpretation, sets it aside, and thus becomes as though he allowed it not. Of those critics who have been less fettered by reverential restraint some have treated the Song as a mere collection of erotic songs or fragments.

We are at last brought to that theory of the Song on which the labours of so many German scholars, mainly of the neologian school, of the present century have been expended; which Ginsburg has sought to naturalize in England, holding the moral lesson thus taught in the Song to be worthy of divine inspiration, and which Renan, denying to the book all sacred character, has, in like manner, transplanted into France. Indeed from the measure of approbation that seems to have been bestowed upon the theory, or at least upon the labours of its advocates, Renan says, not without reason, that it has become in some sort classical in Germany, England, and Holland. From Ginsburg we further learn that it may be also regarded as the view of the Song now generally entertained by the Jews; and, doubtless, he would be entitled to speak on this subject with no light authority, were it not for the contempt with which he decries the defenders of the allegorical interpretation. The theory in question was originally propounded, though in an imperfect form, by Jacobi in 1771: after passing through the hands of Ammon (1790) and Umbreit (1820), it seems to have been matured by Ewald in 1826: since then it has been successively wrought upon by Hirzel (1840), Heiligstedt (1848), Böttcher (1849), Meier (1854), Friedrich (1855), Hitzig (1855), and Vaihinger (1858). By Hitzig it has indeed been considerably elaborated; but it is not likely to be presented in a much more attractive form than by Ginsburg, in English (1857); and to his volume we may accordingly, for the most part, refer, when we come to discuss it. The Song, according to this theory, is viewed as a dramatic poem, in which a country maiden is carried off by Solomon to his harem at Jerusalem; there he endeavours, by commendations and by promises, to attach her to himself; but she, in the strength of faithful love to the shepherd who is the real object of her affections, resists all the king's temptations, and finally, set free, returns with her beloved to her own rural abode.

The advocates of this theory contend, of course, for a purely literal interpretation; but, meanwhile, how strongly the allegorical character of the Song has been felt by even those who have rejected the general interpretation of the Church, is shewn by the views which some isolated scholars of the present century have put forth. According to Hug (1813), the Bride of the Song represents the ten tribes in the days of Hezekiah; according to Kaiser (1825), the new Jewish colony in the days of Zerubbabel; and according to Hahn (1852), Japhetic heathenism.

With less novelty, but with more judgment, Hengstenberg (1853), in a masterly manner, vindicates the meaning of the Song to Christ and the people of God, though he wrongly restricts it too much to the nation of Israel; the American Burrowes (1853), like Gregory of Nyssa, beholds in it the converse of Christ and the soul; and the Scottish expositor A. M. Stuart (2nd edit. 1860), without undervaluing or disregarding its reference to the affections of the individual believer, understands it also, as it was understood by the earliest Christian expositor, of the mutual love of Christ and the Church.

We can hardly fail, in thus pursuing the history of the treatment of the Song, to be struck with the manner in which the original Christian interpretation has, under all opposing influences, continued to assert its own inherent vitality. The contrast between it and all rival interpretations is in this respect very great. Take for example the interpretation of Bossuet,—always remembering that its author would himself have probably not regarded it as conflicting with the primitive interpretation,—how generally has it now died out, in regard of all its distinctive features! Yet it was on this that in the days of Lowth and Percy all the approbation of scholarship was for the time bestowed. Can the advocates of the interpretation which is exhibited in Ginsburg's volume give any good reason for supposing that theirs will be more lasting? It is as yet but in its 93rd year,—not a great age for the fundamental interpretation of a book of Scripture; and already the signs of decrepitude have appeared in the complicated contrivances by which Hitzig has found it necessary to minister to its infirmities.

In the present strife of tongues indeed, as the various influences at work, whether for good or for evil, more and more accumulate, and as it becomes more and more easy for students to acquaint themselves with the various successive views of former ages, it is probable that some of those will, from time to time, turn up afresh. Thus in a late and not unpleasing volume, Weiss, a Scottish converted Jew, has substantially repeated De Lyra by importing into the Church a new adaptation of the Chaldee paraphrase, finding room, like De Lyra, for a portion of the New Testament history towards the end of the Song (1859). The German theologian Hofmann, on the other hand (Appendix to Delitzsch, 1851), advances a view which, though in great measure peculiar, has yet its points of contact with that of Luther. Delitzsch (1851) offers a sort of compromise between the conflicting views of others: he views the Song as based upon a passage in Solomon's history, and rejects all direct allegorical interpretation of it, but at the same time views it as setting forth the idea of marriage, and in this the type of the spiritual relation of Christ to his Church.

It would not seem however, from Hitzig's preface, that this is likely to conciliate the adherents of the dominant literalist school which has been struggling to possess itself of the entire field. Nor indeed, if the first love of the Christian expositors of the Song be true, is there reason why we should in any degree recede from the position which they took. Truth is better than even conscientious compromise; and it is also more convincing. Even though she must defend by controversy the spiritual treasures of her Song of Love, the Church need not be ashamed of that richness of its contents which has nourished the love of so many of the holiest of her children. Let her yet speak out, and that with no uncertain sound. The companions who once may have mocked will then yet listen for her voice; and it is the will of her Beloved that she should utter it forth, that so both he and they may hear it.

§ 3.

In proceeding to discuss the various views that have been entertained with regard to the purport of the Song of Songs, we shall begin with those by which its meaning is most seriously wrested or misconstrued; and with which, in the main, we are only concerned so far as it is needful to refute them.

Foremost and earliest among them is the theory which identifies the Bride of the Song with the Virgin Mary. This was the view of some medieval interpreters. We shall hardly need to dwell long on it. It is fatal to it that the special relation in which Christ stood to the Virgin Mary is not the relation in which the heavenly Solomon stands to the Bride in all but a single passage of the Song. That one passage—the only one from which the theory in its full strictness could derive any shadow of support—is VIII. 5; and curiously enough the mistranslation of that passage in the Vulgate deprived the medievalists of even the one proof which they might otherwise have found for the baseless fabric which they reared. It is however evident that it could only, at best, be allowable to associate the figure of the Virgin Mary with the interpretation of that passage in so far as she might be viewed as representing for the moment the entire community. The same holds good in reference to Rev. XII. 1; or in reference to the case where the painter of a sacred subject, of universal interest, borrows his faces from some living models. It is moreover hardly less fatal to the theory before us that no sanction for it should exist in the writings of any Christian Father. Were it true, it is inconceivable that it should not have been recognized in the Christian Church from the first. But it is younger than Christianity by more than a thousand years. How far it now retains its adherents in the Romish Church is not easily ascertained; especially as much may pass current there among the vulgar that scholars would be ashamed to repeat. Many, probably, who, in conformity with their doctrinal prepossessions, insinuate a special indirect application of the Song to her as foremost of the saints, would yet not contend for any direct reference to her in it.

§ 4.

We advance then to the theory which views the Song as based upon, and as partially celebrating, some historical marriage of Solomon: whether that with Pharaoh's daughter, or one with an Israelitish bride, the critics of Bossuet's school are not agreed. Of this theory we observe, without entering into details, that it introduces many difficulties and explains none. Whatever might have been the case in a short ode, where only a single scene is delineated, it is unlikely that for the purposes of a longer poem, marked by so extensive and orderly a variety of incidents, the story of any one typical marriage could have been found to run exactly parallel to the story of the union of Christ and his Church. Why rather, if the poet, with Psalm xlv. before him, wished to set forth under the marriage-figure the relations of the Church to the future Messiah, should he not draw upon all the varied stores and products of a well-furnished and teeming imagination for the several requisite details of his imagery? For indeed while the course of action of the Song faithfully depicts the successive known relations of the Church to Christ, it is only by shifts and expedients, and by the arbitrary introduction of all manner of supplementary hypotheses, that it can be fitted to the imaginary history of any possible earthly marriage. When Bp. Percy presumes to blame the allegorical interpreters of the Song for neglecting its literal sense, it is evident that his complaint rests upon the false assumption that all the passages of the Song can without violence be worked up into the thread of a literal story. But that is far from being the case: the poet has borrowed his representations from various heterogeneous sources: the unity of his Song lies only in the allegorical sense which he has continually before him. Thus for example the passage IV. 6, "I will get me to the mountain of myrrh, and to the hill of frankincense," sets forth, by a certain imagery of its own, Christ's passion, which is the main theme of the section of the Song in which it is found; and it belongs to the story of Christ's marriage because his act of espousal consisted in his passion; but the moment that the allegorical sense is set aside, that passage loses all connexion with nuptials or with love; for of the sense which Percy presses upon it, the less said the better. One great type the Song admits,—the typical figure of King Solomon: but that there existed any typical original of the Bride has never been proved, and it would only embarrass us to assume it.

The other part of Bossuet's theory, the division of the Song into seven portions corresponding to the seven days of a Jewish wedding-feast, is equally opposed to the tenor of its contents. If it be urged that some of the days are marked by the expressions in II. 17, IV. 6, it cannot be shewn that they are all so marked; and the real division of the Song is, as we shall find, not into seven but six sections, which all begin and terminate elsewhere. Further proof of Bossuet's view we have none; while on the other hand we observe that the passage III. 6—11 belongs manifestly to the great espousal-day, not to a day in the middle of the feast, and that the variety of incident which the Song contains is inconsistent with the unbroken continuance of a nuptial festivity. How shall the passages III. 1—5, v. 2—8, unless all in them be mere dream, be made to harmonize with the first week of a marriage? Then moreover it was a fundamental objection which Michaelis took to this theory, that no mention of nuptial rites is made throughout the Song. Perhaps he somewhat overstated this; but let us listen to Percy's answer. "That the common rites of marriage are not the formal subject of this poem is allowed; nor will it be wondered at, if we consider who is the poet,—a lively and ingenious monarch, who, it should seem, had already gone through all these ceremonies a great many times; and this being the case, what could there be engaging in them? What could there be in them of novelty to excite his genius, or deserve his description?" With this naive defence we may dismiss the theory. Those most adverse to it could hardly have pronounced upon it a severer condemnation.

§ 5.

We have now to deal with that latest treatment which would represent the Song of Songs as a drama displaying the constancy of virtuous love under temptation. It is evident that hardly any theory could, in its method of viewing the Song, more utterly conflict with the interpretation received in the Church for sixteen centuries. Will it bear the test of examination?

It is the fundamental postulate of this theory that there should be two principal male characters, instead of one, speaking either directly or indirectly in the poem. And so certain do the advocates of the theory appear that this is the case, that they actually rely upon the asserted fact as the main proof of the correctness of their view. How do they establish it? "The beloved shepherd," says Ginsburg, "when he speaks, or is spoken to, or is spoken of, is recognised by the pastoral language; the King is distinguished by express allusions to his position;" and "an attentive reader of the original will find nearly as much help from the masterly structure of this Song, as can be obtained from the divisions and initial letters in modern dramas, by which the different speakers are distinguished." This sounds well; but it must be owned that the argument would be more convincing were the advocates of the theory more nearly agreed among themselves as to which parts of the Song should be put into the lips of the King and the Shepherd respectively. Let us take three of the latest, Ginsburg, Renan, and Hitzig; all attentive readers of the original, as will doubtless be admitted. We find that the passage I. 15 is assigned by Ginsburg to the Shepherd, by Hitzig and Renan to Solomon: II. 2 is assigned by Ginsburg and Renan to the Shepherd, but by Hitzig to Solomon: Ginsburg makes the Shepherd the speaker in IV. 1—5, and 7 to middle of 16, with part of V. 1, but Renan gives IV. 1—7 to Solomon, the remainder of the above to the Shepherd, while Hitzig gives IV. 1—5, 7, 9, 10, 12, &c. to Solomon, 6, 8, 11 to the Shepherd: VI. 8 is given to Solomon by Ginsburg and Hitzig, but to the Shepherd by Renan: VI. 9 is given to Solomon by Ginsburg, but to the Shepherd by Hitzig and Renan. How little value is attached by Ginsburg himself to his own argument may be gathered from the circumstance that whereas he assigns IV. 1—5 to the Shepherd, he yet, when this passage is partially repeated in VI. 5—7, VII. 3, puts the identical words into the mouth of Solomon. It is clear that he sees no fundamental difference in the language which his two male characters use. And it is not pretended that they ever address each other; nor indeed is there a single passage in which, according to any probable interpretation[1], they are both addressed or spoken of together. The distinction between them is in fact purely fictitious: there is but one male character in the Song, the true Beloved. As to his appearing sometimes in the full pomp of royalty, sometimes in more pastoral, or at least in simpler guise, that is a matter which can occasion no difficulty to those who take the

[1] For I. 12, see p. 44.

Song in its allegorical meaning. The real unity of the Song lies in the spiritual Story which it sets forth. In the one person of the Lord Jesus Christ all contradictions are reconciled; and the object of investing him with his full royal splendour and with his princely title, Solomon, in III. 6—11, is to signalize his glory in the most solemn act of his incarnate career. He is represented both as a king and as a shepherd elsewhere in the Old Testament; and this even in the same passage, Ezek. XXXIV. 23, 24; Micah V. 2—4. Surely we need not now, in interpreting the Old Testament, go back to imitate the errors of those who sundered the different portions of the Old Testament picture of Christ by distinguishing between a Messiah ben-Judah and a Messiah ben-Ephraim.

So much for the characters with which modern theory presents us. But the supposed plot of the drama will hardly fare much better in the crucible of enquiry. The advocates of the theory explain the situation in the opening of the piece, by informing us that the country-maiden had, in entering a garden near her rural abode, accidentally and unexpectedly found herself in the presence of the king, who, struck with her beauty, had either invited her into his tent, or, as most suppose, carried her off forthwith to his court, where accordingly we discover her. All this rests on an application of the inventive faculty to a mistranslation of VI. 12. They render, in that verse, not "made me the chariots," or "made me like the chariots," but "brought me to the chariots," or "set me on the chariots;" an inadmissible rendering, which even they themselves allow to be doubtful so far as the Hebrew words are concerned. Pass we on. The action has commenced. In I. 9—11 Solomon tempts the maiden. We then learn from Ginsburg that in I. 12 she replies; and that by "my nard" she intends the Shepherd to whom she is attached. Surely "every unbiassed reader" will hardly deem this the natural interpretation. Turn we to II. 4: most expositors would there regard the first clause as explained by, and as helping to explain the similar clause in I. 4. Not so however Ginsburg; for with him they speak of two different persons, Solomon and the Shepherd. Hitzig, it is true, (whose commentary, though published before Ginsburg's and Renan's, evidently represents a later recension of the theory) remedies these awkwardnesses; but how? By introducing a supply of additional speakers, and therewith also a large supply of stage-directions. We shall give his view of the speakers in I. 2—II. 7. First Scene: 2, The maiden. 3, 4, Ladies of the harem. 5—7, The maiden. 8, Ladies of Jerusalem. Second Scene: 9—11, Solomon. 12, A lady of the harem. 13, Another ditto. 14, The maiden (of her absent shepherd). 15, Solomon (to the maiden). 16, first clause, The maiden (to Solomon). 16, second clause, to II. 1, ditto (to her absent shepherd). 2, Solomon (to the maiden). 3, The maiden (of her shepherd). 4, A lady. 5, as 3. 6, as 4. 7, The Poet's moral. It is evident that sufficient ingenuity might make a complicated cross-dialogue of this kind out of almost anything: each difficulty that might arise would only require at most one additional complication, or one additional speaker. On the other hand, in II. 8—17, where the advocates of the theory before us wish to carry on the current of thought more smoothly, the isolated verse II. 15 is a great stumbling-block. Ginsburg will have it addressed to the maiden by her brothers; but he forgets that the אֶחֱזוּ, "take ye," is plural. Renan makes it the fragment of a song which the maiden sings. Hitzig translates, "Hold there! ye foxes," making the verb intransitive, and the noun vocative; but even this is not very satisfactory. It is moreover not only in particular verses but also in whole sections that the plot of these critics stands condemned. The expressions of III. 11 compel them to behold in the section III. 6—11 a marriage procession of Solomon; and indeed Hitzig carries on that marriage into the dialogue of the next chapter. But to the plot of the drama, as these writers understand it, any marriage of Solomon is irrelevant, and worse than irrelevant. It needs only to read Ginsburg's note on III. 11, to be convinced of the absurdity to which it leads; that a king, in the very hour of his marriage procession, and in the very company of his consort, should put on his marriage crown for the sake of dazzling, and so alluring, another woman! Then as to the section v. 2—8: the maiden, says Ginsburg, "relates to the court ladies a dream which she has had, in which she manifests great attachment for her beloved." But our critics have already presented us with either a dream, or something resembling it, and of the same general character, in III. 1—5. Under these circumstances, the new and fuller dream is against all dramatic rule; for as it is but a dream, its details add nought to the development of the plot; while the use of it, as exhibiting the maiden's affection to her beloved, has been superseded by the earlier half-dream, and so the interest in it spoiled. It did not need so full a dream to lead merely to the question in v. 9. Lastly, we have to object to the theory before us the backward manner in which according to it the story of the plot is told. Renan candidly acknowledges this: "Il est certain que dans l'état actuel du poëme, l'ordre chronologique de l'action est tout-a-fait renversé. Ainsi, au chapitre Ier, nous voyons la jeune fille faire son entrée dans le sérail; au chap. III, elle entre pour la première fois dans Jérusalem; au chapitre VI, elle est surprise à Sulem par les gens de Salomon; au chapitre VIII, ses frères semblent former ensemble un complot dont le développement constituerait le nœud du poëme." The only remedy which Renan can see for these difficulties, though he wisely shrinks from applying it, is to transpose some portions of the Song. Ginsburg provides against one particular of the objection by assuming, not very naturally, that the scene in Chap. I. is really prior in order of time to the maiden's being carried off to Jerusalem. But then this renders it only the more improbable that after she has been so carried off, and after the interest of the first temptation scene has been absorbed in that of the second, the maiden should, in VI. 11, 12, explain not how she was brought to Jerusalem, but only how she fell in, originally, and at the first, with the cortége of her royal admirer. We must, by the way, remark that VIII. 9 will not bear the interpretation which the literalists impose upon it: see the commentary upon that passage. They respect its imagery as little as they do the syntax of VI. 12; and they have no more right to the one passage than to the other, as explaining their plot, or as telling in their favour.

It is indeed only by constraint that the Song can be viewed as a drama conforming to the rules of outward dramatic unity. In the internecine warfare of literal criticism, the dramatizing literalists will find it as difficult to withstand the assaults of the idyllizing literalists as the latter to resist the force of the arguments of the former. There is a unity in the Song; but that unity, as we have already observed, lies in the spiritual story which the allegory holds up to view. Do we then deny to the Song all dramatic character? By no means. The Beloved, the Bride, the Chorus of the Daughters of Jerusalem have in it all their several dramatic parts. And in discriminating the speeches of the Beloved from those of the Bride a reference to the original Hebrew will be of great service, because of the distinction in Hebrew between the masculine and feminine forms of the 2nd personal pronoun, which is wanting in English. In fact such reference will at once solve all questions with regard to the structure of the main and simpler part of the dialogue. It is only with respect to a few subordinate and enigmatical passages that any difficulty will then remain in deciding who is the speaker in them:

such for instance as the refrain in II. 7; which, although best put into the lips of the Bride, might also, no doubt, with some shew of probability, be assigned either to the Beloved, or to the Chorus, or even to the Poet himself, though indeed it is through the Chorus that he would, as in the Greek drama, most naturally speak.

The last and perhaps the greatest objection to the theory which we have been discussing is the incongruity of the character of the Song of Songs, so interpreted, with the place which it occupies in the canon of Holy Scripture. Were the theory true, the book would forthwith cease to be in any way sacred. It would not be sacred in itself; nor would it have any special connexion with the sacred history of God's people or of the lineage of the Redeemer, such as belongs to the Books of Esther and of Ruth. It seems moreover questionable whether even that high moral character which Ginsburg earnestly vindicates for it would be conceded to it by all his critical allies; and indeed one may well doubt whether the benefit of the great moral lesson which it is asserted to inculcate would not be fully counterbalanced by the corrupting tendency of the not wholly inattractive pictures of vice which according to the same theory it would contain. Yet let us take it even at the best which this theory can make of it,— as recording "an example of virtue in a humble individual, who had passed successfully through unparalleled" (though, surely, not unparalleled!) "temptations." How then herein does Ginsburg unfold its great importance? He discourses, justly and excellently, on the evils of polygamy and on the true dignity of woman; and then, having worked up his theme, suddenly puts in his plea for the book "which celebrates the virtuous example of a woman, and thus strikes at the root of all her reproaches and her wrongs." Now undoubtedly the debasing effects of polygamy were, even among the Jews, very great; and it is one of the great glories of Christianity that it has restored woman to her rightful position, and that in this respect the influence of its teaching has been felt and has prevailed even beyond its own pale. But where is the proof—no, we will not ask for proof,—where is the faintest indication to be found, that the Song of Songs, as interpreted by the dramatizing literalists, ever in any way contributed to this result? Is it not too strong a claim upon our credulity that we should be required to believe that the increased respect accorded to the female sex since the days of our Saviour was, even indirectly, promoted by a book of Scripture of the right understanding of which, according to Ginsburg, the first traces are to be found in a Jewish commentator of the 12th century, and of which the true meaning was never discovered, with any approach to adequacy, till the year A.D. 1771?

§ 6.

WE shall now offer some evidence in confirmation of the allegorical character of the Song of Songs.

And first, then, we have to notice the tokens scattered through the Song itself, that it is to be viewed as an allegory. Such are the significance of many of the proper names in it, and the references, in some cases unmistakeable, to that significance. Without, of course, insisting on the name Solomon, we may enumerate Bether (II. 17), Amminadib (VI. 12), Shulamith (VI. 13), Heshbon (VII. 4), Bath-rabbim (ib.), Baal-hamon (VIII. 11). Such also is the employment of words, which by their resemblance in sound to other words indicate their own allegorical significance: see the commentary on I. 10, 14. This play on words is of no unfrequent occurrence in Hebrew poetry: we may cite a good instance of it in Psalm LXXXIV. 5—7, where, through the double meanings of three of the terms employed, we have at once both a parable and its interpretation[1]. Another token, —indeed token is here too weak a word,—of the allegorical character of the Song is to be found in the fact that she who is the bride of the Beloved is no less his sister, IV. 10. In vain the literalists attempt to explain this away: see the commentary on the passage. To the same effect run the impossibilities of some of the local descriptions, if literally understood; more particularly IV. 8, where there is no conceivable reason why the Beloved should summon his Bride from the literal Lebanon, or should bid her either gaze or go from the literal summit of Amana. And yet if the Song generally be literally taken, an unbiassed reader will not easily believe that by Lebanon in that passage can be denoted either Jerusalem or indeed any other place than Lebanon itself. In favour also of the allegorical meaning is the

[1] See my *Introduction to the Psalms*, II. p. 71.

character of the similes by which the graces of the Beloved and of the Bride are delineated: IV. 1—5, V. 10—16, VI. 4—7, VII. 1—6. Understood of literal corporeal beauty, these descriptions could hardly appear other than extravagant. Furthermore the allegorical interpretation is able to deal far more satisfactorily than the literal with such passages as V. 2—7. So evident is it that it can be no actual occurrence that is there literally described, that the literalists are obliged to take recourse to the view that that passage contains the relation of a dream. But the allegorical interpretation finds no difficulty in beholding there a direct continuation of the action of the poem.

The indications thus contained in the Song itself are in harmony with the evidence afforded by its superscription. Literally understood, the Song contains nought which should entitle it to be distinctively styled "The most excellent of songs." Neither the beauty of its natural descriptions nor the moral sentiments which it unfolds would justify the special pre-eminence which the title thus accords to it. But let it be viewed as depicting the love of Christ and the Church, and forthwith the justice of the designation becomes evident. The Song is the song of songs, for it celebrates the glories of the Incarnate Son of God and sings of the highest ideal of both nuptial and antenuptial love. It would be a strange anomaly were the title "Song of Songs" reserved for the one book of the Bible which contained no reference to religion.

Our next proof that the Song of Songs is an allegory is supplied by its parallelism with Psalm XLV. The allegorical character of this psalm is generally admitted: for a vindication of it, which need not be here repeated, see Introd. to the Psalms, I. pp. 260 seqq. Further evidence, though of a subordinate kind, to the same effect is contained in the correspondence between the Song and the prophecy of Hosea: see above, pp. 14, 15. The Song has also its points of contact with the remarkable allegory in Ezek. XVI.: compare especially Cant. I. 10, "Comely are thy cheeks in the circlet, thy neck in the necklace," with Ezek. XVI. 11: "I decked thee also with ornaments, and I put bracelets upon thy hands, and a chain on thy neck."

That the Song was viewed as an allegory in the time of our Saviour, is rendered probable by the use made of its images in the apocryphal 2 Esdras V. 23—27; and if the support thence derived to the allegorical interpretation be slight, it is at least more than the literal can boast: "O Lord that bearest rule, of every wood of the earth, and of all the trees thereof, thou hast chosen thee one only vine: and of all lands of the world thou hast chosen thee one pit: and of all the flowers thereof one lily:...and of all the fowls that are created thou hast named thee one dove:...and among all the multitudes of people thou hast gotten thee one people: and unto this people, whom thou lovedst, thou gavest a law that is approved of all." Compare Cant. II. 1, 2: VI. 9.

And now how was the Song viewed by Christ himself, by his forerunner, and by his apostles? The literalists would fain persuade us that there are no references to it in the New Testament. It is indeed there never directly quoted; but, on the other hand, the passages in which its language and its imagery are in various ways embodied, are numerous; the use thus made of it is uniformly allegorical; the cumulative cogency of these repeated dependences upon it in favour of the allegorical interpretation becomes very great; and throughout the New Testament no hint is to be found that it bore or could bear any other than an allegorical meaning. The designation of the Church as the Bride in Rev. xxi. 2, 9, xxii. 17, commends itself the more naturally to us when we allow the preparation which had been made for it by the imagery of the Song. Still more is this the case with John the Baptist's designation, in John iii. 29, of Christ as the Bridegroom: he himself being but the bridegroom's friend, cf. Cant. v. 1. Our Saviour too describes himself by the same title, Matth. ix. 15; and speaks most remarkably of the mourning of the children of the bridechamber when the bridegroom should be taken from them; a contingency which in reference to most bridegrooms would not have been anticipated, but which had been foreshewn in the case of the heavenly bridegroom in Cant. v. 6—8. Then the marriage of the Lamb of Rev. xix. 9—though it here refers to the final union—rests naturally on the bridal union of the Song. The same too is the case with St Paul's description of Christ presenting the Church unto himself, in Eph. v. 27: indeed the language of that passage, "that it should be holy and without blemish," expressly recalls Cant. IV. 7. Of the various further correspondences which we proceed to notice some will be more fully unfolded in the commentary; to which therefore the reader may refer. The image of Cant. V. 2 repeats itself in Rev. III. 20, "Behold, I stand at the door, and knock." That of Cant. V. 1, in the same verse, "I...will sup with him, and he with me;" also in John XIV. 23, "My Father will love him, and we will come unto him, and make our abode with him;" also in Luke XXII. 30, "That ye may eat and drink at my table in my kingdom." On Cant. III. 2, V. 6, rest John VII. 34, "Ye shall seek me, and shall not find me;" and John XIII. 33, "Ye shall seek me; and as I said unto the Jews,...so now I say to you." With the passage Cant. VIII. 8, which speaks of the little sister, who although not yet marriageable, should yet hereafter be demanded as a bride, is connected 2 Cor. XI. 2, in which St Paul describes the Gentile community of Corinth as a chaste virgin whom he had laboured to present to Christ. On Cant. II. 3, VIII. 5, probably, (see the comment on this last,) rests Luke I. 35, "The power of the Highest shall overshadow thee." And Cant. II. 15 prepares the way for our Lord's designation of Herod as a fox, i.e. a waster of the Church. Yet more remarkable, in some respects, is the way in which the language of the Song forms the prelude to certain symbolical actions recorded in the New Testament; just as our Saviour's discourses in John III, VI prepared the way for the institution of the ordinances of the two Christian sacraments. In Cant. II. 4 we have the germ of the teaching conveyed by the miracle at Cana of Galilee, John II. 1—11. Our risen Saviour's bidding to his disciples in John XXI. 12, "Come and dine," stands in a similar relation to Cant. V. 1: he had, in the oblation of himself unto death, visited the mountain of myrrh and the hill of frankincense, and he was now on the very point of coming into his garden, the Church of the new covenant, to eat and to drink with the members of his body at the feast of love which his love had originated. And as it was not only our Saviour's own acts, but also those of others towards him, which, whether so intended or not by their authors, proved to be symbolical, and are, as such, recorded by the evangelists, we cannot from Cant. I. 12 separate the two anointings of our Saviour's feet, Luke VII. 36 seqq.; John XII. 3 seqq., &c.; nor yet from Cant. V. 3, Peter's girding on of his fisher's coat, in his eagerness to hasten to his risen Lord, John XXI. 7. We need only further remark on this subject that as the Song is truly a song, and not a narrative or direct instruction or prophecy, direct quotations from it were not to be expected. A poem which has thoroughly enwrought itself into men's minds is felt too deeply to be formally referred to, though its imagery and language become interwoven with their most familiar thoughts.

Some objections have been raised to the allegorical interpretation of the Song which may here be conveniently noticed, as they have not been touched upon in the preceding remarks.

It has been urged that parts of the passage VII. 1—9

are, when put into the lips of Christ, inconsistent with his dignity and purity. Yet why inconsistent, when allegorically interpreted? Unto the pure all things are pure. The ancient interpreters took no offence at these words; and probably their views of the person of Christ were quite as elevated as those of the mass of interpreters of the present day. Neither the conventions of modern custom, however useful in their way, nor yet the conventions of dress must be taken as marking the absolute bounds of that which may be described without immodesty. The saying in John VII. 38, "Out of his belly shall flow rivers of living water," is not in harmony with the fastidiousness of modern taste, though it proceeded from our Saviour. No parts of the female form are described in the Song but what a sculptor would imitate, in order thereby to display the full symmetry of the human figure; nor would he generally be blamed for this, so long as he sought by it to appeal to the spectators' ideas of beauty, and not to their idle curiosity or impure passions[1]. Those who are jealous for the honour of the Bible should beware of supposing that they uphold it by seeing in the passage under review aught but a genuine commendation of the graces of the Church. The passage particularizes so minutely that, were the spirit of it vicious, the tendency of it would needs be also vicious, from whomsoever it were represented as proceeding. The public exhibition of

---

[1] "Beauty, and the passion caused by beauty, which I call love, is different from desire, though desire may sometimes operate along with it."—BURKE, *On the Sublime and Beautiful*, III. I.

that which is impure does not practically conduce to purity: we can hardly, even in a drama, enter with any fulness of detail into feelings that are immoral, without catching somewhat of their tone of immorality. Moreover it will appear from our commentary that the verses VII. 7—9 are probably to be put into the lips not of the Beloved but of the Chorus; in which case their purport will necessarily be very different from what, even at best, our objectors have supposed.

It has further been urged by the literalists against the allegorical interpretation that the image of marriage had never, up to the date when the Song was written, been employed to denote a spiritual relationship; and that though it was subsequently so used by the prophets, yet even they never gave a spiritual turn to the antenuptial love which the Song delineates. Now were this fully true, it would have very little weight against the allegorical interpretation. In part it is true; and the reason why the Song differs from the prophetical writings in speaking of antenuptial as well as of nuptial love is, as we shall presently see, because in it the Beloved represents not God but the Messiah. In this respect the Song must be compared with Psalm XLV. It may also be conceded that before the date of these two pieces the image of even marriage, as symbolizing a spiritual relationship, had been comparatively undeveloped. It is by that very circumstance that we are driven to the conclusion that the Song was prior in order of time to the prophecies of Hosea: it was the special glory of the Song (following in the wake of Psalm XLV.) to unfold the image which the prophets afterwards so largely employed. But the germs of the image had existed long before in the phrase "to go whoring after other gods," used repeatedly in the Pentateuch and the Book of Judges. It first occurs in Exod. XXXIV. 15, 16. That it there denotes a spiritual departure from the true God is shewn by the word "jealous" in ver. 14, forming part of the same sentence with vv. 15, 16: "Thou shalt worship no other god: for the LORD, whose name is Jealous, is a jealous God;" and this ought not to have been overlooked or denied. The same is evident in Deut. XXXI. 16; Judg. II. 17; also Numb. XIV. 33. It may be that the phrase, as applied to the heathen Canaanites in Exod. XXXIV. 15, involves, along with its spiritual significance, a literal reference to the impure rites with which heathen worship clothed itself, as if in token of its spiritually adulterous origin. Or it may be that even there it refers purely to the spiritual character of the idolatry which, though in partial ignorance of their error, the heathen practised; and it must be remembered that though used of the heathen, it is uniformly addressed not to them as a reproach, but as a divine warning to the instructed Israelites. But on this we decide not: it is to the present argument of no importance, the spiritual purport of the phrase in question being once established.

An objection of a more general character which has been implied rather than expressed against the allegorical interpretation of the Song is that so detailed an allegorical use of the conjugal relationship, with its preludes and accompaniments, to set forth the highest spiritual truths, is altogether unparalleled. Here however, even though we should condescend to argue the question on only the lowest grounds, we have the practices of other Oriental nations to guide us. With the Hebrew Song have been compared various Indian, Persian, and Arabian poems of corresponding character; and amid all the differences which have been pointed out between them the one great fact remains, that the Easterns have been frequently wont, with much fulness of detail, to clothe their religious devotion in the garb of human love. The allegories of the Hindus and Muhammedans may not avail of themselves to establish the allegorical character of the Song of Songs; but they at least render nugatory much of the reasoning that some might be disposed to urge against it.

If, however, argument *à priori* as to the character of the Song be admissible at all, we may venture to conduct it on somewhat higher grounds. Let the question then be, What, on a cursory inspection of the Song, and in the knowledge that it formed part of the Bible, might we reasonably expect it to contain? It seems to speak, —nay, it speaks,—of love; and why should it not? "For my part," said Niebuhr, "I should deem something wanting to the Bible if no expression were there found for the deepest and strongest of human feelings[1]." No Christian need be ashamed to avow his concurrence in the sentiment which prompted this utterance. For nuptial love is older than the fall; and under the con-

---

[1] Related by Bunsen to Renan; Renan, p. 147.

ditions of our present existence, love antenuptial is the almost necessary prelude to love nuptial; and, without doubt, the volume of God's teaching not only recognizes, but consecrates those feelings of which the germs were by him emplanted in our original nature.

But how then does it consecrate them? Not merely by illustrating their workings in the way in which we continually behold them illustrated in the scenes of ordinary life; but rather by setting before us, in love's own language, that highest ideal of love both nuptial and antenuptial, the love of the Son of God to his earthly Church. It celebrates the great archetypal love of which all our loves are but the shadows. It points to the manifestation of that love in the Son of God's incarnation and death. This is what in Scripture we should justly expect; and this is the especial office of the Song of Songs. Like the rest of the Old Testament generally, it speaks of Christ, and prepares the way for his coming. As other books reared up, on the basis of earthly sovereignties, the picture of Christ as universal king, or traced, in the familiar care with which Eastern shepherds tended their sheep, the imaged outlines of the care with which Christ should watch over his people, so the Song of Songs delineated, in the love of a faithful bridegroom to his bride, the supreme and immeasurable love of Christ to those who should be by him redeemed. And thus by singing of Christ it more truly and more effectually honoured human love than if it had sung of that and nothing beyond. Every lesson which the religiously minded literalists would find in the Song is indeed therein implicitly contained; not in the way they would have it, but in a better way. We see light there; but it is in the light of the Son of God.

§ 7.

WE must now bend our attention to some of the main points with respect to which those who concur in holding the Song to be thoroughly allegorical have differed from each other.

And first then, who is the Beloved of whom the Song speaks? With well nigh one consentient voice, for more than a thousand years, Christian expositors answered, The Messiah. De Lyra first introduced into the Church the Jewish view which regarded the Beloved as God not incarnate; a view which since his time has, no doubt, by Christians been not unfrequently held. That this view should prevail among the Jews cannot surprise us. The prophetical representations of the Jewish covenant as a marriage between God and his people imparted to it a *primâ facie* probability; and after Christ had once come, and still more after Christians had expressly interpreted the Song of him, it would take firm root among the Jews from their unhappy opposition to Christianity and to the truth. In order to carry it through, the Targum forbore to identify the Beloved with the Solomon of III. 6—11, whom it regarded as the historical builder of the temple. This severance of the principal personage of the different portions of the Song De Lyra rightly disallowed; but he was thereby drawn to the view which can hardly appear other than repulsive, that by Solomon is signified God: "nomine Salomonis, qui pacificus interpretatur, intelligitur ipse Deus secundum Hebræos; quia disponit omnia suaviter."

For the identification of the Beloved with the Messiah rather than with God not incarnate the following arguments seem decisive. First, the Song speaks of antenuptial as well as of nuptial love: the day of the espousals is not described till III. 6—11. But in respect of the marriage between God and his people, the Jews always regarded it as ratified at Mount Sinai; and though, it is true, the covenant there established was but a shadow of the covenant which was to be sealed on Calvary, yet it could hardly have been set aside, as invalid, in any representation from which the person of the Messiah was excluded. In other words, the antenuptial part of the Song points to the fact that the Beloved had not yet been fully displayed: God indeed he should be, yet not invisible, but manifest in the flesh. Then there is much beside in the Song which forces us to view the Beloved as one of woman born. He seems to stand throughout on the same level with the Bride. He proclaims himself of the same race with her by calling her sister, IV. 9; and she does the same by longing for him as her brother, VIII. 1. The intensely human descriptions of his person harmonize not with the majesty of God except as incarnate, II. 8, 9, 17; V. 2, 9—16; VIII. 14. Especially is this the case where they necessarily represent him as youthful, by setting forth either the darkness of his hair, v. 11, or the nimbleness of his motions, II. 8, 9, 17; VIII. 14. What moreover could we make of " the crown wherewith his mother crowned him," as applied to the invisible God, III. 11? Furthermore we have the correspondence with Psalm XLV., where the words " thy God," ver. 7, sufficiently shew that it is the Messiah who is addressed. And lastly we have the tenor of the whole language of the New Testament; and specially of those passages of it in which the Song is indirectly referred to (see above, pp. 53—55). The words of John the Baptist, which depend so manifestly on the Song, John III. 29, may above all be instanced as proving that by the Bridegroom the Messiah is intended.

But it will be asked, How came it then to pass that the image of the Messiah as the future Bridegroom of the Church was by the Hebrew prophets no further unfolded? The answer will be found in considering the office which the prophets were more directly called upon to fulfil. They had to bring back the people to the observance of that relation which God had established with them before planting them in the land of Canaan. Hosea here, in his opening chapter, strikes the fundamental note which runs through all the prophetical writings from him to Malachi. For this purpose the marriage on which they had to dwell was the marriage of God and of Israel at Sinai; and this particular application of the image of the bridal union naturally interfered with that which the Song had recommended. Still though they diverted the imagery of the Song, they did not altogether lose sight of its contents. There is probably some degree of reference to it in the title which Isaiah bestows upon the Messiah, The Prince of Peace, IX. 6; and it is in allusion either to the Song or to Psalm XLV. that he writes in XXXIII. 17, "Thine eyes shall see the king in his beauty." It may moreover be observed that the Song of Songs embodies the last great religious glow of the Solomonic period of royal splendour as revived in the kingdom of Judah in the days of Jehoshaphat. As years rolled on, the impression made by their subsequent troubles upon the Jewish nation, and the unfolded consciousness of sin, brought the priestly office of the future Messiah more directly into view; and for the purpose of setting this forth representations of a different kind became necessary.

§ 8.

OUR next question is, Whom shall we understand by the Bride? Here De Lyra did better service. He pointed out that through all ages God's Church had been but one; and that if the Song spake of her both before and after Christ's coming, it must needs, though without destroying her ideal unity, speak of her both in her more restricted and in her more catholic form.

An endeavour has however been made to view the Jewish nation, both before and since Christ's coming, as the Bride of the Song; from direct interest in which the Christian Church will thus be in great measure excluded. Had this view proceeded from those who regard the fortunes of the Jewish nation, not of the Church, as the general theme of Old Testament prophecy, the maintenance of it could have occasioned no surprise. It is urged however by Hengstenberg, who thereby in some measure sunders this Book from the rest of the Old Testament, as specially Israelitish in its contents. It obtains moreover a fragmentary support from some Latin expositors of the post-Roman period, who, instead of rigidly maintaining the unity of the female character of the Song, refer some passages to the "Synagogue" rather than the "Church:" e. g. VI. 12, 13.

The first and fundamental objection to this view is that it is unproved; and that without proof we have no right to assume the Song to be more specially Jewish than the rest of the Old Testament. The identification of the Shulamith of VI. 13 with the Jewish nation rests on a misapprehension of the meaning of the words "Return, return:" see the comment on that passage. Moreover the Israelites, regarded in a national point of view, are represented in the Song by the Mother of the Bride, see on I. 6, &c.: the Bride therefore herself must needs be different: she may according to circumstances, as De Lyra shewed, be either Israelitish or Catholic, but she is, in either case, not a nation, but a church, which the Jews now are not. The foundation for Hengstenberg's view seems to be mainly the false assumption that the passage V. 2—8 describes the present spiritual rejection of a great portion of the Jewish nation; a rejection to be followed by the final readmittance of the nation to God's favour. But parts of that very passage are decisive against his view. Ver. 5 implies a true self-denying devotion of heart, such as the Jewish nation generally, since the coming of Christ, has not yet exhibited: see this discussed in the comment on v. 5, 6. So again with respect to ver. 8, "Declare ye to him that I am sick with love:" how can it be said that the Jewish nation in its present state is sick with love to Christ? Are even those expectations of a Messiah which the Jews now erroneously retain either more spiritual in their views of his person, or more universally diffused throughout the members of the nation, than on the day on which they disowned him at his appearing? There is an unfavourable significance even in the fact that the Jewish interpretation of the Song of Songs, unlike in this respect to the Christian, should have uniformly failed to discern the Messiah in it. It will however be borne in mind that our discourse is here only of those Jews who retain their Jewish nationality; not of the numerous converts whom Judaism has given to the Christian Church, and of whom, though not always free at the first from Jewish prejudices on minor points, the Church has numbered many amongst her most illustrious members. May the time come when that number shall be largely swelled; when the witness of the Old Testament to the kingdom of Jesus of Nazareth shall be universally recognized, and when the hope shall be fulfilled which the Christian Church has in all ages uniformly cherished, of the general reception of the members of the Jewish nation into the Christian spiritual fold!

§ 9.

CHRIST being thus the Beloved of the Song, and the Church the Bride, how far may the Song itself be viewed as of a historical or historico-prophetical character? How far does it set forth, with poetical delineation, the events that had already been or yet should be?

That a story runs through the whole seems, when once pointed out, sufficiently clear. It is implied in the consecutiveness of the several pictures which the Song contains; as also in their mutual relations to each other. Compare, for instance, the picture of VIII. 5 with that of III. 6; or again, the picture of VIII. 5 with the longings expressed in VIII. 1. And what else can these pictures well represent than the different conditions of the earthly Church, and the acts of Christ toward it? If some of the psalms be historical, e. g. Psalms CV, CVI, or even historico-prophetical, e. g. Psalm CVII. 33 seqq., why should not also the Song be the same? And why moreover should not a certain historical order reign throughout it? Extravagant then as many of the historicizing interpretations since the days of De Lyra have been, they have erred rather in the application of their fundamental principle than in the maintenance of it. The violence done by them severally to different passages of the Song does not shew that no historical interpretation should be attempted. It only illustrates the need which exists for laying down, at the outset, the limits which such interpretation ought to observe.

Now if the general theme of the Song be the love of Christ and the Church, it may be reasonably presumed that the events of the Israelitish history could only be introduced into it so far as they bore directly on the hopes that were entertained of the coming of Christ at the time that the Song was written. This is our first canon of historical interpretation; and by it most of the narrative which De Lyra, in imitation of the Targum, imports into the Song is at once excluded; for it does not sufficiently illustrate the "Let him kiss me" with which the Church, in the very opening of the Song, expresses her longing for her Lord.

Again as to the future, it is clear that the interest with which the author of the Song would anticipate the details of the evangelic records would be immeasurably greater than that which he would feel for any details of the prospects of the Church after Christ's ascension. We must therefore at once abandon all interpretations which make the Song speak of the establishment of the Church under Constantine, or of its reformation by Luther, and not of the incarnation and death of Christ. And indeed all details of the post-apostolic history of the Christian Church must have been so remote to the hopes of the sacred singer, except so far as they fulfilled any promises already vouchsafed, that it is not easy to believe that they should have been generally in any wise revealed to him.

We must moreover avoid seeking for historical details in the description which the Song contains of the person of Christ and of the graces of the Church. If the direct object of these descriptions be to illustrate the love of Christ and of his Church for each other, we must not substitute a song of history for a song of love, and so deprive the Song of Songs of that which is its especial glory. Nor again must we tear asunder the different parts of such descriptions.

There are some passages of the Song of which, even when viewed by themselves, the meaning is so far clear, that the student who has once apprehended it will never allow himself to be induced, by the exigencies of any scheme, to abandon it. The passage III. 9—11 sets forth the passion of Christ. The passage IV. 16 foretells the descent upon the Church of the Holy Spirit. The passage VIII. 1 represents the longing of the Church for the advent of Christ in the flesh: it might, taken by itself, represent the longing for either the first advent or the second. The passage VIII. 5 represents, almost certainly, that union of the Church with Christ for which in VIII. 1 she had prayed. Only inferior in importance to the above is the passage II. 11—13, which represents the heralding of the gospel. The true interpretation of the Song will necessarily guide itself by these landmarks.

It is fair to presume that the order of events delineated in the Song is generally chronological. Yet it need not be wholly or exclusively chronological. A strict chronological sequence of the events foretold is seldom found in Old Testament prophecy; and we may repeat of the Song what has been said of the latter part of the writings of Isaiah, that in it "each successive scene is described as in itself complete, and the order of events no farther indicated than that some things were to stand in a relation of priority to others[1]." Definite adherence to chronological order would indeed in the Song be at variance with the centralism by which, as will hereafter be shewn, its different sections are distinguished: the leading theme of each being indicated in the central part of the section, and the descriptions which illustrate this being grouped around it. And as regards the mutual relations of the several sections, two contiguous sections may be chronologically arranged in respect of their leading themes, while yet the events of the one overlap those of the other. Or, lastly, two sections may delineate the history of the same period in two different aspects. Even in regard of the past, we probably have the history of the same period of David's life pictured in two different lights in Psalms XXII, XXIII[2]: how much more might two dissimilar, though not (as it should prove) inconsistent, representations be necessary for the purpose of setting forth with any adequacy the dim outlines of the unknown future?

---

[1] Fairbairn on Prophecy, p. 170.
[2] See my Introd. to the Psalms, I. pp. 144, 145.

§ 10.

That which has passed and still passes in the history of the Church is largely repeated in the experiences of individual souls. There is an analogy between the dealings of God with mankind generally and his dealings with men severally; between the illumination and sanctification of the whole Church and that of each of her members. It is this which so greatly extends the bearing of the Bible records. From the history of the nation of Israel the individual believer derives, and rightly derives, lessons of importance for his own conduct. It cannot then surprise us that many among the pious students of Scripture should have beheld in the Song of Songs a picture of the communing of the soul of man with its Redeemer. If moreover the patient waitings, the anxious searchings, the raptures at the joy of his presence, which are here delineated be such as accord with what they themselves have practically known, who will venture to maintain that their application of the Song can be fundamentally illegitimate or unjust?

Still the private history of each soul is not the same. There is no warrant for supposing that the order of each man's experiences must exactly accord with the order of the experiences of the Church. The earthly dealings of God himself with men are various rather than uniform; and one man may, without being on that account less under the influence of divine grace, have to pass several times through trials from which another may be altogether spared. The Song of Songs involves too definite a spiritual history to admit of being applied as a consecutive whole to the progress of every single soul. Its partial accordance with what we ourselves have experienced, or with what we know to have been the experience of others, must not lead us to press the correspondence between its descriptions and our own souls' histories too far. The individual reference of the Song belongs rather to the province of legitimate application than of strict interpretation; and such application is necessarily restricted by certain limiting conditions. So far as the several passages of the Song can be traced as corresponding to passages in the soul's history, so far, and no further, may the existence of a correspondence be determinately asserted.

We are confirmed in this view by certain passages of the Song, e. g. VI. 8, 9, which militate against the absolute identification of the Bride with the soul of any individual man. How, in that case, could the dove of Christ be but one? If we turn to the commentary of Gregory of Nyssa on this passage, we find that he is here constrained to make the individual soul give place to the whole company of the redeemed, and thus, though he does not confess it, to mar the consistency of his general interpretation. His illustration is taken, not unfairly, from our Saviour's words, Joh. XVII. 21, "That they all may be one; as thou, Father, art in me, and I in thee, that they also may be one in us." And perhaps it is a lesson which most of us need in some measure to learn, that solemn as is our own individual standing before God, we have yet to look not only on our own things, "but every man also on the things of others:" that all-important as is our individual acceptance, we yet rise truly highest as we realize our position as humble members in the Church universal. For assuredly, in the declarations of Scripture, it is the whole glorious company of the redeemed that Christ is most distinctly declared to have desired to present unto himself, and that is most plainly honoured with the ennobling name of the Bride, the wife of the Lamb.

§ II.

There is no single word by which the form of the Song of Songs can be adequately described. It is in the main dramatical, yet it does not conform with strictness to the rules of the regular drama; and the most judicious of even the literalizing dramatical interpreters (Ewald, Ginsburg) do not suppose it to have been intended for representation. In fact, the contemporaneousness of some of the events depicted in successive scenes, and the way in which verses like II. 15, IV. 6 break in upon the dramatic action, forbid us to view it as a drama proper. But, on the other hand, if any should still wish to designate the Song a chain of idyls, he must withal remember that these idyls stand to one another in a definite order of sequence, that they tend to a definite conclusion, and that they embody not merely an idea, but a connected history.

In modern times the importance of recognizing the natural divisions of the Song has been undisputedly acknowledged. It has been generally supposed that the Song contains from five to seven main portions. The true number is six. The endings of the first two, as also of the last but one, are easily recognized by the refrain at II. 7, III. 5, VIII. 4. And it is almost universally agreed that another portion ends at v. 1. How far the portion which commences at v. 2 extends has been a matter of less certainty. Some would make it terminate at VI. 9; others at VI. 13; wishing, apparently, that the different portions of the Song should not differ too widely in length. But the poet himself has marked the true termination of this portion at v. 8, by the similarity of the language of that verse to that of the other refrains. At the very end of the Song, the last two verses may be more properly viewed as an epilogue or conclusion to the whole than as belonging to the sixth main portion. Some recent criticism has so viewed them. The Song then thus divides itself: I. 2—II. 7; II. 8—III. 5; III. 6—V. 1; V. 2—8; V. 9—VIII. 4; VIII. 5—12; with the conclusion VIII. 13, 14.

The correctness of this division is confirmed by the centralism which thus discloses itself in the longer groups. A study of the Hebrew psalms reveals the circumstance that it was one of the most favourite artifices of Hebrew poetry to distinguish the central verses of an ode or of a portion of an ode from the rest by some peculiarity of construction, thus directing attention to them as the verses in which was contained or implied the essence or leading thought of the whole. In the Song of Songs the central verses are correspondingly emphaticized by their enigmatical character and by their isolation in meaning from the context around them. This is manifestly the case with the two verses II. 15, IV. 6, which, as a computation of the verses will readily shew, form the centres of the second and third groups of the Song. The centre of the fifth group is in like manner marked by the isolated and highly enigmatical passage VI. 10—13; and hence if that group end at VIII. 4, it must needs begin, by the number of the verses, at V. 9. In the first group the central passage is I. 9—11; though it is, perhaps, not so strongly marked as in the second, third, and fifth groups. In the shorter groups alone, the fourth and sixth, there is no apparent centralism.

Certain relations, not entirely accidental, may moreover be observed between the lengths of the several groups. The first and third are of equal lengths: they contain each twenty-three verses. The second group, of fifteen verses, is as long as the fourth and sixth together; and the fifth, of thirty-eight verses, is exactly as long as the united first and second, or as the united second and third. Again, the fifth and sixth groups together are exactly twice as long as the first or as the third group. It was perhaps also intended that the concluding passage of the third group, IV. 12—V. 1, should stand out as the central passage of the entire Song; which (from I. 2 to VIII. 14) consists of one hundred and sixteen verses.

It will be seen from our commentary that the several groups have all their respective themes; which may here be conveniently set down beforehand. The theme of the first group is the anticipation of Christ's coming: the second represents the waiting for that blessed time: in the third he is arrived, and we have there the description of the espousal and its fruits. The fourth group delineates the subsequent bodily departure of the Bridegroom from his Bride; the fifth his spiritual presence with her; and the sixth their complete and final reunion.

§ 12.

An introduction to the Song of Songs would be defective without some endeavour to trace the historical basis on which its expectations partly rested, and the connexion of its prophetical announcements with the circumstances of the time at which it was written. As regards the former half of the Song the task is not difficult. The anticipations of the Messiah had throughout the earlier period of the Old Testament history been gradually increasing in definiteness. We read them in the promise to Abraham, and in the blessing of Jacob; in the inspired soothsaying of Balaam, and in the solemn declaration of Moses; in the song of Hannah; and, more determinately, in the promise to David through Nathan, and in the psalms composed by David subsequently to the utterance of that promise. They may be said to have culminated for a time in the joyous and triumphant Psalm LXXII, composed by Solomon on his accession to the throne of Israel; and they shone forth very brightly during the prosperous reign of Jehoshaphat in the glorious Psalm XLV, with which the Song of Songs is in much so closely allied. It was mainly from that psalm that the author of the Song drew the image of the nuptials which he so largely unfolded; and it is thus to the hopes which were cherished during Jehoshaphat's reign that the origin of the Song may, through Psalm XLV, be indirectly traced. The influence of the circumstances of that period shews itself markedly in one feature of the Song which it has in common with Psalm XLV. There is in it no direct prophetical exhibition of the sufferings of the future Messiah, or of the severe conflict which in his own person he should have to sustain[1]. His death is veiled under the symbolism of the myrrh, but it is not explicitly declared. Even in the magnificent delineation of his espousal of his Bride in III. 6—11, it is only the glories, not the bitterness, of his passion that are held up to our gaze. Those alone were prepared to receive the doctrine of a suffering Messiah who had themselves been humbled by God's chastening hand, and were penetrated by a deep sense of sin; and of this, during the reign of Jehoshaphat, we find but little trace. There

---

[1] Cf. part of an eloquent passage from Roos, as quoted by Delitzsch, p. 59: "Es wird der Sohn Gottes im Hohenlied als holdselig, freundlich, schön und herrlich beschrieben, aber das Geheimniss seines Kreuzes ist darin nicht deutlich geoffenbaret. Der Sohn Gottes wird König genannt, er wird als ein weidender Hirt, als ein Herr seines Weinbergs und Gartens, als ein Freund der Seelen, die seine Braut sind, und als ein milder Herr aller andern, die einigermassen mit ihm verbunden sind, vorgestellt, von seinem Priesterthum aber wird keine Meldung gethan."

are consequently throughout the Song no open indications of any struggle of Christ unto victory, of any triumph through the power of endurance, such as we find in the psalms of David. The secrets of the mountain of myrrh and of the hill of frankincense exist, but they are not disclosed; nor would it be suspected from a perusal of the Song alone that the crown wherewith the heavenly Bridegroom should be crowned of his earthly mother would be tendered by her to him in scorn, and that she would be but an unwilling agent in bringing out the fulness of glory which now through his endurance of her bitter persecutions rests for evermore upon him.

Shall we deem it a defect in the Song of Songs that it thus veils from our view all that is painful in the earthly career of the Beloved of whom it sings? Rather let us remember that every side of the truth cannot to the apprehension of man be brought out at once. If the Bible teaches us to weep with them that weep, it no less teaches us to rejoice with them that rejoice. There may be piety in gladness as well as in sorrow. And it is one result of the peculiar aspect in which the career of the Incarnate Son of God is in the Song of Songs presented to us, that all lawful earthly grandeur is thereby consecrated as the material type of the moral grandeur of what he accomplished; that so our natural taste for the magnificent may be not rudely cast aside as vain, but rather made a means of leading us to him whose name is above every name, and whose glories we may rightfully adore.

While however in the Song everything connected

with the coming of the Beloved is thus exhibited in unclouded splendour, it is not concealed that dark tribulations and anxious searchings must precede his approach. His advent shall be a summer's brightness, but a winter must first pass away: he shall be found at length by her who hath longed for him, but there must first be a season during which she shall seek him and find him not. Had the Song proceeded from Solomon, all reference to even these heavinesses would perhaps have been wanting; but they could not well be passed over by those who lived in Israel in the days of Ahab and his successors, or even by the singers of Judah after that a Jehoram and an Athaliah sat upon the throne of their father Jehoshaphat. Thenceforth the expectations of the golden days of the Messiah required an exercise of living faith; for many hearts were sick because of hope deferred. And in such living faith, without doubt, the Song of Songs was written; and by its comforts and encouragements we may well believe that many hearts were sustained.

Vivid nevertheless as is the picture contained in the first three sections, or earlier half, of the Song, it presents to us only those glories which older seers had in various ways also heralded. It far exceeds all previous prophecies in detail of delineation; yet there is hardly any essential feature in it which can be regarded as absolutely or strikingly new. With respect to the latter half of the Song the case is different. The distinctness with which it is there unfolded that the coming of the Messiah will not of itself be the final termination of all earthly expectation and **anxiety** is unparalleled not merely in all earlier Scripture, but throughout the whole of the Old Testament. Psalm II. had implied that the enthronement of the Son of God as king upon the holy hill of Zion should still be followed by conflicts with the rebellious and disobedient; but nowhere else in the Old Testament do we find a passage which speaks as Cant. v. 2—8 speaks of a withdrawal of the Messiah from the Church for whose salvation he has once appeared. If it be asked, How was such withdrawal foreknown? our first answer must needs be, that it pleased God to reveal it. Yet as divine revelations were never inopportunely made, the question still arises, Had the Poet been previously fitted by any historical teaching to accept such revelation, and to recognize the withdrawal which it announced?

One event then there was, unique of its kind, which, if the date that we have assigned to the Song be correct, would undoubtedly serve as the basis whereon the picture of the withdrawal of the Beloved Messiah might be reared. In the mysterious disappearance from earth of the prophet Elijah, the Christian Church still beholds the type of the subsequent ascension of the Saviour of the world into heaven. It was an event marked with unusual solemnity, not only by the manner in which it was divinely accomplished, but also by the communications which the sons of the prophets had previously received, that Elisha's master would that day be parted from him. It was an event moreover which could not fail to excite the deepest marvel; so that the sons of the prophets, notwithstanding the previous warning to them, and despite the remonstrances of Elisha, insisted on seeking for him who had disappeared; and for three days accordingly fifty of their number sought for him, "but found him not." The phrase used of this their unsuccessful search is, it may be observed, almost precisely that which recurs in the Song, as put into the mouth of the Bride after that her Beloved has departed, "I sought him, but I did not find him." Again, neither the removal of Elijah nor that of the Lord Jesus Christ from earth was intended as a judgment on those whom they quitted: in each case it was for the master's glory and for the disciples' welfare that he should depart. All things therefore being duly weighed, we can hardly tear the translation of Elijah and the passage Cant. v. 2—8 asunder; and if no subsequent prophecy unfolded further the teaching of that passage, it may with equal justice be remembered that no subsequent prophet of ancient days was parted from this world otherwise than by death.

That the Bridegroom who was to be thus outwardly withdrawn from his Bride would nevertheless be in some way present with her, strengthening her for all the earthly conflict which she should yet have to sustain; and that at the last they would be completely and eternally united;—these are truths the early announcement of which can, if the withdrawal itself were announced, excite no surprise. By whatever dispensations the pathway of salvation might be chequered, the prospect of full ultimate victory and blessing must remain unimpaired.

§ 13.

THERE is probably no part of Holy Scripture with which the great mass of educated Christians are now so little familiar as the Song of Songs. In the Church of England it is never publicly read; and the authoritative exclusion of it from the Calendar of Lessons leads naturally to the general avoidance of it by the clergy in their teaching. Many, probably, are well content to pass it thus by; and some who are not so content find a difficulty in preaching upon texts of Scripture of which the greater part of their audience are ignorant. The same lack of acquaintance with the book prevails also doubtless among other Protestant communities. Thus we find the nonconformist expositor, Matthew Henry, speaking in his preface of those who rarely read this book, and in a tone which seems to imply that he himself was one of that number. In our own day Prof. Moses Stuart, writing from the point of view of an American Congregationalist, holds that general usage among the more intelligent Christians has decided against occupying their public or family devotions with such parts of the Old Testament Scriptures as this; and even urges that it should be altogether withdrawn from ordinary use.

It is by no means plain how far this depreciation of the practical value of the book can plead the sanction of Christian antiquity. We find Theodore of Mopsuestia asserting, indeed, that it was never publicly read[1]; nor

---

[1] Ap. Concil. Constant. II. See Labbé, v. p. 453.

do the oldest lectionaries exhibit any lessons taken from it and appropriated to particular occasions. On the other hand, in the days before lectionaries existed, we find it enumerated in the decrees of councils as one of the books which were to be generally read in churches[1]; nor was the discretion of the clergy fettered in choosing their lessons from it. We find Augustine interrupting the course of his sermons on the Gospel of St John, in order to unfold the meaning of a passage in the Song which seemed to him to illustrate a passage in that Gospel[2]. Moreover, the many commentaries which were written upon it, and the frequent references to it in the patristic literature, shew that it could not have been so strongly eschewed as is now the case. When, for instance, Ambrose makes use at considerable length of its language to eulogize the character of the emperor Valentinian (whether wisely and rightly or no we need not now enquire), it is plain that his procedure implies a familiarity with that language on the part of the people at large whom he was addressing. The Song of Songs must in short in some measure have served to the ancient Church not as a book to excite curiosity, but as spiritual food and sustenance: the extreme neglect which it now receives is of comparatively modern date.

Those who desire to shut up the Song of Songs to the people at large seldom fail to quote in their favour the Jewish custom which forbade the reading of it to any under thirty years of age. To such-like maxims

---

[1] See Bingham, Book XIV. Sec. 15.
[2] In Joannis Evang. Tract. LVII.

however of the Jewish doctors too much weight must not be attached. The same prohibition extended to the opening chapters of the Book of Genesis: the very chapters of the Old Testament which are probably, by many Christians of the present day, put the earliest into children's hands.

The pleas that have been urged for avoidance of the Song may be reduced to two; viz. the difficulty of understanding it, and the immoral tendency which, it is alleged, would wait on any general perusal of it. The former of these, it may be safely asserted, arises in no slight degree from the lack of general acquaintance with it. The Christian Fathers, who read it more, understood it, in spite of all the drawbacks of their imperfection of scholarship, far better than we. A comparatively slender key to its meaning, such as a general traditional interpretation would supply, would render it more easily intelligible than a large part of the Prophets. The true remedy for ignorance of its meaning is that the Song itself should be more generally read.

The other plea would carry more force were it possible to banish love between the sexes entirely from the world, or at least from among the youthful. But while the tendency to such love exists (and that it was designed for a blessing we cannot doubt), the true office of religion must surely be not to ignore it, but to purify and refine it. What means can be deemed more efficacious for this end than to set before it the heavenly ideal to which it must strive to conform? The theme, no doubt, must be delicately and reverently handled, not rudely profaned. But in this it stands not alone among the themes which Holy Scripture brings before us. The story of the incarnation and wondrous birth of our blessed Saviour involves details which most would refrain from making the topics of easy and familiar conversation; yet which few would on that account desire to expunge from the public reading of the gospel-narrative. It is, as a general rule, with reverent solemnity, that such themes are practically listened to even by the thoughtless and careless; a holy teaching is conveyed by them which, though not lightly repeated from lip to lip, is nevertheless felt and appreciated; and though the danger of possible abuse exists, it should not deter us from opening out to the use of all that which God has provided for our spiritual comfort and edification.

To maintain that some will be better prepared to profit by the reading of the Song of Songs than others, is but to maintain that which in a lower degree is true of the entire Scriptures. Personal holiness of life will always remain the first and greatest requisite to the due appreciation of it. But when it is therefore sought to confine the use of it to the "few that have reached the lofty heights of a Baxter or an Edwards," we cannot fail to remark the similarity of the argument to that by which some have defended the withholding of the entire Scriptures from the great mass of the people. There seems, no doubt, at first sight, a gain in withholding from them that which they may wrest unto their own destruction. But experience has shewn the evil of such procedure. In locking up the word of danger we of necessity lock up also the word of life; and are thus led into direct opposition to the spirit of our Saviour's teaching, "Freely ye have received, freely give." We cannot lay a practical interdict on the perusal of any book of Scripture without thereby inflicting a grievous injustice on many to whom it might be of the highest profit. The Church must needs publicly offer to all the treasures of her writings equally with the treasures of her sacraments, if she would not incur the responsibility of shutting out from the enjoyment of them those for whom they were designed.

What seems to be really needed is that the special solemnity of that which is specially solemn should be publicly marked. For this the Church has surely the means of providing. Those who regret the entire exclusion of the Song of Songs from the Church-calendar of Lessons would not necessarily desire that it should be read through in regular course, like other books, at ordinary seasons; nor yet is it absolutely needful that it should be read in its entirety. Its theme evidently imparts to it a festal character: let that which itself is festal be appropriated to festal occasions. Furthermore let, if possible, the occasions on which it is read be such as of themselves to throw light upon its meaning. The two opening chapters of the Song would be far better suited in every way to the festival of the Annunciation than the two chapters taken in course from the apocryphal book of Ecclesiasticus, which are assigned to that day in our present Calendar. The latter part of the third chapter (6—11) might in like manner be read on one of the days in Passion-week. It is in this same general spirit that some have fittingly desired to connect the teaching of the Song of Songs with the seasons of administration of the Holy Communion. Indications of this may be found in some of Dr Watts' hymns drawn from the Song. The eminent German preacher Dr Krummacher, in one of his sermons on the Song (seventh edition, p. 146), says, "It seems to me indeed as though the Song of Songs were adapted by special pre-eminence for our Church sacramental meditations; nor am I the first to entertain this view. The communion-hymn 'O Fels des Heils,' which we so justly love, flowed almost entirely, verse for verse, in regard both of contents and of form, out of the Song of Songs." It need scarcely be added that the festal use of the Song in church would give its tone to the spirit in which it would be approached in private; and that this is precisely what we ought to desire.

In the following translation of the Song it has been deemed proper to indicate the different speakers, viz. the Beloved (or Bridegroom), the Bride, and the Chorus of the Daughters of Jerusalem. The reasons for assigning any passage to any particular speaker will, when not immediately apparent, be generally found in the Commentary. In designating the speakers, the term Bride has been employed throughout for the sake of convenience: it is not however strictly applicable till the Third Section, nor is it found till then in the Song itself. This the reader is respectfully requested to remember.

The numbering of the chapters and verses is, throughout this volume, that of the English Bible, in which Chapter VI. extends one verse further than in the Hebrew. Our VI. 13 is the Hebrew VII. 1: our VII. 1—13 is the Hebrew VII. 2—14. Neither in the English nor in the Hebrew do the chapters correspond with the natural divisions of the Song.

The Song of Songs, which is of Solomon.

THE ANTICIPATION.

I. 2—II. 7.

Von Anfang, da die Welt gemacht,
Hat manches Herz nach dir gewacht;
Dich hat gehofft so lange Jahr
Der Väter und Propheten Schaar.
GERHARD.

2 *Bride.* Let him kiss me of the kisses of his mouth;
  For better is thy love than wine.
3 Goodly for odour are thy ointments:
  As ointment thou art, by thy name, poured forth:
  Therefore do the virgins love thee.
4 Draw thou me! Let us run after thee!
  The king hath brought me into his chambers:
  Be we glad, and rejoice we in thee,
  Let us remember thy love more than wine:
  The upright love thee.
5 Black am I, yet comely, O daughters of Jerusalem;
  As the tents of Kedar, as the curtains of Solomon.
6 Look not disdainfully on me that I am dark,
  That the sun hath fiercely scanned me:
  My mother's sons have been angry with me,
  They have made me the keeper of the vineyards:
  My vineyard, that which is mine own, I have not kept.
7 Tell me, O thou whom my soul loveth:
  Where feedest thou thy flock, where restest it at noon?
  For why should I be as 'a veiled one by the flocks of thy companions?
8 *Chorus.* If thou knowest not, O fairest among women,

Go thy way forth in the footsteps of the flock,
And feed thy kids beside the shepherds' tents.

9 *Beloved.* To the steeds in the chariots of Pharaoh
Have I compared thee, my love:
10 Comely are thy cheeks in the circlet,
Thy neck in the necklace:
11 A circlet of gold will we make thee
With studs of silver.

12 *Bride.* While that the king at his table sitteth
Sendeth forth my nard its fragrance.
13 A bundle of myrrh is my beloved unto me
Which resteth in my bosom.
14 A cluster of henna is my beloved unto me
From the gardens of Engedi.

15 *Beloved.* Behold thou art fair, my love,
Behold thou art fair, thine eyes are doves.
16 *Bride.* Behold thou art fair, my beloved, yea lovely,
Also verdant is our couch:
17 The beams of our house are cedars,
Our boardings are firs.

II. 1 I am the daisy of the meadow,
The lily of the valleys.
2 *Beloved.* As the lily among the thorns
So is my love among the damsels.

3 *Br.* As the citron-tree among the trees of the wood,
So is my beloved among the youths:
In his shade I sat down with delight,
And his fruit was sweet to my taste.
4 He brought me into the banqueting house,
And love was his banner over me.
5 Strengthen me with grape-cakes, strew me with
 citron-leaves,
For I am sick with love!
6 His left hand shall be under my head,
And his right hand shall embrace me.
7 I adjure you by the gazelles, or the hinds of the fells,
O daughters of Jerusalem,
That ye upstir not and that ye disturb not
The play of love, till it will it.

The first section of the Song, I. 2—II. 7, contains the Anticipation of the Beloved's presence. It consists of twenty-three verses. The central three verses are I. 12—14: they are enclosed by two other well-marked portions of three verses each, I. 9—11, 15—17.

Vv. 2—4. *Let him kiss me,* &c. The Church of Israel desires the very presence of her Saviour. She had, as the Greek Fathers express it, been instructed and wooed through the messages of prophets, as Moses and Samuel: she desired now that her promised Messiah should pour into her mouth words from his own mouth:

she desired to hear him speaking, and to behold him teaching, and to handle with her hands of the Word of life. *Than wine.* Wine "maketh glad the heart of man": the love of Christ, once manifested, should be to the heart a source of far deeper gladness. *Goodly for odour are thy ointments, &c.* It has been deemed proper, in translating, to abide by the received Hebrew text, which is upheld by the Syriac version and the Targum. Little confidence can however be placed in its correctness. The LXX. have καὶ ὀσμὴ μύρων σου ὑπὲρ πάντα τὰ ἀρώματα; while Jerome, translating rather freely, gives *fragrantia unguentis optimis.* Neither of these agrees with the Hebrew: moreover the Hebrew words לריח שמניך טובים are of very awkward construction, nor can the text represented by the Greek well have sprung from them. What if the original reading were לריח שמני קטורים "Like as the scent which cometh from incenses," "art thou, even thy name, as ointment poured forth"? From this all the other texts can be easily derived. Those of Jerome and of the Hebrew editors would be obtained by the alteration of ק into מ or ב (note the evident uncertainty with regard to this letter) and the annexation of it to the preceding word, and by the consequent change of the unmeaning טורים into טובים. In the Hebrew text of the LXX, the same words would be corrupted and amplified into וריח שמניך מני קטורים. But the mistake here in respect of the first letter was afterwards perceived; and for καὶ ὀσμὴ μύρων σου was noted, either in the margin of a Greek MS. or in a column of Origen's Hexapla, the correction εἰς ὀσμὴν μύρων σου, which was subsequently dragged by a transcriber into the Greek text, but inserted by him in the wrong place, viz. in ver. 4[1]. The strongest commendation of the Hebrew reading now submitted for trial as the original is the homœophony it exhibits between the etymologically unconnected words שְׁמָנֶי, שֶׁמֶן, and שְׁמֶךָ, and also between תּוּרַק and קְטוּרִים (the latter being strictly the past participle from קטר, used in the Piel and Hiphil). Such homœophony is in full accordance with the genius of Hebrew poetry: we have a remarkable instance of it in IV. 2, שֶׁכֻּלָּם and וְשַׁכֻּלָה: see also IV. 4; VI. 2; VII. 2 (3); VIII. 6. Our E. V. rendering of the verse before us is necessarily inadmissible; for תּוּרַק cannot, as the 3rd pers. fem., agree with שֵׁם, which is masculine. *Thy name.* The name of God is, in Scripture, the manifestation of God in his dealings with men, and above all, with his chosen people; for it is by those dealings that he has made himself known to them, and it is in that by which a person is known that the essence of his name consists. The name of the Messiah, at the time that this Song was written, constituted itself out of the prophetic declarations of what he as the future Ruler, Prophet, and Saviour of Israel should at his coming accomplish. To him were all the hopes of Israel directed:

---

[1] A similar explanation is to be given of the words ἐπὶ τὰ ὄρη Βαιθήλ in II. 9, which have no claim to a place there, but are evidently intended as a correction of the ὄρη κοιλωμάτων in II. 17.

witness the prophecies of Jacob and Moses, the song of Hannah, the promise by Nathan, and the psalms of David and Solomon. There may also be in this passage a reference, as Bossuet remarks, to the circumstance that the name Messiah signifies Anointed. *The virgins.* The mention of the virgins, at the very outset of this Song, as the lovers of the Bridegroom, precludes any other than an allegorical interpretation. The same conclusion follows from such alternations of the singular and plural, *me — us*, as that which we have in the next verse, and on which it will be sufficient here once for all to remark. The virgins are in effect identical with the Bride: they represent in their severalty the communities and individuals of whom the Church consists, while the Bride is the Church in her ideal entirety. The same remark applies to Psalm XLV, where, moreover, the mere external distinction between the virgins and the Bride is greater than in this Song, the former there appearing as the attendants of the latter. *Draw thou me.* An anticipation of the great Christian doctrine that it is Christ who must draw us unto himself; and this both by his name, i. e. by the display of his love, cf. Joh. XII. 32, "I, if I be lifted up from the earth,"—on the cross,—" will draw all men unto me;" and also by the gracious influence of his Spirit, cf. Joh. VI. 44. *The king.* This title, as Origen rightly judges, is here made prominent in order to shew the richness of the chambers into which the Bride is brought. *Hath brought me.* The prophetic preterite: the Bride anticipates the time when she should be brought. *Into his chambers*. In other words, he hath made known to me the riches of his grace: see especially Eph. I—III. And this again in two ways: first by his own personal presence in the flesh on earth, Matth. XIII. 17; and secondly by the teaching of his Spirit, 1 Cor. II. 10. It is in a king's chambers that his costliest treasures are to be seen. *Be we glad, &c.* For the honour put upon them, in the close intercourse with Christ into which they have been admitted. *The upright love thee.* This interprets the last line of the preceding verse, "the virgins love thee." The "upright" and the "virgins" are one and the same.

Vv. 5, 6. The Church describes her own present state. *O daughters of Jerusalem.* The daughters of Jerusalem come before us again in II. 7; III. 5, 10; v. 8, 16; VIII. 4. The exact phrase is not found elsewhere in the Old Testament. It is evidently of importance that we should determine whom the Daughters of Jerusalem represent. Origen took them for the rejected Jews, the daughters of the Jerusalem that "now is, and is in bondage with her children"; "enemies" "as concerning the gospel," but "as touching the election, beloved for the fathers' sakes"; but looking with disdain on the new Gentile Church. This view is unsustained by sufficient proof; and it does not harmonize with the early period at which the Song of Songs was written. On the other hand, Hengstenberg supposes the Daughters of Jerusalem to be the Gentile nations, allying themselves as spiritual daughters to Jerusalem their mother-church. In support of this he refers mainly to Ezek.

XVI. 61 and Psalm LXXXVII. But these are both of later date than the Song of Songs, and could not therefore have furnished the foundation on which the imagery of the latter rested; while neither do they recall it with sufficient definiteness to be accepted as interpretations of it. The circumstance that the phrase "daughters of Jerusalem" is confined in the Old Testament to the Song of Songs will lead us to seek the explanation of it primarily from the Song itself. Now in six of the seven passages in which they are here mentioned, they plainly play the part of spectators of what is otherwise passing: they are in short strictly the chorus of the drama, the visible exponents of the feelings of the audience. The reason of their appearance in III. 10, where the same is not so manifestly the case, may be best considered when we arrive at that passage. Guided by the other six passages, we shall properly assume them to be the members of the Church of Israel in their contemplative capacity; not necessarily different persons, in their outer being, from the virgins of ver. 3, but yet representing them in a different point of view, with reference solely to their intelligent and emotional survey of what is passing, and without regard to their own spiritual state. Any allusion to the latter would have required that they should be styled not Daughters of Jerusalem, but Daughters of Zion; the fundamental difference between the terms Jerusalem and Zion being that the one denotes only the inhabited city, the other the seat of the Lord's presence. For the sake of variety they are, of course, interchangeable, but where the one term is definitely and systematically preferred to the other, its strict import should be observed. The above explanation of the "daughters of Jerusalem" is thoroughly confirmed by Our Blessed Saviour's use of the phrase in the only other passage of Scripture in which it meets us, Luke XXIII. 28. He was addressing the company of people that followed him with lamentation to Calvary: "Daughters of Jerusalem, weep not for me, but weep for yourselves and for your children." Such words from him who knew all hearts shew plainly that their grief was not of the highest order: it was the grief of passionate excitement rather than of spiritual anguish; the grief of spectators who felt a natural and spontaneous sympathy with the sorrows which it was their lot to witness, but not necessarily of believers who recked that those sorrows were fraught to themselves with deep and lasting interest. And it may be well to bear in mind that it is possible to survey, as Daughters of Jerusalem, the loving intercourse of the Bridegroom and Bride, possible to peruse the Song of Songs with an outward appreciation of its various beauties, without being truly drawn, as virgins, to him who must, if loved at all, be loved in the spirit. *As the tents of Kedar, as the curtains of Solomon.* That is, I am black as the one, yet comely as the other. They stand in mutual contrast, like the blackness and the comeliness in the preceding line. The descendants of Kedar, one of the sons of Ishmael, were probably among the Arabs with whom the Israelites were best acquainted. The special mention of them here is particularly appropriate, because the name Kedar signifies *black*. The blackness of their tents mainly arose from their being covered either with goatskins, or with cloths of goats' hair. In such materials there is an appearance of gloominess, but no essential deformity; and accordingly blackness is here the emblem of tribulation, not (as it has been too generally taken) of sin. The following verse will more fully explain this. Respecting any curtains of Solomon we have no details. It may be that we are simply to assume them to be some definite hangings of great beauty and richness; the curtains, for example, of a palanquin, such as that in which in III. 6—11 the heavenly Solomon is represented as approaching. On the other hand, the meaning may be that darkness and loveliness might co-exist, even as in tent-hangings, which notwithstanding their sombreness of hue, were yet for richness and costliness worthy of a Solomon. *That the sun hath fiercely scanned me.* The sun, from its scorching power, is used in various passages of Scripture as the emblem of tribulation: see Psalm CXXI. 6; Isaiah XLIX. 10; Matth. XIII. 6; Rev. VII. 16. *My mother's sons.* The Mother of the Bride is here the nation of Israel. As it was through the medium of the national institutions of the Israelites that their churchly character was brought to light, and on their national unity that their privileged pre-eminence as the elect of God rested, the Church might be not improperly represented as the daughter of the nation. The mother's sons will then evidently be the several members of the nation, from the king, his nobles, and his officers, downwards, viewed however only in their civil dealings, in their relation to the State, not in their relation to the Church. For this reason the Bride, although she calls them her mother's sons, abstains from speaking of them as her brethren: their immediate relation to herself does not come under consideration. We must in analysing the imagery of this Song refrain from extending its details, and from drawing inferences which, inasmuch as they would be unsuited to his purpose, the author of the Song has avoided. *Have been angry with me.* We have in this passage one important clue for the determination of the date at which the Song was written; and upon this subject we have already spoken in the Introduction. The starting-point of those civil proceedings of the Israelites whereby the Church had so grievously suffered was the rebellion of the ten tribes against the sovereignty of the house of David. Upon this had followed the erection of the rival kingdom, with its own separate head; and then upon this the measures whereby Jeroboam had made Israel to sin: the public establishment of idolatry at Dan and at Bethel, instituted with the avowed object of preventing the resort of the people to the mountain where the Lord had fixed the seat of his presence; the unauthorized consecration of a new body of priests to minister in the high places; and the ordinance of a new feast in the place of those enjoined by the law of Moses. On the accession of Ahab to the throne, and his alliance with the Tyrian Jezebel, yet worse had succeeded, the public sanction of the worship of Baal. And although, in respect of this latter, a general reformation had been made by the remorseless severity of Jehu, yet the sins originally introduced by Jeroboam still held their way with unabated power: Israel still kept aloof from the courts of Zion, and the worship which the Lord had enjoined was still publicly disregarded. Which things being so, the Church of Israel might well complain of the treatment she had received from the rulers and princes of the nation. *They have made me the keeper of the vineyards: my vineyard, that which is mine own, I have not kept.* The vineyard, the enclosed and cultivated plat within the limits of which lie the scenes of the vine-dresser's labour, represents the organized sphere in which the ministrations of the Church are to move. Had the Church been doing the work entrusted to her in the way ordained and enjoined of God, had she been nurturing the religious life of Israel from her own appointed metropolis on Mount Zion, she would then, in the language of the Song, have been keeping her own vineyard. But from this the political condition of the nation had hindered her. Israel would not come up to worship in the courts of Zion. And therefore the Church must find for herself other means, adapted to the special exigencies of the times, of labouring in the holy cause; and the means on which she lit consisted in the establishment of colleges of holy disciples, "the sons of the prophets," at different centres in the kingdom of the ten tribes, to act as unobtrusive nurseries of piety, and to minister instruction in God's law, as opportunity might offer, to the districts around. The spheres of action of these several centres of religious life were the vineyards in which the Church was now toiling, being no longer able to cultivate to its full extent the vineyard originally assigned her. We read of such colleges at Bethel, at Jericho, and at Gilgal (2 Kings II. 3, 5; IV. 38). They had doubtless been principally established through the zeal of Elijah and Elisha. Earlier germs of them have been sometimes traced in the days of Samuel; but it is doubtful whether the prophetical companies of his time continued to exist through the reigns of David and Solomon, when all the organization of religious ministry and worship was concentrated at Jerusalem. It has, in the Introduction, been already observed, that it was probably from a member of one of the prophetical colleges that the present Song proceeded. There is much interest in comparing the interpretation given of this passage by Cassiodorus and Bede. They take the "vineyard" of the primitive Christian Church at Jerusalem: the "vineyards," of the many churches which were planted abroad in consequence of the dispersion to which the persecution of the church at Jerusalem gave rise. This interpretation, as it stands, is not admissible, for two reasons: first, because its point of view belongs to the history of the New Testament, not of the Old; and secondly, because that multiplication of the vineyards of which the Bride speaks in the Song is evidently to her a theme of mourning, rather than of rejoicing: she has lost the vineyard which she most prized. Still the interpretation harmonizes in some respects so remarkably, and yet so undesignedly, with ours, that it does, in effect, substantially confirm it.

Vv. 7, 8. The Church longs for her Saviour's presence; and this all the more, because of her present comparatively forlorn condition. *Tell me, O thou, &c.* She apostrophizes her promised Lord. *Where feedest thou thy flock, where restest it at noon?* The force of the question lies in the "where": she desires to find and to behold the object of her love. As for the rest, she knows that the office of Christ will be both to sustain and to refresh his people; in other words, to feed them, and to rest them. These are two main parts of the shepherd's task. Noon is mentioned simply as the season of rest; the season, when, in the heat of the day, rest for the sheep is necessary. Others, as Cassiodorus, press it to symbolize the heat of persecution or temptation. Observe that although the Church had not yet beheld her Beloved, she nevertheless represents him as already engaged in his pastoral work. *Why should I be as a veiled one?* That is, Why should I be forced to wear the semblance of a harlot (cf. Gen. XXXVIII. 14, 15), wandering about to seek for a lover when there is none that beareth any genuine love to me? The whole period of the schism, from the days of Rehoboam to those of Hezekiah, was, more especially among the ten tribes, a bitter time of trial for the Church of Israel. The severance of the ten tribes from the dominion of the house of David, from which house it had been declared that the Messiah should spring, made all the promises of a Messiah appear delusive and visionary; and in longing after her promised Saviour the Church seemed like a wanderer, sighing after one that had no existence. Various interpretations have been given of the word עְטִיָה, but on the whole *veiled*, as explained above, seems the most probable. *By the flocks of thy companions.* The companions or fellows of Christ (cf. Psalm XLV. 7) are the false shepherds of Israel (cf. Ezek. XXXIV.); oppressive rulers, self-consecrated priests, lying teachers. So, substantially, Cassiodorus and Justus Orgelitanus, who, following Augustine, take them of the heretics "qui gregem deceptorum hominum sibi aggregant." It was by such, and by their flocks, i.e. by those under their influence, that the Church, when she came in contact with them, was liable to be mocked and despised. *If thou knowest not, &c.* Some take this as the reply of Christ himself. But it may with more dramatic propriety be regarded as the wholesome counsel of the Chorus of the Daughters of Jerusalem, through whom, as in the Greek drama, the author utters the lessons which he himself desires directly to enforce. *Go thy way forth in the footsteps of the flock.* The way in which the Church must look and watch for her promised Lord is by diligently and patiently pursuing meanwhile her own proper work. Her flock had strayed from her: she must not on that account abandon it, but must rather follow after it, to the end that she may recover it. Most interpreters explain these words of following in the exemplary footsteps of the righteous that have gone before; but they thus separate the flock of the present clause from the kids of the next, whom it is the office of the Church to feed. *Beside the shepherds' tents.* That is, beside the tents of the false shepherds, of whom the fair one had spoken in the preceding verse, and whose rude gibes and contemptuous looks she keenly felt. Even in the presence of such rudeness and contempt, she must still labour on at the charge assigned her: if her kids had strayed to the evil shepherds' tents, even by those tents she must not hesitate to seek them: she must not shrink from encountering wickedness if only so she may win back the unwary to the truth: like Elijah she must not fear to stand before Ahab, like Amos she must, despite the threats of Amaziah the priest, continue to lift up her voice at Bethel, if only so she may turn the heart of the children to the fathers, and may tend, even in the dark and cloudy day, the kids for whom she is responsible.

Vv. 9—11. These and the six following verses, which form altogether the centre-piece of the first portion of the Song, do not follow in strict dramatical sequence upon what had preceded. They are rather to be taken by themselves, as a picture of the inner intercourse of the Church and Christ. In the midst of her loneliness and sorrows, which the preceding dramatic passage had exhibited to us, the Church has a gracious vision of Christ's succouring love; which accordingly stands in the same relation to what had gone before as the communion of an individual soul with Christ does to the man's outward history. *To the steeds in the chariots of Pharaoh have I compared thee.* As regards the לססתי, the word סס is here collective; and the י is paragogic. The words are those of Christ addressing the Church. The general sense is: Notwithstanding thy apparent loneliness and distress, divine might from on high so waits upon thy watchings and thy efforts, that thou mayest compare and successfully compete with the proudest array of worldly force. Horses were, in the sacred language of the Old Testament, one of the standard symbols of worldly, and therefore presumptuous, strength. It had in Deut. XVII. 16 been commanded that whenever the Israelites should have a king over them like the nations round about, he should refrain from furnishing himself with a multitude of horses; and in particular, that he should not "cause the people to return to Egypt, to the end that he should multiply horses." The remembrance of this, and also of the fact that the strength of the Pharaoh of the Exodus had been displayed in his horses, chariots and horsemen (Exod. XIV. 9, 17, 23), naturally gave rise to the associations which the mention of horses subsequently suggested. Hence the continual repudiation in the Old Testament of trust in horses for safety: cf. Psalm XX. 7; XXXIII. 17; CXLVII. 10; Prov. XXI. 31; Isaiah XXXI. 1; Hosea I. 7. *Comely are thy cheeks in the circlet.* "The circlet or coiffure here intended was probably similar in character to the modern Persian head-dress; which is described as consisting of two or three rows of pearls, worn round the head, beginning on the forehead, and descending down the cheek and under the chin, so that the face seems, as it were, set in pearls." (Olearius, ap. Harmer's Outlines, p. 205.) It is rightly observed by Ainsworth and Hengstenberg, that in the word תורים, used in this and the following verse, and signifying literally strings or rows of beads or the like, there is an allusive reference to the word תורה "law," with which it is etymologically connected. The same thing was evident to the Targumist. It was the Law, the Commandments of her God, that formed the distinguishing glory of the Church of Israel: cf. Deut. IV. 5—8. It is that Law with all its varied provisions that is here represented under the two images of a circlet and a necklace. Like a row of many beads, in that all its ordinances fitted on the one to the other; like a chain of many links, in that all its precepts contributed to its restraining force, it was at once an ornament and a bond. And it must be remembered that at the date of the composition of this Song, the Law itself remained, in all its integrity, the precious heirloom of the Church of Israel; and however much its various provisions might be slighted or set at nought by the members of the nation, the Church in her deepest needs had still the treasure in her possession, a criterion by which she might recognize the truth, and a fountain whence she might draw her rills of instruction. Various passages in the Proverbs have been adduced in illustration of the imagery under which the Law is here represented. So Prov. I. 8, 9; "My son, hear the instruction of thy father, and forget not the law of thy mother: for they shall be an ornament of grace unto thy head, and chains about thy neck." Similarly III. 3, 22; IV. 9; VI. 21. Compare the ordinance in Deut. VI. 8. And all these prepared the way for the more elaborate passage Ezek. XVI. 11, 12, in which is described God's early mercy to Israel in adorning her with the precepts of the Law. *A circlet of gold will we make thee with studs of silver.* The glories which the Church had displayed in the days of the old dispensation were to be exchanged for higher glories under the new. So in Isaiah LX. 17, "For brass I will bring gold, and for iron I will bring silver." The handwriting of ordinances, written and engraven in stones, was to give place to the perfect law of liberty, written by the Spirit on the fleshy tables of the heart. The Targumist explains this verse, equally with the preceding, of the Law given by Moses at Sinai: he knew not that in his day the glory of that law had already become dim by the side of "the glory that excelleth," 2 Cor. III. 10. All through the sacred period of their history, as this Song shews, the Israelitish people had viewed the glories put upon them as but the preludes and earnests of something better: it was not till they had finally rejected their promised Messiah, the Lord of glory, that they came to view the Mosaic dispensation as perfect in itself, and so to invest it with praises which it had never really claimed.

Vv. 12—14. The central verses of the first portion of the Song. The Church, cheered by spiritual communion with her promised Lord, testifies how all-precious he is to her. *While that the king at his table sitteth.* The table is the symbol of the communion betwixt Christ and his people; and this symbolism, easy of comprehension from the first, has been now permanently and definitively fixed by Christ himself in the ordinance of the Lord's supper. It was seated with his disciples at the table that he enjoyed his last solemn intercourse with them before his death; and to partake at his table of the appointed tokens of his body and blood is for ever in the Christian Church the highest outward act of communion with him. It is implied moreover that at his table Christ spiritually feeds his Church with his word and his graces. It was at the conclusion of his last supper with his apostles that the fullest promises were given of the presence of the Comforter to abide with them for ever. *Sendeth forth my nard its fragrance.* By the nard of the Church are signified "the sweet-smelling fruits of repentance, faith, love, prayer, thanksgiving, &c. which the Church sheweth forth by the communion of Christ with her." Here too the symbolism of the Song of Songs was outwardly acted, as is recorded in the Gospels, in the earthly life of the Lord Jesus, and is also permanently embodied in the worship of the Christian Church. It was while he sat at table that the feet of our Saviour were, on two separate occasions, anointed; and it may be added that if the one anointing, that in Luke VII. 36—50, represented more especially the offering of repentance, the other, that in Joh. XII. 3 seqq. &c. represented emphatically the offering of the pure communion of love. And it is in the celebration of the Lord's supper that the Church still most solemnly presents her sacrifice of praise and thanksgiving which she beseeches God of his fatherly goodness to accept. *A bundle of myrrh, &c.* As a bundle of myrrh, treasured up for its fragrance in the bosom (the Hebrew phrase "between the breasts" signifies no more than this), such is Christ to all that receive him, and to the Church generally. He dwells in their hearts by faith. It must be further noted that myrrh is the emblem of death; and it was as a sacrifice to God that Christ gave himself for us for a sweet-smelling savour. Cassiodorus: "Fasciculus myrrhæ dilectus meus mihi factus est, quia propter me mortuus et sepultus est...In cordis mei memoria æternaliter habebitur, et nunquam tantorum ejus beneficiorum obliviscar." *A cluster of henna.* "Henna is an Egyptian shrub, not unlike to our privet, nursed by the Easterns with great diligence for the sake of its sweet-smelling flowers. These are of a pale yellow colour, and stand in spikes of the length of a span, but not very close, so that leaves appear between them: they smell somewhat like musk. The leaves of the plant are extensively used for staining the hair and the nails red. The plant has to be warmly protected during the winter, as it cannot endure the frost; and it is frequently watered with soapsuds or manured with lime in order to make it earlier sprout, which it would not naturally do before August." (Rauwolff, ap. Harmer's Outlines, p. 220.) The Hebrew word for this plant, כפר, signifies also ransom, propitiation; of which the henna accordingly becomes the emblem. Thus as the last verse had testified of the preciousness to the Church of Christ's death, so this testifies of the preciousness of the redemption wrought by his death. *From the gardens of*

Engedi. Engedi, a spot of remarkable and luxuriant fertility on the generally barren western shore of the Dead Sea, was known for its palms and its balsam. The mention of it here seems to be mainly intended to express, in a lively manner, the richness of the henna to which the Bride compares her Beloved.

Vv. 15—17. The Bride and her Beloved address each other. *Behold thou art fair, my love.* Christ speaks the first. It is almost needless to observe that it is the spiritual beauty of the Church that he here commends. In what this spiritual beauty consists, the succeeding words shew. *Thine eyes are doves.* So again, IV. 1. The dove is the emblem of meek innocence and peaceful love: the eye is the symbol of joy. The source therefore of the beauty of the Church is that it is in peaceful love to Christ that her joy consists. In simplicity of mind she looks to Christ alone for life and salvation: on him rest all her hopes and all her desires; and this direction of her whole soul to him constitutes her beauty. *Behold thou art fair, my beloved, yea, lovely.* The Church replies. She assigns the reason why all her thoughts are directed to him. Cf. Psalm XLV. 2; Isaiah XXXIII. 17. *Also verdant is our couch.* The couch is the symbol of the union of the Bridegroom and the Bride. Its verdure or freshness denotes therefore the freshness of delight with which the Bridegroom and the Bride are both continually attracted the one toward the other. Each never ceases to commend the other's fairness: in the eyes of the Church Christ is permanently and unfadingly lovely, and on him never palls the charm of her continual devotion to him. *The beams of our house are cedars, our boardings firs.* It is a matter of controversy whether the ברוש, for which ברות is merely a dialectic variation, represents the fir or the cypress. We may, till the matter be decided, adhere for convenience' sake to the received rendering; but there can be little doubt that the tree was one whose wood was held in some esteem. It grew upon Lebanon, and was reckoned one of the ornaments of that range (Isaiah XXXVII. 24; LX. 13); and, along with the cedar, was used in the construction of the temple (1 Kings V. 8, 10; VI. 15, 34). In this last circumstance must be sought the key to the interpretation of the passage before us. The temple was the standing outward embodiment of the presence of God with his people. The permanence of the union of Christ with his Church might accordingly be symbolized by the imagery of a building bearing a certain relation to the temple, and constructed of similar materials. In order however to testify not only to the established permanence but also to the continual living freshness of the union, the poet describes the building as framed not merely of the wood of the trees which Lebanon supplied, but of the trees themselves; and this the more appropriately, since, as Hengstenberg remarks, both the trees were evergreens.

II. 1—7. The glow of the preceding verses does not altogether fade from what succeeds; nor does the dialogue between the Bridegroom and the Bride altogether cease. Yet on the whole the verses on which we now enter, instead of delineating the actual bliss of communion between the Church and her Lord, describe rather the feelings with which the former surveyed it. *I am the daisy of the meadow, the lily of the valleys.* The Church modestly disclaims for herself all pretensions to native dignity or splendour: the humblest flowers, set in their own lowly places, are the meetest emblems of her. The first-named of the two flowers, הבצלת, has been occasionally, and perhaps rightly, identified with the autumn crocus, or meadow-saffron. The word שרון, meadow, has been frequently treated as a proper name, Sharon; and if this be allowed, it is not without reason that Hengstenberg takes עמקים, valleys, as a proper name also, explaining it of the valley of the Jordan. But the word is not elsewhere, in the plural, applied to that valley; and the better course therefore seems to be to take both terms in the verse as common nouns. *As the lily among the thorns, &c.* Christ replies. He accepts the comparison which the Church had drawn of herself: it is just in her resemblance to the lily that her true beauty is discerned; the beauty of modesty, purity, and grace. And this all the more when she is contrasted with those in the midst of whom, like the lily among the thorns, she is often set. Thorns are the emblems of the wicked: David in his last words says, "The sons of Belial shall be all of them as thorns thrust away" (2 Sam. XXIII. 6: the Hebrew word for thorns is not the same as that in the passage before us, but it need not essentially differ from it in meaning). The character here ascribed to the Church was well exemplified in that privileged member of the Church, the virgin-mother of our Lord; the handmaiden whose low estate God did not pass unregarded, when, putting down the mighty from their seat, he exalted the humble and meek. *As the citron-tree among the trees of the wood, &c.* The Church, commended by Christ, shews forth in return his praise. It is now generally agreed that the תפוח is the citron rather than the apple. The former corresponds to all that may be gathered of the tree from the notices of it in Scripture. The citron-tree is shady and beautiful: its fruit golden-coloured, and fragrant. By the trees of the wood are denoted the wild trees, emblems of men in their natural state, with whom Christ is here contrasted. In drawing out the primary contrast, it is evidently right that we should remember it to be the contrast between Christ such as he is in himself, and men such as they are in themselves: the graces which they have received from his fulness, and whereby they have been partially transformed into his image, not entering in the first instance into consideration. *In his shade I sat down with delight.* Even before the coming of Christ into the world, when he was as yet known only by promise, the Church was able to take refuge in that spiritual presence of him which was revealed to her by promise. Those who looked forward to the time when "a man" should be "as an hiding-place from the wind, and a covert from the tempest; as rivers of waters in a dry place, as the shadow of a great rock in a weary land," must themselves have been comforted by the anticipation of the comfort which they foretold. *His fruit was sweet to my taste.* The fruit represents that food which is the sustenance of each individual soul, and wherefrom also the entire Church derives her appropriate nourishment. Of the trees which appear in the vision of Ezekiel it is said, XLVII. 12, "The fruit thereof shall be for meat, and the leaf thereof, for medicine." The words before us declare that the meat supplied to us by Christ is not only nutritious, when received, but also delicious, while the act of receiving it is being performed. *He brought me into the banqueting house.* So in Prov. IX. 1—5, Wisdom, having built her house, is represented as inviting the simple to turn in, and to eat of her bread and drink of the wine which she has mingled. Isaiah LV. 1 may be also compared. "The characteristic of wine," remarks Hengstenberg, "in its relation to man is the cheerfulness of disposition which it produces. Cf. Psalm CIV. 15; Prov. XXXI. 6, 7; XV. 15. The banqueting house (literally, house of wine) is accordingly, as observed by J. H. Michaelis, the symbol of all the benefits which conduce to the salvation and the comfort of the sinner, and the sentiment intended may be expressed in the declaration that the gospel furnishes the richest motive to comfort and joy. We have, in the passage before us, the motto to the gospel-narrative of the marriage in Cana, Joh. II. 1—11; of which, as also in the present case, the fundamental thought is, 'Christ, the Joy and the Comfort of the Church during her pilgrimage through the vale of misery.' The image of the verse before us is there acted out. The scene there displayed stands in precisely the same relation to our present passage as the entrance of Christ into Jerusalem to Zech. IX. 9. Nor is it accidental that it should have been just at a wedding that that symbolical representation took place: the inferior wedding is, in the symbolical action, an image of that higher wedding in which Christ is the bridegroom." *And love was his banner over me.* Or perhaps, *And love was a banner over me*[1]. A banner represents by some device, directly or indirectly, the cause to which we have professed our determination to adhere; and being presented before our eyes it strengthens in a lively manner our resolution to abide by that to which we are bound. And what can more effectually seal our previous vows, and unite us more closely and permanently to him who is the very Fountain of love, than an abiding sense of the love which he has shewn, and a corresponding feeling of love in return? *Strengthen me with grape-cakes, strew me with citron-leaves, for I am sick with love!* The general thought is that the Church had long been ardently desiring her Lord's very presence. She had sought him, she had spiritually conversed with him; but face to face she had not yet beheld him. And thus her longing was at present unsatisfied;

---

[1] The received reading ודגלו, "and his banner," is substantially confirmed by the versions of the LXX, the Syriac translator, and Symmachus, though they pointed and rendered the word as a verb. But Aquila and Jerome (ἔταξεν, ordinavit) seem to have read simply ודגל, or דגל; and this, pointed and treated as a substantive, commends itself in preference. The Targum (Latin Version, et vexillum praeceptorum ejus) might have been framed on either reading.

and she was consequently sick with love[1]. In this her languor she craves some immediate refreshment. If she may not yet obtain the presence itself, she asks that she may at least be indulged with glimpses of it. If she may not yet drink of wine, the juice of the grape in all its richness, she may at least be strengthened with cakes made of grapes dried and pressed together: if she may not yet eat of the rich golden fruit of the citron-tree, she may at least have citron-leaves strewn under her as she lies down to repose. Doubtless there were seasons before the coming of Christ at which this craving of the Church was especially indulged. We meet with a great historical period of religious refreshment, about a century after the date of this Song, in the reign of Hezekiah of Judah, when many of the Israelites of the ten tribes were brought back to the appointed seat of worship at Jerusalem, and when, through the occasion furnished for them by the piety of the reigning monarch, the anticipations and predictions of the coming of Christ attained strength and clearness in a more than ordinary degree. The eighty-fourth and following psalms, and the thirty-second chapter of the prophecy of Isaiah, present us with reminiscences of this period of refreshment. *His left hand shall be under my head, and his right hand shall embrace me.* In other words, The time shall come when that sickness of love of which I now complain

---

[1] The right meaning was perceived by Augustine, although the translation used by him scarcely represented the original. "Vulneratam se dixit charitate: amabat enim quiddam, et nondum tenebat; dolebat, quia nondum habebat" (In Psalmum XXXVII).

shall be ministered to, and solaced, and satisfied by the presence of him on whom my affections are set. For that in these words the Church describes the full enjoyment of the presence of her Beloved is evident from the manner in which they are again introduced, before the refrain, in VIII. 3. In the following refrain itself the Church, enwrapped in visions of love, charges the by-standers, the spectators of her transports of delight, that they break not in rudely upon that bliss which she is enjoying. *I adjure you.* It is the Bride who still speaks: as is shewn by the circumstance that the corresponding charge in v. 8 unquestionably proceeds from her. *By the gazelles, or the hinds of the fells.* In translating this verse an endeavour has been made to preserve some approach to the structure of the original, where the word יְרוּשָׁלַםִ, as originally pronounced, i. e. יְרוּשָׁלֵם, would approximately rhyme to אֶתְכֶם. The reason why the gazelles and hinds are here introduced is their peaceful tenderness. The very existence of natural tenderness among animals should be a memento to the children of men to display, by moral restraint upon themselves, a tenderness no less pure and lovely. *O daughters of Jerusalem.* See above on I. 5. Although it is the Daughters of Jerusalem that are here addressed, the gender both of the pronoun "you" and of the verb "that ye upstir not" is, in the original Hebrew, masculine. The reason of this is probably to be sought in the general indefiniteness of the character which the Daughters of Jerusalem, as members of the chorus, here sustain. *The play of love.* In the Hebrew this is expressed (excluding the particle and article) by a single word, אהבה, love; but as the thing intended is love in its activity, love as it flows peacefully forth towards its object, it seems necessary to render it in English by a paraphrase. *Till it will it,* i. e. till the soul which is now wholly absorbed in love desire it. Not that contemplation is altogether to supersede outward service, or that the "Master, it is good for us to be here," is to be indulged to the neglect of the labours wherein, during the season of this world, love to Christ is to display itself. But rude assaults by which the faith of the Church is tried, or distractions and schisms whereby her singleness of aim is enfeebled, she may lawfully deprecate; all, in short, which evilly upstirs or disturbs the love to Christ which she is seeking to cherish.

THE AWAITING.

II. 8—III. 5.

Veni, veni, Emmanuel,
Captivum solve Israel,
Qui gemit in exilio
Privatus Dei Filio.
Gaude, gaude, Emmanuel
Nascetur pro te, Israel.

8 *Bride.* The voice of my beloved! Lo he is come,
   Leaping over the mountains, bounding over the hills.
9 Like to a gazelle is my beloved,
   Or like to a young hart:
   Lo, he standeth behind our wall,
   He looketh through the window,
   He glanceth through the lattice;
10 And he taketh and speaketh, even he, my beloved,
         to me:
   'Rise now, my loved one, my fair one, and come thou!
11 For lo, the winter is past,
   The rain is over and gone:
12 The flowers appear on the ground,
   The pruning-time is come,
   The voice of the turtle-dove is heard in our land:
13 The fig-tree matures her green figs,
   The vines are in blossom, they yield forth a fragrance:
   Rise now, my loved one, my fair one, and come thou!
14 My dove in the clefts of the rock, in the hiding-place
         of the cliff,
   Let me see thy countenance, let me hear thy voice,
   For sweet is thy voice, and thy countenance comely.'

15 Take ye us the foxes, the little foxes,

The destroyers of the vineyards; for our vineyards
  are in bloom.

16 My beloved is mine, and I am his,
  His who feedeth his flock among the lilies.
17 Against the day breathe cool, and the shadows flee
    away,
  Turn, haste thee, my beloved, like a gazelle or a
    young hart
  Upon the mountains of Bether.
III. 1 Upon my couch by night
  I sought him whom my soul loveth:
  I sought him, but I found him not.
  2 I resolved to rise, and to go about the city,
  Through the thoroughfares and the streets,
  To seek him whom my soul loveth:
  I sought him, but I found him not.
  3 The watchmen found me that go about the city:
  Have ye seen him whom my soul loveth? I asked.
  4 Scarcely had I passed from them
  When I found him whom my soul loveth:
  I held him and would not let him go
  Till I had brought him into the house of my mother,
    into the chamber of her that conceived me.
  5 I adjure you by the gazelles, or the hinds of the fells,
  O daughters of Jerusalem,
  That ye upstir not and that ye disturb not
  The play of love till it will it.

THE AWAITING.

In the previous section of the Song the Church had exercised her faith by anticipating her Lord's coming. But that coming was not to be immediately. There must be a previous season, and that a long season, of deferred hopes; of dark storms, of baneful attacks, and of anxious searchings. Through all these the Church must be prepared to persevere, and must learn patiently to await the advent which in imagination she had already realized as present. Hence this section may be fitly designated as the Awaiting. It consists of fifteen verses. The principal division in it is formed by the central verse, II. 15, which stands by itself, alone.

Vv. 8—14. The storms which should precede the Bridegroom's coming are not directly described; but his coming itself is represented as occurring at the close of a comparatively dreary period. *The voice of my beloved.* Hengstenberg notices the allusion to this passage in Joh. III. 29. *Leaping over the mountains, bounding over the hills.* The mountains and hills are apparently mentioned because in nature they would form the furthest visible separation between us and one whom we desired to behold, but who was far removed from us. Mountains are indeed in Scripture the general symbol for kingdoms. But there is no sufficient warrant for applying here any interpretation based upon this known symbolism, as the choice of the imagery may be adequately explained by its correspondence with the comparison of the Bridegroom to a gazelle or young hart, and with the description of natural scenery in the succeeding verses. To the former of these the leaping and the bounding unmistakeably point. Furthermore this passage explains the image in Psalm CXXI. 1, "I will lift up mine eyes unto the hills, from whence cometh my help." *Like to a gazelle is my beloved, or like to a young hart.* The points of comparison are, first, the graceful tenderness; and secondly, the ability to surmount any height, however steep. Hab. III. 19 will here serve to guide us: "The LORD God is my strength, and he will make my feet like hinds' feet, and he will make me to walk upon mine high places." *He standeth behind our wall.* Notice again the "our," used by the Church in speaking of herself. The general idea is that the Church has been imprisoned within her wall by the wintry storms, cf. Lam. III. 7, 9: her Lord now graciously appears to summon her forth to the joys of the spring. The window and the lattice are consequently those of the wall within which the Church had been immured. *He glanceth.* The sense conveyed by the verb in the original Hebrew is that the Bride beholds the beaming joy depicted on his countenance. *He taketh and speaketh,* lit. He answereth and saith, reminding us of the phrase so constantly employed by the evangelists in introducing the words of the Lord Jesus in the Gospels: e.g. Matth. XI. 25, Joh. V. 19. By answering they intended not merely the replying to words previously uttered, but also, more generally, the seizing occasion of discourse from anything that was or had been passing. *The winter is past, the rain is over and gone.* "Temporalis tribulatio finem accepit" (Justus Org.) "The winter and the rain are here," observes Hengstenberg, "an image of calamities and judgments. In Psalm CXLVII. 16, 17, the psalmist beholds in snow, hoar-frost, and ice a type of the season of suffering which had lasted up to that date; in the spring, ver. 18, a type of salvation which was just returning. We have there the explanation of the symbolical representation in the passage before us. And as winter here denotes a certain state of external circumstances, so in Joh. X. 22 it appears as an emblem of a certain moral state. The 'it was winter," like other analogous expressions in that Gospel, implies more than at first sight appears. Every one knew that the feast of the dedication fell in the winter season. But as there was winter without, so too was there winter in the heart, in spite of the festal celebration; and thus the words prepare the way for the wintry scene which follows. Rain, which is in Palestine more closely bound up with the winter than in our countries, appears as an image of calamity in Isaiah IV. 6; also in Matth. VII. 24, 25. One cannot stand out of doors in the rain, Ezra X. 13." *The flowers appear on the ground.* One of the various tokens of the spring; which would sufficiently warrant the poetical mention of it here. It is probable however that the flowers themselves were intended to indicate the spiritual graces which should accompany, and even in occasional instances herald in, the advent of the gospel. Such were the fruits of repentance which John the Baptist invited: such also were the faith of the shepherds of Bethlehem, and the earnestness of Peter, and the guilelessness of Nathanael.

The pruning-time. The Hebrew word occurs but in this passage; and many render, with our E. V., the time of the singing (of birds). But the root of the word, though applied both to pruning and to singing, is never used of the singing of birds; and in the imagery before us any other singing than that of birds would hardly be in place. The key to the true meaning of the imagery is to be found in Joh. xv. 2: "Every branch that beareth fruit, he purgeth it, that it may bring forth more fruit." At the introduction of the gospel all that there was good and honest and true among the children of men was to be nursed and quickened and stimulated into new and higher life. *The voice of the turtle-dove.* The turtle-dove appears in Psalm LXXIV. 19 as an image of the meek, or of the congregation of God in its defenceless meekness. And in the gospel history we recognize the voice of the turtle-dove in the hymns of Mary, of Zacharias, and of Simeon; hymns in which, from meek and chastened souls, the lyrical psalmody of Israel seemed after the lapse of many hundred years to be poured forth anew in order specially to herald in the new era of evangelic blessedness. *The fig-tree matures her green figs, the vines are in blossom, they yield forth a fragrance.* Two more images of the preparatory signs of the evangelic fruits of righteousness which were speedily to follow; and the imagery here drawn from trees with which, of all fruit-bearing trees, the Jews were most familiar. To sit under one's own vine and under one's own fig-tree, was with them a proverbial expression to denote the enjoyment of peace, prosperity, and abundance (1 Kings IV. 25; Micah IV. 4; Zech. III. 10); and, independently of this, we find in other passages the vine and fig-tree associated together, as trees from which throughout the land the people expected their annual produce of fruit (Hos. IX. 10; Micah VII. 1, in which latter passage, equally as in the former, the first-ripe is the first-ripe of the fig-tree). It will be noticed that the passage before us does not speak of the ripe figs of the fig-tree, nor yet of the grapes of the vine: those were not to be expected till the influence of the gospel itself had been felt; and it was as yet but spring-time: the summer was nigh at hand, but was not yet arrived. The green figs and the vine-blossom were the proper indications of it. It was for the green figs that our Saviour sought on the fig-tree on the way from Bethany to Jerusalem, and sought in vain. That tree was a type of the Jewish nation, which as a whole had failed to shew forth in due season the desired effects of God's past nurture; and which thus brought down the doom of desolation on its head. But though the nation had proved barren as a whole, there was yet a remnant of grace that realized the anticipations of the verse before us, and became the nucleus of the Christian Church. *My dove in the clefts of the rock*, &c. Hengstenberg translates "in the refuges of the rock," understanding the rocks themselves to form the refuge, and arguing that this is the only admissible interpretation in the parallel passages Obad. 3, Jer. XLIX. 16, where the same Hebrew phrase is found. Whichever rendering we adopt, the general purport of the passage is substantially the same. The rock is but another image for that which was in ver. 9 expressed by the wall. It is a place of protection, but withal a place of confinement. And in the days of Israel the Church of God was all along confined as well as protected; confined by the heathen antagonism of the nations that hemmed in the little people of Israel around, though protected by the watchful power of the Lord against their violence and their malice. *Let me see thy countenance, let me hear thy voice.* Christ at his appearance upon earth summoned the Church forth from this her previous retreat. She was thenceforward to walk abroad into the world around. Knowledge of the truth, and with it discipleship, was to spread through all nations. The Church, with her acknowledgement of membership and with her outward organization, was to display herself to view in every region of the inhabited world; and from all nations were the strains of Christian worship to ascend up on high. And then should he who, as Saviour of the Church, was to see of the travail of his soul and be satisfied, gaze, as Lord of the Church, on the comeliness of her countenance and listen to the sweetness of her voice.

Ver. 15. *Take ye us the foxes.* Who speaks in this verse? Probably the Church, in her corporate capacity; yet so as that these words are not dramatically connected either with those which precede or with those which follow; and this the use of the plural pronoun of the first person helps to indicate. It will be noticed moreover that the "ye" and the "us" are alike plural. The drama is in fact interrupted for the moment by this, the central verse of the second portion of the Song; which describes by means of a general command, expressed with as little definiteness as possible, the work which the various members of God's people, the various labourers in the vineyard, must be continually pursuing during the period that shall elapse ere the Lord of the Church arrive. Foxes are common animals in Palestine. They are described as very numerous in the stony country about Bethlehem; as abounding also near the convent of St John, in the desert, about vintage-time; and as destroying all the vines unless strictly watched (Hasselquist, ap. Harmer's Outlines, p. 256). They thus form an appropriate general designation for those who from within rather than without waste the heritage of God: who by the evil influence of their authority and example lead the people into sin, and so prevent those fruits of righteousness from appearing for which the blossoming of the vines had given encouragement to hope[1]. Evil kings, unworthy priests, lying prophets, all belong to this class; Jeroboams, Ahabs, and Manassehs, Hophnis, Amaziahs, and Urijahs, Zedekiah-ben-Chenaanahs, and Hananiahs. And as regards the circumstance that the warning against all such misleaders of the people should form the central flower of a poetic garland that is mainly occupied with the expecta-

---

[1] In the Apostolical Constitutions, VI. 13, heretics are compared to foxes who crouch on the ground, the ruin of the vineyards: through them, it is said, the love of many waxes cold.

tion of the coming of Christ, we have to mark how analogously in the Prophets it is the very contemplation of present kingly, priestly, or prophetical ungodliness that leads to the delineation of Christ as the future worthy ruler and shepherd. Cf. Isaiah XXXII; Jeremiah XXIII; Ezekiel XXXIV. Nor is the comparison of the internal wasters of God's heritage to prowling foxes peculiar to the Song of Songs. It is found also in Ezek. XIII. 4: "O Israel, thy prophets are like the foxes in the deserts." It was moreover with allusion, as Hengstenberg has acutely pointed out, to the passage before us, that our Lord, when warned by certain of the Pharisees to depart, because Herod would kill him, replied, "Go ye, and tell that fox, &c." (Luke XIII. 32). "It is maintained by Bengel that Herod is here called a fox on account of his craftiness and his hypocritical timidity. There is however here no trace of any craftiness; nor does aught beside lead us to the conclusion that craft was a feature in Herod's character. Nor is there any other passage of Scripture in which the fox appears as the symbol of craft. The appellation can only rest upon the fact directly related of Herod, that he wished to kill Jesus; and the true connexion is only brought out when we refer back to the passage in the Song of Songs: our Lord's meaning being, Go ye and tell that destroyer of God's vineyard."

Vv. 16, 17. In these and the ensuing verses is more definitely delineated the anxiety with which, ere her Lord arrive, the Church awaits his presence. She first virtually declares, in the full confidence of faith, her conviction that he will eventually come to receive her; she then prays for his coming; and thirdly, shews how her anxiety must continue till she actually welcome his presence. *My beloved is mine.* And therefore it cannot be that he will absent himself from the Church for ever. *And I am his.* And therefore if the Church thus feel that it is to him that she belongs, she must never be so undutiful, however long his approach be delayed, as to lay her thoughts of him aside. She must expect him till he come: she must live for him, and in hope of him. How deeply the most pious of her members connected each crisis through which they had to pass with their expectations of the coming of the Messiah may be illustrated by the example of the prophet Daniel. *Who feedeth his flock among the lilies.* Lilies are the emblems of holy purity. Even before his coming, Christ was, through the prophets, and through the ceremonial training of the Law, nursing his people in holiness. Still more has he so nursed them since his coming, cf. VI. 3. *Against the day breathe cool, and the shadows flee away.* That is, before the evening set finally in. The approach of the natural evening is known by its signs; viz. first, the gentle breeze springing up before sunset; and secondly, the gradual elongation of the shadows and consequent retreat of their outline, cf. Psalm CII. 11. But that natural evening here represents the evening of the season of grace of God's ancient people. It was just as the transgressions of the Jewish nation, as a nation, had nearly reached their full, that Christ appeared, bringing salvation to them that had waited for him. And long before his coming, the faithful, beholding the multiplied provocations wherewith Israel was vexing God, might well pray that the advent of the Messiah might not be delayed till the day of probation should have finally passed away, and the tidings of redemption should be too late. Hengstenberg remarks that in the words of the disciples at Emmaus, Luke XXIV. 29, "Abide with us: for it is toward evening, and the day is far spent," there was an allusion, through a probably unconscious reminiscence, to our present passage. "The reference to it," he adds, "was deeper than they could have intended: they themselves were a type of their nation, whose sun was on the point of setting." And we may further observe that the symbolism involved in their words has probably been recognized and felt by many who have been comparatively unacquainted with the passage whence it was originally drawn: the more especially since it has been transferred to other Christian writings, such as the German hymn, "Ach bleib bei uns Herr Jesu Christ," or the evening-hymn in the "Christian Year." The New Testament has brought out to many the significance of the Old: Christian poetry has further unfolded to many the significance of the New. *Turn.* That is, turn thee hither, come to me. Others take the word in the opposite sense, of departing. But the former accords better with the context. *Like a gazelle or young hart.* See on ver. 9. *Upon the mountains of Bether.* Bether (from the root בתר "to divide") denotes separation: the mountains were those which separated the Church from her Beloved, see above, on ver. 8. It may be that the Bithron, mentioned in 2 Sam. II. 29 as lying to the east of the Jordan, was the name of a mountain-district, and that it was the hills of this district that the poet had in view, and thus worked up into his imagery.

III. 1—5. *Upon my couch by night.* The night here mentioned has no connexion with the close of day of the imagery of the preceding verse. In fact what was day there is night here; for that which was in one respect to the Church a season of grace, through which she was being divinely nursed with the hope of ultimate redemption, was yet in another respect a season of darkness, because troubles floated thick around, and her Lord was still absent from her. There is a natural harmony between night-time and sorrow, which causes the mention of the one to be often introduced in Scripture in connexion with the delineation of the other: e.g. Psalm LXXVII. 2 (for a list of other passages, see Hengstenberg). For the like reason, since "weeping may endure for a night, but joy cometh in the morning," the morning-time is in Scripture the natural emblem of gladness, and as coming from God, of salvation. The couch, again, naturally associates itself with the darkness of night. *I sought him.* In three different ways. First, by simple longing, on her couch: nor can we wonder that in the depth of her afflictions the Church should long more earnestly for her appointed deliverer. Secondly, in the streets of the city, through which, during the darkness, she should hardly have spontaneously roamed: we have here indications of the impatience which led Israel, when "howling upon their beds," to "call to Egypt," and "go to Assyria," and to picture to themselves phantom deliverers, forgetting that he who made darkness created also the light, and that "his going forth" was "prepared as the morning" (Hos. VI, VII). Still, in the Song, it is primarily after her own true Lord, albeit with some impatient rashness, that the Church is represented as searching. Thirdly, she seeks by enquiring of the watchmen who found her in her rambles. In these watchmen we may recognize the various Hebrew prophets raised up of God. It was the prophets, from Hosea onward, that faithfully rebuked the impatience to which the Church was too apt to give way, and that yet at the same time upheld and quickened her hopes of the eventual coming of her Messiah. Most truly may it be said that they "found" the Church roaming; for they began to be raised up just at the time when Israelitish impatience was most strongly unfolding itself, and they were, in fact, the contemporary witnesses of all the vain endeavours which the Israelites made to obtain deliverance from their troubles by alliance with the empires of the world. Of these then, as they successively found her, the Church enquires—"Watchman, what of the night? Watchman, what of the night?" Nor were her enquiries fruitless, when a Daniel was commissioned to declare even the time of the Messiah's coming. *Scarcely had I passed from them.* Nearly nine centuries elapsed from the period when this Song was written, four centuries from the period when the last Old Testament prophet spoke, to the time when Christ actually appeared. But prophecy does not in general measure the distance in time between future events. It views them as linked together by sequence of connexion rather than of time. The speediness with which Christ's advent is here represented as following on the enquiries made by the Church of the watchmen finds its parallel in those anticipations of the speediness of Christ's second advent with which the New Testament abounds, e. g. Phil. IV. 5, James V. 8, Rev. I. 1. *I found him.* The season of expectation is at an end: Christ has come unto his own. *I held him,* &c. The phrase expresses the deep ardour with which they that had long waited for him welcomed him. There was a literal verification of the words when the aged Simeon took up the infant Saviour in his arms. *Till I had brought him into the house of my mother, into the chamber of her that conceived me.* No stress must be laid on the "I had brought him," except so far as the Church had prevailed thereto by her prayers: rather we may say that the bringing him is poetically represented as the act of the Church, in order thereby to express the welcome with which she received him. We are said to bring a person into our house when we go out to meet him as he enters, though it may be that he enters spontaneously, and even by his own right: in like manner we are said to bring him on his way when we escort him forth, even though we may not be rendering him any actual assistance. The mother of the Bride is here, as elsewhere in the Song (see on I. 6), the Israelitish nation; and by Christ's being brought into her house is denoted his being born into the world of the stock of Israel. It was of Israel that "as concerning the flesh Christ came, who is over all, God blessed for ever;" and thereby were all the promises to Israel fulfilled, and the glory of Israel consummated. The Church beheld therein a crowning proof of God's faithfulness, and rejoiced that her Lord should spring of the privileged race to which all her own members had up to that time belonged. *I adjure you, &c.* See on II. 7. Again brought to the point where through faith she beholds her Beloved as actually arrived in answer to her longings, the Church again charges the bystanders that her enjoyment of the blissful prospect may not be rudely disturbed.

THE ESPOUSAL AND ITS RESULTS.

III. 6—V. 1.

Vexilla Regis prodeunt,
Fulget crucis mysterium,
Quo carne carnis Conditor
Suspensus est patibulo.
     VENANTIUS.

6 *Chorus.* Who is this that cometh up from the wilderness
   Like to columns of smoke,
   Perfumed with myrrh and frankincense,
   With every fragrant powder of the merchant?
7 Lo! it is the bed of Solomon:
   Around it are threescore valiant men
   Of the valiants of Israel;
8 All practised swordsmen, men expert in war,
   Each with his sword upon his thigh
   Ready against nightly alarm.
9 A palanquin hath King Solomon made for himself
   Of the wood of Lebanon:
10 Its pillars hath he made of silver, its back of gold,
   Its seat of purple,
   Its middle tesselated with love because of the daughters of Jerusalem.
11 Come forth, ye daughters of Zion, and gaze on King Solomon,
   And on the crown wherewith his mother hath crowned him,
   In the day of his espousal, and in the day of his gladness of heart.

1 *Beloved.* Behold, thou art fair, my love,
   Behold, thou art fair, thine eyes are doves

Behind thy plaits;
Thy hair is like a flock of goats
Hanging down the slope of Mount Gilead:
2 Thy teeth are like a flock of shearing-sheep
Coming up from the wash-pool,
All appearing in pairs,
And not a lone one amongst them:
3 Like a crimson brede are thy lips,
And lovely to behold is thine utterance:
Like a slice of pomegranate are thy temples
Behind thy plaits:
4 Thy neck is like the tower of David
Built with projecting parapets,
Whereon are hung the thousand shields,
The whole of the targes of the valiants:
5 Thy two breasts are like two young twins,
Fawns of a gazelle, that feed among the lilies.

6 Against the day breathe cool, and the shadows flee
   away,
   I will get me to the mountain of myrrh and to the
   hill of frankincense.

7 Thou art all of thee fair, my love,
   And there is not a blemish in thee.
8 From Lebanon, spouse, with me,
   From Lebanon with me shalt thou come,

Shalt gaze from the summit of Amana,
From the summit of Shenir and Hermon,
From the dens of lions, from the mountains of panthers.

9 Thou hast ravished my heart, my sister, my spouse,
Thou hast ravished my heart with one bend of thine eyes,
With one chainlet of thy necklace.

10 How fair is thy love, my sister, my spouse,
How goodlier is thy love than wine,
And the scent of thy ointments than all spices!

11 Thy lips drop honeycomb-drops, my spouse;
Honey and milk are under thy tongue;
And the fragrance of thy attire is as the fragrance of Lebanon.

12 A garden enclosed is my sister, my spouse,
A garden enclosed, a fountain sealed:
13 Thy shoots a paradise of pomegranates,
With precious fruits,
Henna and spikenard;
14 Spikenard and saffron, calamus and cinnamon,
With all trees of frankincense,
Myrrh and aloes,
With all choicest aromatics;
15 A bubbling fountain,
A well of living waters,
And streams from Lebanon.

16 *Bride.* Awake, O north wind! and approach, thou south!
Blow on my garden that its perfumes may flow out!
Let my beloved come into his garden
And eat his precious fruits!

v. 1 *Beloved.* I am come into my garden, my sister, my spouse;
I gather my myrrh with my spices;
I eat my honeycomb with my honey;
I drink my wine with my milk:
Eat, O friends! Drink and enjoy ye, O beloved!

The third section of the Song, in which all the interest of its earlier portion culminates, consists, like the first section, of twenty-three verses. Of these the first six, III. 6—11, evidently run together, and form the description of the Espousal. Correspondingly the last six, IV. 12—V. 1, have a close mutual connexion: they describe the Bridegroom's garden, and his entry into it to gather its precious fruits. The intermediate verses are mainly occupied with setting forth the graces of the Bride; and their appropriateness to the place in which they stand will appear as we examine the whole section in order. But among them one verse, IV. 6, remarkably interrupts the flow of the rest; and the very isolation in which it apparently stands renders its meaning in the first instance obscure. It is the central verse of the whole section, as a computation of the verses will readily shew. It comprises in itself, as we shall find, the essence of the whole; and to this we have an outward testimony in the circumstance that the myrrh and the frankincense of which it speaks appear at once in the opening verse of the section, III. 6, and again, substantially, in the concluding verse, v. 1, "my myrrh with my spices." If therefore we were to follow the phraseology of the Song itself, "Myrrh and Frankincense" would form the most proper designation of the present section: it may however be otherwise described, less enigmatically, as "The Espousal and its Results."

Vv. 6—11. *Who is this that cometh up.* The pronoun is feminine, so that it is the Bride whose approach is here described. The Hebrew will bear also the translation, "What is this that cometh, &c.;" which accordingly some interpreters have been led by the context to adopt. But against this is the analogy of the corresponding passage VIII. 5, where the subject of the question is plainly the Bride herself. We can hardly tear asunder two passages which stand in so manifest a mutual relation; and of which the one describes the satisfaction of all the Bride's earlier longings, the other her complete and final blessedness. No direct answer is given to the question here asked, nor indeed is any needed; the purport of it being simply to draw attention to the honour which she who so long had sought her Beloved was now at last receiving. In this and the following verses it is the Chorus of the Daughters of Jerusalem, and through them the poet, that speaks. *From the wilderness.* As symbolical of a state of pilgrimage and toil which now at last was ended. The Church had arrived at the goal of her Old Testament journey, and the beauty of the LORD her God was now manifested upon her. *Like to columns of smoke.* The Hebrew word for "columns," תימרות, is of uncertain etymology, and is found elsewhere in the Bible only in Joel II. 30. The correctness however of the meaning usually assigned to it has been recently vindicated by Rödiger in his completion of the Thesaurus of Gesenius. The LXX. rendered it στελέχη, intending thereby "stems" or "branches:" so also Jerome, "virgula." These come sufficiently near to the received translation. The general purport of the image is that the Bride was so richly provided with perfumes that they curled up in dense columns of smoke, visible at a distance as the procession moved along. The following words shew the nature of these perfumes. *With myrrh.* It had been mentioned once before in the Song; and that (observe hereby the importance attached to it) in the central verse of the first section, I. 13. Here, as there, it is the emblem of Christ's death; and to the death of Christ for her the Church owes all her honour: "Ye were not redeemed with corruptible things, as silver and gold,...but with the precious blood of Christ." In the myrrh offered to the infant Saviour by the wise men of the east the Church has ever recognized the unconscious token of his future passion; and it was also one of the substances used for his burial. What was thus offered in devotion to him comes back from him to the Church as an emblem of the virtue that has gone forth from him for her purification. *And frankincense.* Frankincense is, throughout Scripture, the emblem of prayer, ascending upwards, like the fragrant wreaths of its smoke, towards the throne of God. The symbolism was necessarily recognized in the Mosaic ritual, where the regular use of a sacred incense, partly compounded of frankincense, was prescribed. It is also recognized in Ps. CXLI. 2, Rev. V. 8, VIII. 3, 4. Here, where frankincense is conjoined with myrrh, the one, so to speak, qualifies the other: the myrrh symbolizes Christ's death: the frankincense expresses the priestly character of that death; the death itself constituting that act of devotion wherein he made offering to God. Thus then the Church is represented as perfumed with the sweet-smelling savour of that offering and sacrifice which her Lord made to God for her (Eph. v. 2). The older view of the import of the frankincense in this place, as given by Theodoret, and in part also by Philo of Carpasia, was that it represented prayer made *to* Christ, and so expressed the Church's acknowledgement of his divinity. But the perfume spread over the Church must, according to all analogy, proceed from some *act* of Christ's; not merely from her acknowledgment of his perfections. *With every fragrant powder of the merchant.* That is, with every fragrant powder which can be procured: myrrh and frankincense themselves were both articles of commerce, and were brought to Palestine from Arabia. The words before us give expression to the truth that in whatever aspect, main or subsidiary, the death of Christ be viewed, it is still for the Church that it was endured, and it is she to whom accrue *all* benefits of his passion. In the composition of the holy anointing oil of the Mosaic ritual there were used, besides myrrh, cinnamon, calamus, and cassia: in that of the holy incense there were mixed with the frankincense stacte, onycha, and galbanum (Exod. XXX.). In Psalm XLV. 8 we have mention, along with the myrrh, of aloes and cassia (different from the cassia of Exodus); and in the description of the garden, at which we shall in the Song presently arrive, we have aloes again associated with the myrrh, and calamus and cinnamon with the frankincense. *Lo! it is the bed of Solomon*, to wit, in which the Bride is being borne along. The succeeding verses shew that a travelling litter is here intended. But the fact of its being Solomon's shews also that it is as the bride of her Beloved that the Church is being here conveyed and escorted. This is the first passage in the Song (for we can scarcely take the like view of I. 5) in which the Beloved is designated as Solomon. Vv. 9, 11, in which he is again so designated, are obviously connected with this: after which the name does not occur again till at the close of the Song, VIII. 11, 12. The first and most obvious respect in which the Beloved here appears as the antitype of Solomon is his royal splendour. There is however a second and no less important point of comparison: both in this chapter and in Chapter VIII. the Beloved comes before us as the "Peaceful One," whose advent is to introduce a period of glorious repose to the Church after her long previous struggles. The question now arises, What is it precisely that is here symbolized by the bed of Solomon? In the commentary of Philo of Carpasia the Church herself is supposed to be intended; and it is beautifully observed that she was the chosen resting-place of Him who, before he took her unto himself, had not where to lay his head. So sudden a representation however under the figure of a bed of her who throughout the rest of the Song appears as the Bride would be violent and unnatural. It is no sufficient answer to this to say that in IV. 12 seqq. the Church is described under the figure of a garden. An additional metaphor is there avowedly introduced, and that without setting aside the ordinary allegory of the Song; for it is not the Church directly that is there compared to a garden, but rather the Bride by whom, throughout the Song, the Church is represented. No poet however could well institute a comparison between a bride and the bed wherein she was being conveyed. Besides which, there is no room to doubt that the "bed" of the present verse is substantially identical with the "palanquin" of vv. 9, 10; and to interpret that palanquin of the Church is fairly impossible. The fact is that the bed of ver. 7 is mentioned mainly as an anticipation of the palanquin of vv. 9, 10; and we must wait for its full interpretation till we proceed to those verses. We may however at once observe that the Bride is being conveyed in her Lord's litter, and that thus is set forth her union with him. *Around it are threescore valiant men, &c.* The image is taken from the corps of heroes who, having been the early companions of David in his wanderings, formed eventually the nucleus and the élite of his army (2 Sam. XXIII.). A similar body may have shone around the court of Solomon. The number of David's heroes, "thirty and seven in all," was exactly thirty exclusive of those who stood superior to the rest in rank; and if the number threescore have any definite meaning in the present verse, it is probably to be taken as the double of the number of the heroes of David's reign. A comparison however of this verse with VI. 8 may furnish ground for regarding sixty as a determinate number used for an indeterminate. The general idea conveyed by the image is the all-efficient guard with which Christ watched over those whom he had come to ransom. It is the same idea which is expressed by the words of his own final prayer: "While I was with them in the world, I kept them in thy name: those that thou gavest me, I have kept" (Joh. XVII. 12). The fact that Christ's was mainly a spiritual protection precludes our thinking of any visible antitypes of Israel's older valiants. *Ready against nightly alarm.* Nightly alarm is sudden alarm which comes upon us in the hours of darkness. It was an outward testimony of Christ's readiness to defend his Church against such alarm, when, suddenly confronted with Judas and the band that had come to arrest him, he bade them, if they sought him, let his disciples go their way: " that the saying might," adds the evangelist, "be fulfilled, which he spake, Of them which thou gavest me have I lost none." The more general lesson is that Christ's grace is sufficient for us under every temptation. *A palanquin hath King Solomon made for himself.* In this and the following two verses there is no direct mention of the Bride. Her happiness has been already described: henceforth the bed or palanquin is viewed solely in its relation to the Bridegroom himself. To this the "for himself" of the present verse points. The word אַפִּרְיוֹן, LXX. φορεῖον, Jer. "ferculum," i. e. a triumphal wagon or car, is best derived, with Gesenius, from the unused root פרה, "to be borne;" but there can in any case be no doubt, from the ensuing description, of the general character of the object intended. It is the vehicle on which the royal Bridegroom is being conveyed to the solemnities of his espousal, and to the fulness of his glory and his joy. If now it be asked by what outward means Christ united his Church unto himself, and entered into his glory, we must at once answer, By his career of suffering. "Through sufferings" he was made "perfect;" and the unshrinking endurance of each temptation and agony added a precious jewel to the crown of unperishing glory which now rests upon him. That which was once his shame is seen, in its true light, as his glory by us. And as all his sufferings culminated in his death upon the cross, so is that cross become to us the outward symbol of all his patient mortal pilgrimage: it was the outward instrument on which all was finally accomplished, and is accordingly invested in our eyes with the reflexion of the glory into which by it Christ entered. Hence the correspondence between the palanquin of the Song and the cross of the Gospels: each is, in its own proper sphere, the outward symbol of the same inward reality. The palanquin was, by Cyril, interpreted of the cross; and it was probably not without some reminiscence of the description of the one that the passion-hymn of Venantius thus apostrophized the other:

> Arbor decora et fulgida,
> Ornata regis purpura,
> Electa digno stipite
> Tam sancta membra tangere.

Of the wood of Lebanon. As the palanquin is to be represented as of the utmost magnificence, the best of materials contribute to its construction. It is not necessary to suppose that any significance is intended in the assignment of separate materials to particular parts of the vehicle: the object is simply to embrace in the description all the richest. *Its pillars.* The pillars support the canopy of the palanquin. *Its back.* LXX. ἀνάκλιτον, Jer. "reclinatorium," the part against which the back of the rider leaned. *Its middle tesselated with love.* It is not quite clear what we are to understand by the middle; whether the interior panelling of the vehicle, or its floor. Happily in respect of the symbolical meaning this is of little importance. That we must here allow a symbolical meaning is evident from the fact that it is "with love" that the vehicle is represented as tesselated; and it was probably to make the symbolical meaning clearer that the phrase "its middle" was employed. The truth symbolized is this; that Christ's manifold love to the Church was the great central secret of his death. "He loved the church, and gave himself for it." *Because of the daughters of Jerusalem.* It has been shewn above, on I. 5, that the Daughters of Jerusalem represent the members of the Church simply as spectators of the scenes that are passing, and irrespectively of their spiritual condition. The truth then here enigmatically set forth is the love of Christ to all, even to those who might be looking with comparative indifference upon him. The passage amounts to a direct denial of the doctrine that Christ died only for the elect. Of those who followed him to Calvary, and who stood round his cross, how many must there have been who entered not at all into the real depths and purport of his sufferings, but on whom meanwhile he was gazing with the tenderest love and pity, and for whom he was offering himself up an obedient sacrifice unto God! Nor vainly offering himself; for it was to those very persons, who had looked upon his sufferings with comparative ignorance and indifference, that the pentecostal discourse of Peter was addressed, stirring them up to a sense of what had been wrought on their behalf, and bidding them be themselves baptized "in the name of Jesus Christ for the remission of sins." *Come forth, ye daughters of Zion, and gaze, &c.* Remarkable here is the use of the phrase "daughters of Zion" in contrast to the "daughters of Jerusalem" of the preceding verse. It occurs but thrice in Scripture beside, viz. in Isaiah III. 16, 17, IV. 4, which verses all form part of one connected passage; and in which the prophet is engaged either in delineating the sins of the members of the church, as aggravated by their privileges, or in shewing that from the consequent judgment a remnant shall be preserved holy unto the Lord. It is thus distinctly as members of the Church that, even elsewhere in Scripture, the Daughters of Zion are contemplated. The same is here the case. The invitation is not here to all, to go forth and gaze on the Divine King of Israel, merely as outward spectators of the course by which he enters into his glory; but rather to those who have been taught to feel the deep connexion between his wondrous career and the salvation and glorification of the Church, to go forth and gaze on him in true devotion, and to admire and to adore his matchless love. And this invitation is renewed each time that the Church summons us, whether by lesson of Scripture or by observance of holy day, or in any other manner whatsoever, to the contemplation of the passion of our Redeemer. *And on the crown wherewith his mother hath crowned him.* That is, Gaze on him as crowned. His mother, identical with the mother of the Bride (see on III. 4), is, as has been shewn on I. 6, the Israelitish or Jewish nation; and it was she who crucified him. This was in early times, so far as we can learn, the universal Christian interpretation. Philo of Carpasia says, tersely enough: "His mother crowned him, when the Synagogue of the Jews placed the crown of thorns upon his head. It is she who is here called the mother of his flesh, because it was of the Jews that, according to the flesh, he sprang." Replace "synagogue" by "nation," and this observation is excellent. Similarly Cyril. Theodoret writes: "He was crowned with love:...greater love hath no man than this, that a man lay down his life for his friends. Now it was his mother that thus crowned him. By his mother is intended Judea, in reference to his human nature. It was she who, unwillingly, presented him with this crown. She, to do him dishonour, crowned him with the crown of thorns: he, through the thorns, received the crown of love, by voluntarily enduring the dishonour." If the early interpreters thus agreed in recognizing in the Jews the mother of the Bridegroom, it is evident that they also further agreed in connecting the Bridegroom's crown with the crown of thorns. The interpretation naturally commends itself to us; and it is hardly improved upon by Theodoret's additional observations respecting the crown of love, at least in the form in which he puts them, since that cannot strictly be said to have been presented to the Bridegroom by his mother. Let us see then how far the parallel between the nuptial crown of the Song and the crown of thorns of the Gospels holds good. It may be at once premised that, as in the case of the palanquin and the cross, the one cannot be directly treated as a symbol of the other: each, in the light in which it here comes before us, is itself but a symbol, and must therefore not be mistaken for the object symbolized. The two may however correspond in being alike symbols of the same thing. And be it here observed that each coronation was essentially of the nature of an exhibition or display; a summing up, so to speak, in outward show, of what was otherwise passing; not a means to an end, not a ceremony which in itself contributed to any result. The nuptial crown of the Song was the public token of the personal rejoicing of the Bridegroom on the arrival of that day of union to which he had long been looking forward: "Come forth,...and gaze...on the crown...in the day of his, &c." The crown of thorns of the Gospels, imposed in mockery by the soldiers after they had observed the temper of the Jewish populace, was the public token of our Saviour's pretensions to royalty. "Then came Jesus forth, wearing the crown of thorns, and the purple robe. And Pilate saith unto them, Behold the man!" Now wherein, by his own account, did our Saviour's royalty consist? In bearing witness to the truth. It was for this that he had been born and had come into the world; and this he had, that day, in the presence of Pilate, emphatically had the opportunity of performing. Amid the sorrows that on that day surrounded him, and of which the thorns of his crown were no inappropriate emblems, he was accomplishing that which had been the purpose of his whole earthly life; the day had arrived wherein he should, by his sufferings, summon most touchingly and most effectually unto himself all that were of the truth and that heard his voice; and it was the very intensity of the trial that was to bring out into full relief the moral grandeur of his triumph. Henceforth, by being lifted up, he should draw all men unto him; and thus by his sufferings and death would both his union with the Church and his dearest joy be accomplished. Each crown thus witnessed, in its own peculiar way, to the heavenly Solomon's successful achievement of his cherished purpose. And as it is evidently on the exposure of his glory to the public gaze that the chief stress is here laid, so let it be remembered how essentially public was our Saviour's death, by reason of his being lifted up upon the cross for all men to behold. The more public the shame intended for him by his crucifiers, the more public the display of his real glory. No other form of death would have rendered him so completely a spectacle unto men as the death of the cross; and therefore in no other form of death would his love to all mankind have been so openly and effectually manifested. *In the day of his espousal.* The death of Christ was the act of espousal: it was herein that he "loved the church, and gave himself for it," "that he might present it to himself." With his life was his troth to the Church irrevocably plighted: with his blood was his love to the Church irrevocably sealed. In no way could he give himself more determinately to the Church than in this: "greater love hath no man than this, that a man lay down his life for his friends." And so also correspondingly, for the marriage-bond must be mutual, in no way more effectually than in this could he bind the Church unto himself. No force can be given to any human covenant or engagement more sacred than that which is imparted to it by the death of one of the contracting parties. There remains no power of alteration when he who alone could alter it, even if he had the will to alter it, has been once lastingly removed. And thankless and ungracious as it might be to repel the voluntary devotion of a friend so long as there remained to him the power of withholding it, it would be a disregard of all that is sacred among men to dishonour our obligation to one who in our best and truest interests had once surrendered, past recall, his all. It is because Christ and his Church are thus mutually bound by his passion, that our outward sacrament of communion with him still consists, by his appointment, in partaking of the tokens of his body and blood that were given and shed in death for us. *And in the day of his gladness of heart.* The extremity of grief was also the fulness of rejoicing. Beneath the sorrows that weighed upon him lay the joy with which the Redeemer of the world welcomed the consummation of the purpose for which he had come into the world. "I have a baptism to be baptized with," he once had said; "and how am I straitened till it be accomplished!" And with this accord his words to his apostles at the last supper: "With desire I have desired to eat this passover with you before I suffer" (meaning, "with desire have I desired to enter upon this prelude of my approaching sufferings." The words "before I suffer" do not qualify the desire, but rather interpret the passover[1]). It was with kindred

---

[1] Aponius eloquently writes: "Diem lætitiæ cordis Christi esse Spiritus sanctus edocuit diem qua lugubriter gaudebat Judæus, et lætitiæ lachrymas in morte Christi fundebant apostoli, lugebant et elementa pendere in patibulo condemnatum: sed lætabatur qui pependit; quum mors pendentis omnibus credentibus vitam et gaudia adportavit. Cordis utique erat lætitiæ dies Domini Christi quando meretrix lachrymas fundendo, raptor quadruplo male direpta restituendo, publicanus relicto

feelings that an apostle of the Lord wrote respecting himself, " Yea, and if I be offered upon the sacrifice and service of your faith, I joy, and rejoice with you all. For the same cause also do ye joy, and rejoice with me." In fact the joy wherewith so many of the early Christian martyrs welcomed, sometimes even to excess, the day of their martyrdom, was, in its purest form, the genuine reflexion of the gladness wherewith their Master had previously humbled himself to his appointed death upon the cross. They rejoiced inasmuch as they became "partakers of Christ's sufferings." It is only one taken at random, out of innumerable testimonies on this subject, when Ignatius is described as commencing his journey from Antioch with much readiness and joy, through desire of his suffering; μετὰ πολλῆς προθυμίας καὶ χαρᾶς, ἐπιθυμίᾳ τοῦ πάθους.

IV. 1—5. *Behold thou art fair, my love.* It is written in the New Testament, that Christ loved the Church and gave himself for it, " that he might sanctify and cleanse it," "that he might present it to himself a glorious church, not having spot, or wrinkle, or any such thing; but that it should be holy and without blemish." The graces of the Church are therefore the fruits of her espousal to her Lord. Not that as yet they are perfected: the picture on which we now enter is

telonio præsentibus lucris contemptis sequendo, latro vociferando regnum cælorum a se longe alienum pervasisse monstratur. Sic quippe coronatus a matre pacificus, quæ eum secundum carnem genuit synagoga, rex Christus, verus Salomon." It is furthermore interesting to observe that the day of our Lord's suffering, being that of the Passover-feast, was emphatically the great day of all Jewish rejoicing.

but an ideal, not to be attained by the Church till the results of Christ's love to her shall be complete. Still as it is out of the espousal that that future spotlessness shall spring, the description of the one properly follows on that of the other. The words before us are those of Christ addressing the Church whom he has espoused: in her he surveys the graces which his love has wrought. The allegory describes in succession seven features of the Bride's loveliness: her eyes, her hair, her teeth, her lips, her temples, her neck, her bosom. The very remarkable character of some of these comparisons, e. g. that of the neck to the tower of David in ver. 4, as also the utter dissimilarity and even inharmoniousness between the several natural or artificial objects to which the Bride's features are compared, shew that each image must have its own distinct allegorical import. The comparisons would be as extravagant on the allegorical as on the literal interpretation, if the former were not to be carried out into details; and in fact that interpretation is virtually literal which refuses to see any allegory except in the general words, "Thou art fair." We are confirmed in viewing even the details as allegorical by observing that different features of the Bride's person are here described, where she is contemplated in her general beauty, to those which are selected for delineation where the special object is to represent her as going forth into the world on her evangelizing work, VII. 1—6. *Thine eyes are doves.* This commendation had been anticipated in I. 15: see the note there. Meek simplicity had been in fact a grace as much demanded from the Church before Christ's coming as since her espousal unto him; though it is through him and through the manifestation of his love that every grace is perfected. The quality symbolized is in great measure that expressed by the Hebrew word עָנִי, "poor," of so frequent occurrence in the Psalms, e.g. IX. 12; XXXIV. 6; LXX. 5. The patient, peaceful expectation of the Lord's salvation involved in it was at the Incarnation rewarded by the honour conferred upon Mary, wherein God "regarded the low estate of his handmaiden," and "exalted them of low degree." That it was to continue emphatically a Christian virtue was shewn by our Saviour at the commencement of his ministry by the two beatitudes, "Blessed are the poor in spirit," and " Blessed are the meek." And it was the ornament of a meek and quiet spirit which the apostle Peter pronounced as, in the sight of God, of great price. *Behind thy plaits.* The word צַמָּה occurs again in ver. 3, in VI. 7, and in Isaiah XLVII. 2. The meaning, "veil," which is now assigned to it by most interpreters, has in its favour the Greek translation of Isaiah. But for the rendering "plaits of hair" (so Hengstenberg: others give simply "locks"), we have the admitted meaning of the root צָמַם, "to twine or weave," and the asserted meaning of the corresponding Arabic root, لَمّ, "torsit crines."

The design here seems to be to set forth the natural beauty of dovelike eyes by contrast with the more artificial ornament of plaited tresses. The latter, viewed merely in themselves, might cover hideous and beautiful

11

features alike: whatever attractiveness they possess is purely superficial. And hence, since every Christian bride may well take as her model the graces described as appertaining to Christ's bride, the Church, St Peter, in the passage above referred to, enjoins that wives' adorning be not the mere outward adorning of plaiting the hair, 1 Pet. III. 3. Similarly St Paul, 1 Tim. II. 9. For as plaited tresses without when compared with eyes within, so is all outward decoration whatsoever when compared with the hidden man of the heart: the one does but excite disgust if the other be found wanting. *Thy hair is like a flock of goats, hanging down the slope of Mount Gilead.* Here we have to deal not with artificial plaits, but with the hair itself in its own natural beauty. It is compared to a flock of goats browsing all over the inclined side of a mountain, and so seeming, when viewed from a distance, to be hanging suspended to it. So Gesenius, &c.; and so Renan, "comme un troupeau de chèvres suspendues aux flancs du Galaad." The comparison is the more appropriate, as each goat, or line of goats, would represent a separate lock. Gilead is specified on account of the pastoral character of that country. The beauty for which the Bride's hair is praised would naturally consist in its length and thickness: it represents the numerousness of the people by whom the Church should be thronged. Such, substantially, is the interpretation of Philo of Carpasia among early, and of Hengstenberg among recent commentators. The former quotes the saying of the apostle, "If a woman have long hair, it is a glory to her: for her hair is given her for a covering"; and remarks that the hair of the Church is the multitude of people, with whom she covers herself according to the words of the prophet, "Lift up thine eyes round about, and behold: all these gather themselves together, and come to thee. As I live, saith the LORD, thou shalt surely clothe thee with them all, as with an ornament, and bind them on thee, as a bride doeth" (Isaiah XLIX. 18). The point on which Philo might have more definitely insisted is that this covering, like hair, is not extraneous, but springs from the Church's own richness. *Thy teeth are like a flock of shearing-sheep.* The usual translation is, "of shorn sheep." But Ginsburg with good reason observes that sheep are shorn not before they are washed, but after; and also that a comparison of VI. 6 shews that קצובות is but a poetical epithet for רחלים. He thus understands it of sheep that are shorn periodically. *All appearing in pairs.* "That is, each upper tooth has its corresponding lower one; thus they, as it were, appear in pairs, like this flock of white sheep, each of which keeps to its mate, as they come up from the washing-pool. The Hiphil of תאם, 'to be double,' 'to be pairs,' is 'to make double,' 'to make pairs,' 'to appear paired'" (Ginsburg). This is far better than the old translation, as given in our English Version. Again, it is better to render "all appearing, &c." than "which all appear, &c." For the relation expressed by the ש is quite indeterminate: it may introduce what occurs in the imagination equally with what occurs in fact: cf. Psalm CXXXIII. 2, 3. It is thus immaterial whether sheep usually came up from the wash-pool in pairs or not. The two beauties then for which the Bride's teeth are commended are their whiteness (cf. Gen. XLIX. 12) and their regularity. Now by the teeth of the Church seems most properly to be represented her power of rightly dividing that word of truth which is her bread of life; that so not being thrust down her hardly and crudely, but rather being thoroughly and effectually digested, it may serve to the ultimate sustenance and invigoration of all her members. And this power is obviously one which rests mainly with the ministers of the Church; so that the Targum was not altogether remote from the truth when it interpreted the teeth of the priests and Levites of the older dispensation. The above explanation is mentioned (though not adopted) by Ainsworth; and it is not unlikely that the interpretation of Origen accorded with it[1]. The whiteness of the teeth will denote the purity with which the dividers of the word of truth are to discharge their commission; not handling the word of God deceitfully, nor polluting or adding to it as it passes through them. The regularity of the teeth will denote the regular organization of Church ministers, all helping each other and working with each other in the discharge of their office. As regards the distribution of teeth in pairs, it is to be remembered that Christ, when he sent out his

---

[1] For he applies the following words to the double way in which the word of truth was to be taken, and consequently prepared for digestion "Ἄπασαι διδυμεύουσαι." διὰ τὸ διττὸν τῆς νοήσεως τῆς τε ῥητῆς καὶ τῆς πνευματικῆς.

apostles, and again when he sent out his seventy disciples, sent them out in each case two and two. Nor, for the most part, did the apostles depart from the example which their Master had set: we are all familiar with the companionship of Peter and John, of Paul and Barnabas, of Barnabas and Mark, of Paul and Silas. Even with reference to the testimony of the Church in times of severe persecution, it is worthy of note that while in the Old Testament we have Elijah complaining, "I, even I only am left," in the New Testament the witnesses that prophesy in sackcloth are two in number. We have on this verse further merely to observe that the Fathers, Philo, Theodoret, Augustine, all explained the wash-pool of the laver of baptism. But for this there is perhaps hardly sufficient need or warrant. *Like a crimson brede.* It is at least curious that the same expression should be used of the line which Rahab the harlot suspended from her window in Jericho, and in which the Fathers, from Clement of Rome downwards, so delighted to trace a symbolical meaning. The colour intended is that produced from the insect *coccus ilicis*, or cochineal, a rich and beautiful hue, deeper than that of lips generally. *And lovely to behold is thine utterance.* Not as English Version, "thy speech is comely," for the whole description in these verses applies to what is seen, not to what is heard. On the other hand, there is no authority for understanding by מדבר, as do recent translators, either the tongue, the mouth, or the palate; nor is such rendering necessary. It is for the gracefulness with which she opens her lips that the Bride is here praised: such commendation forms the natural sequel to the commendation of the beauty of her lips themselves. The general interpretation of the earlier eulogy may be given in the words of Origen: "it sets forth the blood-rich and living character of the words which come forth through her lips, words dipped, as it were, in the genuine potion of the blood of Christ." In the name of Christ her Saviour, delivered unto death for her, are all her prayers offered to the throne of grace above; "Worthy is the Lamb that was slain" is the burden of all her praises; and similarly, "Christ crucified" is the burden of all her preaching, wherewith she addresses herself to those whom God hath purchased with his own blood. And sweet and beautiful it is to hear her putting forth, alike to God and to man, the glory of the salvation with which she has thus been enriched and quickened. *Like a slice of pomegranate are thy temples.* The reference is probably to the delicate colours of the pulpy grains which only fully appear when the fruit is cut or when it is bursting: it was from these that it derived its European name, "pomum granatum," or grained apple. As the half-concealed hues of the pomegranate, such also were the blushing hues upon the temples of the Bride, partially concealed behind her plaits of hair: the whole betokening, in the Church, "her reverend and modest countenance, as fearing and taking heed lest she should speak or do amiss, or blushing if she had failed" (Ainsworth). Theodoret, and probably Origen, took nearly the same view, though they were both much embarrassed by the eccentricity of the Greek translation. *Thy neck is like the tower of David built with projecting parapets, whereon are hung the thousand shields,* &c. Our first business is here with the controverted word לתלפיות, our translation of which, "with projecting parapets," is in partial accordance with, and derives support from, that of Symmachus, εἰς ἐπάλξεις (al. ἐπάνω ἐπάλξεων). The word תלפיות, or rather its singular תלפיה, is regularly derived from the root לפה. That root is, according to Buxtorf, actually found in Chaldee in the Targum of Jonathan on Lev. VI. 5; although in the Targum, as printed by Walton, we read not ילפי but יוסף. However, whether the root be used or no, its meaning may be assumed to be identical with that of לפף, which is found in other places in the Targum of Onkelos. The meaning is "to add on," "to join on." The substantive derived from it, when applied to a building, would thus naturally denote the projecting parts of the building, which seem, as it were, to be added on to the rest. We have an analogous term in the Chaldee לופין, derived from the same root as תלפיות, and used in the Talmud of strongly marked eyebrows. The projecting parapets of a tower are in fact its eyebrows. And that ancient towers were built with such projecting parapets, and moreover that shields were hung, by way of display, on the exterior of the parapets, is established in the most satisfactory manner by a representation on a bas-relief at Kouyounjik, given by Layard, and also in Smith's Dict. of the Bible, s. v. Gammadims. Of the current explanations of תלפיות, the only one which seems to call for notice is that which derives it from תלה, "to hang," פיות, "edges," and makes it mean "an armoury." Against this lie the objections, 1st, that it unnecessarily treats תלפיות as a composite word; 2nd, that an armoury would be more naturally described as a "hang-weapons" than a "hang-edges;" 3rd, that the figure before us is not that of an armoury, but of a building with shields hung on its exterior; 4th, that any etymological connexion between the words תלפיות and תלוי in the two adjoining clauses is improbable, as it would destroy the charm of the studied homœophony. With respect to this last, see on I. 3. Of the history of the tower here alluded to comparatively little is known, as it was never rebuilt after the captivity, and is consequently not mentioned (so far as we can judge) by Nehemiah; for none of the several towers specified in his account of the walls of Jerusalem seem to be of the importance that would attach to a tower known as "the tower of David." It was in all probability the chief ornament of that part of Jerusalem which was called by David after his own name the City of David, and which lay immediately to the north of the temple (see my Ancient Jerusalem). Doubtless it either formed part of, or else adjoined, the royal residence constructed for David by the workmen of King Hiram of Tyre; and it is worthy of note that the castles of the bas-relief referred to above, which it resembled, both in its shape and in its display, were those of some maritime, possibly Phœnician, people. There are two other passages of Scripture in which we may trace some allusion to this tower. The one is Micah IV. 8: "Thou, O tower of the flock, the strong hold of the daughter of Zion," a passage fully explained by Hengstenberg in his Christology, where he shews that the tower was a symbol of the royal dignity and authority of the house of David. The other is Isaiah v. 2, where the tower in the midst of the vineyard is outwardly this tower of Zion, the symbol of that Davidic sovereignty, which formed, and through Christ the Son of David still forms, the safeguard and salvation of the heritage of God. In the absence of any description of the tower, it may help us to estimate aright its architectural dignity, if we refer to the description which Josephus has given of the three great towers of Herod, named by him Hippicus, Phasael, and Mariamne; towers which, according to Josephus, exceeded in magnitude, beauty, and strength all that the world could produce, and which, in the destruction of the city by Titus, were spared as memorials of its splendour and of its fortifications. The style of Herod's towers was, of course, not that of the tower of David; but they stood, in some measure, in the same relation to the rest of the buildings of the city. *The whole of the targes of the valiants.* For the valiants, see above on III. 7. If it be intended that anywhere near a thousand shields had been suspended on the tower, they could only well be the shields of several successive generations of warriors. This would imply that the date of the Song is considerably later than the age of Solomon. The practice of suspending shields on the exterior of walls is not only illustrated by the bas-relief already mentioned, but also referred to, in the case of Tyre, in Ezek. XXVII. 11. What now are the points of resemblance between the neck of the Bride and the tower of David? First, the erectness: secondly, the majestic gracefulness involved in lifting high that which is conspicuous at the top, the tower carrying its projecting parapets, the neck carrying the head: thirdly, the decoration with ornaments, the value of which, whether jewels or shields, depended on their historical interest. The whole betokens the stedfast and majestic boldness with which the Church ever lifts aloft her head; and this through faith. It was by like faith that "the elders obtained a good report;" and their memories are therefore still dear to her, and their deeds of faith in former time are her encouragement and her boast, and, through her familiarity with them, the shields of faith whereby in their day they quenched the fiery darts of the devil may still be said to hang as holy memorials on the defences of her walls and the heights of her battlements. Before we part from this picture, let it be remarked how inappropriate and highflown would be the comparison to the tower of David of any mere earthly bride; and what a testimony is borne by this to the exclusively spiritual character of the Song *Thy two breasts.* The fountains of nourishment: cf. Isaiah LXVI. 11; 1 Pet. II. 2. *Like two young twins, fawns of a gazelle.* The gazelle is mentioned, as before, for its graceful tenderness; and the youth of the gazelle adds to its tenderness. The fawns are twins to the end that they may be pictured to the imagination as exactly corresponding in size; and that so the Church may lie under no suspicion of deformity. *That feed among the lilies.* Lilies are, as before, the emblems of purity; and the feeding may denote the original imbibing of the doctrine which the Church is afterwards in turn to impart to her children. The substance of the whole therefore is that the Church tenderly and regularly nourishes her children with the milk of that pure and sound doctrine which she herself has derived from a heavenly source. Let us now, in conclusion, sum up our interpretation of the beauties of the Bride's person. The first three qualities surveyed in her are her meekness, her prolific richness, and her power of rightly dividing the word of truth. The last three are her reverent modesty, her boldness of faith, and her power of nourishing with pure doctrine. In the middle and therefore most prominent place stands her testimony to redemption though the blood of Christ; the same testimony with that which, in the Apocalyptic vision, the elders and angels in heaven utter forth before the throne of God (Rev. v).

Ver. 6. This, the central verse of the section, stands out in striking contrast to the rest. The position however which it occupies, in the midst of the Bridegroom's address, leads us naturally to infer that its words must be his; and this was the view of the older interpreters. The theme of the verse will thus be

Christ's surrender of himself for the Church in sacrificial death before that her season of grace have passed away. This is in fact the general theme of the entire section of which this verse forms the central gem; and the verse must be regarded not as posterior in logical or chronological sequence to what has immediately preceded, but as embodying with enigmatical brevity the purport of the whole. In order however that the representation in this central verse may be rendered as general as possible, the image of the espousal is not directly introduced into it. There is another, though on the whole less probable, view which may be taken of the precise meaning of the verse by those who deem that the analogy of its language to that of II. 17, VIII. 14 furnishes sufficient ground for putting it into the mouth of the Bride. The import of the words, regarded as hers, and translated into Christian language, would be this: that ere the season of darkness, wrath, and desolation set finally in, the atoning death of Christ should be her refuge. With this would substantially accord the words of Isaiah, XXXII. 2: "A man shall be as an hiding-place from the wind, and a covert from the tempest." And we should then have to observe that, as in the earlier sections of the Song Christ was the comfort of the Church in expectation, so here he is her comfort in very act. It will be seen that whichever view we take of the verse in its dramatic relations, its general bearing in reference to the contents of the section of which it forms the centre remains substantially the same. It wraps up in itself the death of Christ for the

Church's sake. *Against the day breathe cool, &c.* See on II. 17. *To the mountain of myrrh, and to the hill of frankincense.* For the import of the myrrh and the frankincense, see on III. 6. The mountain seems to come before us either as a place of nearer communion with God; or else as a place where the myrrh-tree grows, and where the perfume is consequently to be obtained in full abundance. From the days of the Targumist downwards it has been frequently assumed that in the mountain of myrrh, מור (*mor*), there is an allusive reference to the name Moriah, מוריה. Such reference would be in full keeping with the general practice of the Song; and it would also be appropriate, as the name Moriah had in previous Scripture been exclusively associated with the offering of Isaac (Gen. XXII.), by which the sacrifice of Christ had been so remarkably foreshadowed. But can we trace any similar allusion in the hill of frankincense, לבונה (*lebonah*)? For this the correspondence seems almost in that case to require. Our thoughts naturally turn first to Lebanon, לבנון, more especially as it is mentioned in the next verse but one; but the associations of that mountain seem ill-suited to our present passage. More probably the Poet may have had Shiloh in his mind, and may have mentally styled it the hill of Lebonah, or frankincense, from the village Lebonah, between two or three miles distant; which village may perhaps even itself have been so named as being the place where the frankincense for the use of the tabernacle was in earlier times prepared. Shiloh, equally with Zion, was within the limits of the mountain-range of Moriah; this latter name not having been restricted to any single hill till a later period (see my Ancient Jerusalem, pp. 44—48). And though its glory had never returned to it since the days of the high-priest Eli, and though its subsequent desolation passed into a proverb, its olden associations may have floated for the moment before the mind of the Israelitish Poet, who has, in his Song, uniformly avoided all mention of the Jewish temple. But we must not speculate too far. The general import of the verse before us is independent of any plays on words which it may contain, and may be treated as certain, while these remain uncertain.

Vv. 7—11. These verses resume the Bridegroom's address to his Spouse. He first briefly sums up all his previous praises: he then proceeds to describe the rich prospect of triumph and delight which, through their mutual espousal, opens out before them. *Thou art all of thee fair.* As had been shewn in detail in vv. 1—5. *Not a blemish in thee.* From this the words of the apostle in Eph. v. 27 seem to be almost directly borrowed. *From Lebanon, spouse, with me.* We have, for convenience' sake, throughout this commentary spoken of the object of the Beloved's affections as the Bride. This is however the first time that she is so addressed in the Song itself; obviously with reference to the fact that the espousal has been accomplished, and that she is now about to share the triumphs of her espoused Lord. The word כלה is used here and in the ensuing verses without any suffix; it is not "my spouse," but simply "spouse";

mainly, perhaps, because the object was to mark not whose bride she was, but rather the fact that her espousal had been solemnized. *From Lebanon with me shalt thou come, shalt gaze from the summit of Amana, &c.* It is not easy to improve on what Hengstenberg has written on this passage: it may be allowable therefore to translate and abridge his comment on it. "The heavenly Solomon, such is the thought, assures his bride of freedom from the dominion of the world. Mountains are, in the holy Scriptures of both the Old Testament and the New Testament, the symbols of kingdoms, cf. Psalm LXV. 6, LXXVI. 4; Jer. LI. 25; Zech. IV. 7; Rev. VIII. 8, XVII. 9. This symbolism is frequently extended by a further representation, in which the mountain-chain of Lebanon and Antilibanus, which separated the heathen territory on the north from the seat of God's people, is treated as the image of the heathen world-power. So in Psalm XXIX, of which David was the author, where the wilderness of Kadesh is coupled by way of correspondence with Lebanon and Sirion, it is the symbols of the world-power on the north and on the south of the Lord's territory that are represented as seized with terror at his voice, and as unable to endure the thunder of his might. So again in another psalm of David's, Psalm LXVIII, Bashan repeatedly appears as the border of Canaan towards the heathen world beyond. In Isaiah XXXVII. 24 the King of Assyria knows no higher boast than that he has ascended the highest summit of Lebanon: his meaning being that he has thus the whole world-power beneath his feet. And in Isaiah x. 34, Hab. II. 17, Lebanon appears as the image of the Assyrian kingdom. Now in the Song of Songs it is fundamentally assumed, in accordance with the representations which we find in the Davidic psalms, that Israel will, at the time of the appearance of the heavenly Solomon, be in a state of subjection to the power of the world, and will through him be exalted to the glorious liberty of the children of God. The expressly repeated 'with me' of the present passage points to the fact that freedom from subjection is only possible for the people of God through union with the heavenly Solomon: 'Without me ye can do nothing,' Joh. xv. 5. The Bride however, through her union with the heavenly Solomon, is not only to be freed from the power of the world, but is also to have it under her feet, and to look down in security from its heights; in fulfilment of the promise, Messianic in its ultimate reference, of Deut. XXXIII. 29: 'Thine enemies shall be found liars unto thee; and thou shalt tread upon their high places.' This assurance of dominion over the world along with deliverance from the world is contained in the words 'Shalt gaze from the summit of Amana, &c.' The summit of Amana is identical with the summit of Shenir and Hermon: it is the summit in which the Amana, or Abana (see the Keri on 2 Kings v. 12), had its rise. The name is here specially employed because the river Amana flowed through the first great world-city, Damascus, on which the Bride looks proudly down; a city which was, in early times, of even greater importance than afterwards, when it was thrown into the shade by the side of Nineveh and Babylon. The Amana serves to mark the direction in which, from Hermon, the Bride is to gaze: it carries her eye to Damascus, and forms the link which connects the symbol with the thing symbolized. So that, to sum up: Deliverance from the world is represented as a coming from Lebanon: Dominion over the world as a gazing downward from Hermon." *Shenir and Hermon.* "Shenir was the Amoritish name of Hermon, Deut. III. 9. As such it is here placed before the more usual name, in order to indicate that the mountain comes into view as the symbol of the heathen power." Only one mountain is intended: it is that magnificent summit in which the whole Antilibanus range culminated, the modern Jebel esh-Sheikh. *From the dens of lions, from the mountains of panthers.* "Lions and panthers form a frequent symbolical designation of the fierce enemies of the people of God: cf. Jer. v. 6; Nah. II. 12; Hab. I. 8, &c." *Thou hast ravished my heart.* Lit. "Thou hast behearted me;" and in truth it would be. better could we altogether avoid the various words of expediency to which translators have here had recourse, "vulnerâsti," "ravished," "taken away," &c., all of which introduce somewhat of a foreign element into the simple phrase. The expression is to be interpreted by the help of such passages as 2 Kings X. 15, "Is thine heart right, as my heart is with thy heart?", and Prov. XXIII. 15, "My son, if thine heart be wise, my heart shall rejoice, even mine." It implies the answering of heart to heart and the consequent union produced by the mutual engagement of the affections. Compare the well-known apophthegm of Niebuhr, "Kein andrer Gott als der Gott der Bibel, der Herz zu Herz ist." *My sister, my spouse.* More literally, "my sister, spouse:" but this sounds so awkward in English that it becomes necessary to supply the pronoun. As the pronoun is equally omitted in Hebrew where we have the word "spouse" by itself, in ver. 8, it is only by an unjustifiable refinement that some translators seek here to combine the two words together, and to render "my sister-spouse." The import of the appellation "spouse" has been already unfolded. The appellation "sister" rests partly on the fact that Christ and the Church have sprung of the same earthly mother, the Jewish nation, cf. I. 6, III. 11, and partly also on the more general fact that Christ has taken human nature upon him. The union of the two appellations is of itself an almost decisive objection against all literal interpretation of the Song. When it is urged by the literalists that the term sister is merely used as an expression of endearment, it may be at once replied that that is the very last term which, in chaste love, a bridegroom would ever think of applying to his bride. The passages referred to by Ginsburg in support of the literalist view will hardly much help him. In Prov. VII. 4 there is a metaphorical use of the term "sister," but it does not proceed from either a bridegroom or a lover. In Tobit VII. 12 Tobias is called his bride's ἀδελφός and vice versâ, but this is with reference to their previous consanguinity. In the Apocryphal Esther XV. 9, Ahasuerus says to Esther, "I am thy brother, be of good cheer." But why? He was the lord of a harem, the obligations of conjugal affection sat loosely upon him, and his being Esther's husband afforded no guarantee that her life would be spared: accordingly he resorts, in order to assure her, to a term of endearment of a different kind, just as an untruthful man, when he wishes to obtain credence, resorts to an oath. The very use of the term shewed how little, in his case, conjugal relation went for. Finally appeal is made to the use of the Latin "soror." This word is employed by heathen poets to denote the object of an illicit attachment: it has yet to be shewn that it ever designates a lawful partner. Chaste love, which is not ashamed to call a bride a bride, and a wife a wife, has no need of such equivocal disguises. Thus then the following observations, in a Homily printed with the works of Athanasius, still retain their full force: "Wherefore does he style her both spouse and sister? A bridegroom generally does not give the name sister to his spouse. That name however he here bestows, in order to shew that it is before no carnal bridechamber that the hymeneal song is here being sung. In styling her spouse, he means that the Word has wedded to himself the human soul" [better however if the Church Catholic, not the individual soul, had here come under view]: "in styling her also sister, he testifies that he himself has worn our human flesh. Let none then deem these words to be of carnal meaning." Cassiodorus neatly writes: "Sponsam et sororem suam sanctam dicit ecclesiam, quæ et sponsa est, quia eam sibi Christus incarnatus despondit eamque, emundatam sordibus peccatorum, dote Spiritus sancti sibi conjunxit; soror vero est, quia propter eam incarnatus." *With one bend of thine eyes, with one chainlet of thy necklace.* Of the two parts of the Bride's person described in vv. 1—5, it is just her eyes and her neck that symbolize the direction of the thoughts of the Church to Christ. Her eyes represent the meekness of her waiting upon him: her neck the boldness of her faith in him. We found moreover that her necklace, which, though not directly mentioned, was implied, represented the monuments of the faith of the most illustrious of her members. The import therefore of the passage before us must be this: that a single act of waiting on Christ, a single act of faith in him, is accepted before him, and fails not to draw forth from him the manifestation of his love. A doctrine full of comfort to thousands who tremble for the ignorance, rudeness, and imperfection of their devotion! Yet withal how abundantly illustrated by the narratives of the Gospels, where the single cry, "Have mercy on us, O Lord, thou Son of David," the single determination to touch the hem of the Saviour's garment, the single half-expressed willingness to be made whole, and even that not spontaneously put forward, drew forth this or some corresponding gracious answer, "Thy faith hath saved thee: go in peace!" *How fair is thy love, &c.* The heavenly Bridegroom now addresses the Bride in terms similar to those in which, in the very beginning of the Song, I. 2—4, she had addressed him. "By loves" (the word in Hebrew is plural) "are meant not only the affections, but the actions also and fruits of love, which the Church manifesteth towards Christ, by her 'work of faith, and labour of love, and patience of hope;' and by keeping 'his commandments,' 1 Thess. I. 3; 1 John v. 3" (Ainsworth). And this it is that Christ desires. How ought such representations as this, of its welcomeness before him, to quicken the zeal of our devotion! *And the scent of thy ointments.* The ointments of the Church are the graces wherewith she has been endued. *Thy lips drop honeycomb-drops, my spouse; honey and milk are under thy tongue.* The outward idea in both clauses is the same, viz. that the mouth is full to overflowing with the richness that streams forth from it. This richness consists in honey and milk, the two rich products for which the land of Canaan was praised by Moses. The worth of honey is its sweetness: that of milk its nutritiousness, cf. 1 Pet. II. 2. And we shall hardly be going too far in thus interpreting: that the same discourse of the Church which is pleasing in the sight of Christ is full of nourishment also to her own children. *And the fragrance of thy attire is as the fragrance of Lebanon.* The fragrance of Lebanon is, at least in part, the fragrance of the wine of Lebanon, cf. Hos. XIV. 7. The attire of the Bride represents the condition of the Church in the sight of God. The like is the case with the wedding-garment of the parable, and with the fine linen of the Lamb's wife, which "is the righteousness of saints," Rev. XIX. 8. Compare also Zech. III. 3, 4. The meaning therefore is that the state of the Church is a state of acceptance before God, a state in which the favour of God rests upon her. For the former cannot be separated from the latter: even in Gen. XXVII. 27, the fragrant field is the field "which the LORD hath blessed."

Ver. 12—v. 1. In these six verses, of which one, ver. 16, is uttered by the Bride herself, the Church is compared to a garden, filled with the richest and most fragrant plants. That Christ may delight himself in the garden as is meet, it must yield forth its perfumes; which it can only do through those quickening gales that by an easy symbolism represent the gracious influences of the Holy Spirit. The summons of ver. 16 to those gales to blow implies that the time for them to blow is arrived. In other words, the passion of Christ being now complete, the life-giving Spirit is poured forth from on high upon the Church, to the end that she may abundantly bring forth the fruits of righteousness to her Redeemer. *A garden.* A pregnant remark has been made by Dr Wolff (Autobiography, I. pp. 248, 249) to the effect that when Jesus after his resurrection first appeared to Mary Magdalene, and she took him for the gardener, "the mistake was not great; for our Blessed Lord was a gardener, because he planted the garden of God, the Church, where the fruits ripen, and are made fit for the kingdom of heaven." That St John should have mentioned the fact of Mary's mistake renders it highly probable that he had this symbolism directly in view: symbolism attaches in general to all the minuter circumstances that he records. Christ had watered the garden with his blood: he was now risen from the dead, and henceforth all the treasures of the garden were, beneath his fostering care, to unfold themselves with new and sympathetic life[1]. *Enclosed.* Shut out, as Cyril observes, to the world, but open to the heavenly Bridegroom. Very little did the world without understand of the inward life of the Church of Christ: very little was the world able to interfere with its development and spread. *A garden enclosed*, second time. The received Hebrew text here gives not גן but גל, which our E. V. renders "a spring." But the word never occurs elsewhere in this sense; nor is it indeed, in the singular, applied to aught but a heap of stones. The LXX, Syriac and Jerome read גן, as before; the same either is or was the reading of one-ninth of the manuscripts; and this ought on every account to be preferred. The reading of the Targum is uncertain. *A fountain.* There can be no doubt that as in the former part of this verse the Church is compared to a garden, so here she, the same, is compared to a fountain. This may be seen from the verses that follow. The one comparison is expanded in vv. 13, 14: the other in ver. 15. The Church then is at once both garden and fountain; and the two images must be kept asunder; not mixed up together, as though by a fountain nothing more than a watered garden were intended. The Church is a fountain, as being the proximate source whence grace is derived to the faithful. Water appears

---

[1] Cassiodorus writes, on VI. 1: "In horto sepeliri voluit, et primum Mariæ Magdalenæ in horto apparuit, ibique quodammodo primitias ecclesiæ consecravit."

as the symbol of spiritual grace in John IV, and elsewhere; and there is a substantial accordance in doctrine between our present passage and the prophecies in Joel III. 18 and Ezek. XLVII, in which waters are represented as issuing from beneath God's holy dwelling. If it be asked how the waters first came there, it is easily answered that the Church is the appointed receptacle of the grace of God, the fulness of him that filleth all in all. But this does not here come immediately into view. *Sealed.* A fountain is said to be "sealed" or "stopped," when its waters, instead of being raised at once to the surface of the ground above, are diverted by a subterranean channel to some other place for which they are needed. Such is the case with the fountain which supplies the Pools of Solomon, south-west of Bethlehem. The general import of the figure is that the grace with which the Church abounds is not wasted upon those that value it not, like pearls cast before swine, but is conveyed by appointed means to those for whose benefit it is bestowed. *Thy shoots a paradise of pomegranates, &c.* The image of the garden is unfolded. Its products consist, first, of fruit-bearing trees; and secondly, of aromatics. The distinctive import of the several trees and plants enumerated either has been or will be noted at other passages of the Song; see on I. 12—14; III. 6; VIII. 2. Two observations only seem needful here. First, that the garden is described as a paradise of all that is most precious: "precious fruits," "all trees of frankincense" (i.e. every species of such tree), "all choicest aromatics" (lit. "all chiefs of aromatics"). Secondly, that the Church is here commended, in the main, for the same glories for which she herself had commended Christ. It is the highest glory of the Church of Christ that she is being made like unto him, and that her members are being conformed to his image; that by her own sufferings she is entering into the fellowship of his sufferings, and that the triumph of his death is being continually repeated in her career. Christ himself indicated this beforehand. "The disciple is not above his master, nor the servant above his lord. It is enough for the disciple that he be as his master, and the servant as his lord." "Ye shall drink indeed of my cup, and be baptized with the baptism that I am baptized with." *A bubbling fountain.* The image of the fountain is unfolded. The Hebrew text has מעין גנים "a fountain of gardens." This seems inappropriate; partly because the introduction of the "gardens" tends to confusion with the previous image, partly because as that spoke of "a garden," in the singular, we should hardly here have mention of "gardens," in the plural. Houbigant conjectured, with unusual felicity, that for גנים we should read גלים; and this, though unconfirmed by external authority, has so strongly the appearance of being the true reading, that we may, without much rashness, venture to accept it. The error in transcription might be naturally connected with the reverse change of גן into גל in ver. 12. The word denotes the waves of the fountain, continually welling upwards; and this harmonizes with what follows. The fountain is perennial. *And streams from Lebanon.* That is, writes Delitzsch, as fresh as though they came from Lebanon. But we may even go further, and allow it to be the streams of Lebanon itself that are here in imagination represented as irrigating the garden. The whole scene is one of imagination, not of outward fact; and to the introduction of the streams of Lebanon we have a close parallel in Psalm CXXXIII. 3, where the dew of Hermon is pictured as descending upon the mountains of Zion. These streams are introduced partly, perhaps, to call up the remembrance of the rich and beautiful scenery through which the course of many of them lies, e.g. that of the Kadîsha, which runs through the valley of Kanôbîn; partly, because, unlike too many of the torrents in the parched regions of the south, they flow all the year through. "The fertility of this upper region of Lebanon," writes Robinson, speaking of the scenery round the Kadîsha, "is mainly caused by the great abundance of water. Fountains and streams are everywhere bursting forth; and even the high declivities of the hills are richly irrigated" (Later Bib. Res. p. 595). *Awake, O north wind! and approach, thou south! Blow on my garden,* &c. The Bride, continuing with a slight modification the image of the garden, prays now that it may be made meet for him to whom it rightfully belongs. The latter part of the verse, "Let my beloved come, &c." is indisputably spoken by her. A few critics have however contended that the earlier portion of it cannot be put into her mouth, because the words "my garden" would then be inconsistent with the fact that she herself, and not anything separate, had been described as the garden. They consequently desire to retain this part of the verse for the Beloved: urging moreover that the "my garden" and the "his garden" indicate a change of speaker. Still such a change in the middle of a verse would require to be more clearly and more definitely marked; while on the other hand the modification of the image from a garden with which the Bride is identified to a garden of which she is the keeper is so easy that little stress can be laid upon it. It was the more readily made, that so the garden might not be represented as speaking. The fact that the great majority of commentators have put the whole verse into the Bride's mouth, may be taken as a decisive proof that that is the more natural view. The address to the north wind and the south wind is, in effect, an address to the wind generally: Ginsburg well illustrates this by referring to the poetical expansion of Num. XI. 31 in Psalm LXXVIII. 26. And the wind is the emblem of the Holy Spirit. It may not be too much to assert that the present passage prepared the way for the outward manifestation, in the mighty rushing wind, of the descent of the Holy Spirit on the great day of Pentecost. On that day began to be fulfilled the prayer to which the Bride here gives utterance. Her position in this verse is that of the apostles, waiting for the promise of the Father. But in the dramatic form in which the Song of Songs is cast, the utterance of the desire implies, of course, its accomplishment. The wind of the

Spirit blows upon the garden of the Church, and the perfumes of its deeds of holiness flow forth, pleasing and acceptable to Christ the Redeemer. For the symbolical import of wind, as representing the Holy Spirit, we may compare Ezekiel's vision of the dry bones (XXXVII. 9), and our Saviour's discourse with Nicodemus (Joh. III. 8); nor should we forget the fact that alike in Hebrew, Greek, Latin, and English, the Third Person of the Blessed Trinity is designated by a word signifying, etymologically, wind or breath. *Let my beloved come into his garden and eat his precious fruits.* Which Christ does, in a spiritual manner, by looking on the holy works of his Church. That which is "good and acceptable in the sight of God our Saviour" (1 Tim. II. 3) is good and acceptable also in the sight of Christ; viz. that the Church should walk "unto all pleasing, being fruitful in every good work" (Col. I. 10). The Apocalyptic epistles illustrate this. To the angel of the church of Ephesus Christ says: "I know thy works, and thy labour, and thy patience." To the angel of the church in Thyatira: "I know thy works, and charity, and service, and faith, and thy patience, and thy works." Similarly, *mutatis mutandis*, to the rest. The translation "and eat its"—for "his"—"precious fruits" is admissible, but not so good as the other: if the garden be "his," the fruits would also naturally be described as "his." *I am come into my garden.* The earthly career of the Church of the latter days in the sight of her ascended Redeemer has commenced: Christianity is, through the abiding grace of the Holy Spirit, bringing forth its fruits throughout the world. The myrrh and the spices, the honeycomb and the honey, the wine and the milk, which serve to represent the various acts and affections of devotion of the Church to her Lord, had all been either enumerated or implied in IV. 10, 11. *Eat, O friends! Drink and enjoy ye, O beloved!* Philo of Carpasia, who like the older Christian commentators generally, looks rather to the outward parallel than to the relation symbolized, explains these words of the sacramental passover supper, and of the "Take, eat; this is my body," and the "Drink ye all of it; for this is my blood of the new testament," which were to form a perpetual and binding ordinance on the New Testament Church. Nor is he fundamentally wrong. That very ordinance was to be a witness that by the same act wherein the Christian faithful presented themselves, a reasonable, holy and lively sacrifice, unto their Saviour, they were to hold communion with him and with each other. The words before us are plainly an invitation from Christ to all the faithful to participate in the joy wherewith he welcomes the devotions offered by the Church unto himself. Doubtless that is their greatest joy, to rejoice with him in the honour which he receives: doubtless at this present time there is nought which so gladdens the hearts and strengthens the spirits of the individual members of the Church, as to behold the continual efforts of the Church, as a body, to yield forth unto her espoused Lord that which he rightfully claims from her. A similar representation is to be found in the New Testament, in the parable of the marriage of the king's son, where the members of the Church sit down, as guests, to the wedding-feast of Christ and of the Church his bride. Other passages in which the faithful are represented as eating with Christ are Luke XXII. 30, "That ye may eat and drink at my table in my kingdom": Rev. III. 20, "And he [shall sup] with me." For the use of the word "friends," compare John XV. 15, "Henceforth..... I have called you friends." The occurrence of the word here affords a confirmation of the correctness of the primitive rendering of רעיך by "thy friends," not "thy thoughts," in Psalm CXXXIX. 17. The word דודים elsewhere in the Song signifies "love:" the parallelism however shews that it is here to be taken as a concrete, "beloved."

THE ABSENCE.

v. 2—8.

Jesu dulcis memoria.
                    BERNARD.

2 *Bride.* Asleep am I, but my heart is awake:
There soundeth the voice of my beloved knocking,
'Open to me, my sister, my love,
My dove, my own one,
For my head is filled with dew,
My locks with the drops of the night.'

3 I have put off my vesture,
How shall I put it on?
I have washed my feet,
How shall I besoil them?

4 My beloved thrust in his hand through the door-hole,
And my bowels were disquieted with yearning for him.

5 Up I arose to open to my beloved,
And my hands dropped with myrrh,
And my fingers with liquid myrrh,
Upon the handles of the bolt.

6 Forthwith I opened to my beloved,
And my beloved had turned and was gone;
My soul failed me for what he had spoken:
I sought him, but I did not find him;
I called him, but he did not answer me.

7 The watchmen found me that go about the city,
 they smote me, they wounded me,
They stripped me of my covering mantle,
The watchmen of the walls.

8 I adjure you, O daughters of Jerusalem,
  If ye shall find my beloved,
  O! declare ye to him,
  That I am sick with love!

We now enter upon the second half of the Song. In the former half the delineation of the career of the ancient Church had been carried up to the epoch when her longings were satisfied by her espousal with the Messiah, and when by the pouring down of the Spirit from on high the new period of righteousness and of peace, of devotion and of joy, was inaugurated. But the end was not yet. The Christian Church, the Church now wedded to Christ and sanctified by his Spirit, was to pass through a new career of expectation and of trial, the counterpart of the career of the Church of the older dispensation; a career to be terminated only by his second and final appearing, even as his first appearing had formed the close of the earlier period. He, the Bridegroom, was to be taken away for a time from the children of the bridechamber, and they were to mourn because he was no longer present, in the body, with them. This forms the theme of the fourth and present section of the Song, which we may accordingly entitle The Absence. But though outwardly separated, Christ and his Church were not to be spiritually parted; the promise, "Lo, I am with you alway, even unto the end of the world," was to have a real and undeniable fulfilment. The glory which accrued to the Church in consequence of this presence of her Lord with her is set forth in the fifth section, which we shall thus appropriately designate The Presence. One further section, the sixth, was needful to the completion of the Song: Christ was to appear again in the flesh, and love was then to reap her final and manifest triumph.

The section now before us is the shortest in the Song, containing but seven verses. The Bride speaks in it throughout: what had been uttered by the Bridegroom is recounted by her.

Asleep am I, but my heart is awake. The great resemblance which this whole section bears to the passage III. 1 seqq., enables us to refer back to that for guidance in the interpretation of the present symbolism. It is in the first place evident that it is the night-time during which the Bride here represents herself as sleeping: indeed at the end of the verse the "night" is expressly mentioned. The night here must, like that of III. 1, be the night of suffering and sorrow. Then again, inasmuch as it is night, we must not be surprised at finding the Bride asleep: night is the natural season of sleep. She was not, it is plain, sleeping either soundly or unconcernedly, for her heart was awake, agitated by the remembrance of the object of her desires, and by the apparent disappointment of her hopes. From which it follows that no great stress is to be laid on the mention of her sleep: in simply recognizing that it is night-time, we have recognized the point of main importance. And even so far as any interpretation is to be given to her sleep, it must be borne in mind that sleep has, in

Scripture, two distinct meanings. It represents both the blameworthy neglect of duty, and the repose of peaceful confidence in God. The former, viz. neglect, and with this the spiritual deadness which is the judicial consequence of neglect, is its import in Prov. xx. 13, xxiii. 21; Isaiah xxix. 10, lvi. 10; Rom. xiii. 11; 1 Thess. v. 6, 7, &c. For the other meaning we may refer to Psalm cxxvii. 2, "He giveth his beloved sleep;" also to Psalm iii. 5; Prov. iii. 24; Jer. xxxi. 26; and, in the New Testament, to the parable of the ten virgins. In this parable, which has in respect of its bridal imagery an obvious analogy with the Song of Songs, it will be remembered that the wise sleep along with the foolish, and yet are ready when their Lord comes. Their sleep is that calm, healthy sleep of peacefulness with which, whether in life or in death, as God shall appoint, they await the Bridegroom's promised approach; and for a delineation of the true spirit of such sleep as this, in connexion with the announcement that "the Lord is at hand," we may compare Phil. iv. 5—7. Now it is possible that the sleep of the Bride may, in spite of the wakefulness of her heart, have had in it some elements both of undue negligence, and of peaceful trust: still whatever such ethical meaning be attached to it can only be admitted as subordinate. The scene of anxiety which the Song here depicts represents, from the minuteness of the description, a definite epoch in the history of the Church. It is the night-time of heaviness wherein she is plunged into mourning for the loss of her Lord; the Great Sabbath, during which, to her inexpressible grief and bewilderment, he on whom all her hopes had been set lies lifeless in the grave. She had trusted that it had been he which should have redeemed Israel; but he is gone, and as yet she understands not fully why: he sleeps, and, through sympathy with him and through amazement at his loss, she sleeps also. This is the primary and most important reason of her slumber. There may, as we have remarked above, be a degree of negligence in her sleep: we know that during the hour of the Lord's agony in Gethsemane the three most privileged apostles were overcome with drowsiness, against which, although they were sleeping for sorrow, they should more diligently have guarded. And again her sleep, as we have also above remarked, may not be altogether devoid of peaceful confidence: those who in the full tide of sorrow for their departed Saviour rested, even from outwardly honouring him, the sabbath-day, according to the commandment, could not surely have been without calm trust that God was ordering all for the best, and that his gracious purpose should not fail. But while the Church thus slept, her heart was awake, for thinking of him whom she had lost. Would he return? Should she behold him yet again? *There soundeth the voice of my beloved knocking.* Literally, "The voice of my beloved knocketh." The meaning conveyed by the words is clear enough, but the compression of the language is too violent to be retained in English. The imagery of this passage is employed, with a more extended and general meaning, by the Lord Jesus Christ himself, Rev. III. 20. *Open to me.* It is no mere dream that the Bride here relates. The speed with which the Beloved soon disappears might indeed induce the suspicion that he had never really been present, but on the other hand we must take account not only of the distinctness with which the Bride asserts his presence, but also of the extent to which her own subsequent conduct is dictated by the assurance that he had been truly there. So too it is not only in the recorded testimony, but also in the consequent course of action, of the apostolic company that we read the evidence of the truth of Christ's resurrection. *My sister.* It was on his resurrection that Christ first openly and unreservedly spoke of his disciples as his brethren, Matth. XXVIII. 10; John XX. 17, cf. Psalm XXII. 22. *My love.* All terms of endearment are here crowded together, in order that the Bride may be assured that her Beloved, thus returning to her, claims her indeed as his own. *My dove.* Her eyes had been previously compared to doves, I. 15, IV. 1. *My own one.* Literally, "my perfect one," i.e. mine perfectly or entirely. Compare the Homeric use of the Greek φίλος. *For my head is filled with dew, my locks with the drops of the night.* The most ancient Christian interpretation, as found in Origen and Philo of Carpasia, beheld in this passage a definite allusion, or more than allusion, to the early morning-hour at which Christ rose from the dead. It would be wrong to press this too far; but it must at the same time be admitted that the present imagery legitimately serves to recall with vividness the fact of the Redeemer's early rising. It was while "it was yet dark," "as it began to dawn toward the first day of the week," that Mary Magdalene came to the sepulchre, and found the stone removed. The dominion of death was not in any wise to extend into the season of new joy and life: it was upon a triumph already won that the sun of the first Lord's day of the Christian Church was to rise. The "dew" is here, as in Dan. IV. 25, the token of affliction endured; and the mention of the "head" indicates that no part had been spared, that the cup of misery had been drunk to the full, and that the affliction had fallen where it would be the most severely felt. *I have put off my vesture, how shall I put it on?* The Bride recounts her ponderings on hearing her Lord's voice. The general import of these and the following words is, that for the sudden triumph of Christ's resurrection from the dead the body of the faithful had not been prepared. It is evident from the language held by the two disciples on their walk to Emmaus, that even the tidings brought by the women as they returned from the empty sepulchre had failed to remove the desolate sadness into which the death of their Redeemer had thrown them. They were therefore off their guard: they were taken by surprise, and were at a loss how to receive their Master as he appeared to them anew. But it must not be inferred from this that there was any real reluctance to receive him. The subsequent verses of the Song shew rather that the Bride, when once she had realized the fact of her Lord's presence, was anxious in the highest degree, and at any cost to herself, to welcome him and to fold him to herself again. It was thus that Peter in his fishing-boat on the sea of Tiberias, when assured by his companion that it was the Lord who, risen from the dead, stood upon the shore, forthwith, in the impetuosity of his zeal, "girt his fisher's coat unto him, (for he was naked,) and did cast himself into the sea," John xxi. 7. The evangelist, by the minuteness with which he relates this incident, shews that he recognized its coincidence with the imagery and symbolism of the present passage of the Song. There can be the less reason for doubting the symbolical meaning attaching to Peter's girding himself with his coat, since the same action was of sufficient importance to furnish the starting-point for our Lord's subsequent warning respecting his girding himself when he was young, and another girding him when he was old. *I have washed my feet, how shall I besoil them?* The feet, especially as besoiled with dust, indicate a journey. When the Lord Jesus yielded up his life upon the cross, when those sacred feet whereon he had travelled after men in the days of his ministry were transfixed with the nail, it seemed as if the ministerial journeys of the disciples had come to an end along with those of their Master. But it was not so. The forty days during which "he shewed himself alive to them after his passion by many infallible proofs" conveyed to them the lesson, that they who had hitherto witnessed to him only in the land of Israel were henceforth to go into all the world and preach the gospel to every creature. Their feet would thus be besoiled with missionary wayfaring far more than they had ever been besoiled before: a work of which they had suspected not the magnitude must be performed ere they could rightfully rest from their labours. *My beloved thrust in his hand through the doorhole.* This, it will be observed, is the only glimpse which the Bride's eyes catch of her Beloved's presence. The hole is that through which, according to the fashion of Eastern doors, a person from without thrusts in his hand in order to insert the key and so to open it (see Thomson, The Land and the Book, Chap. XXII.). We must therefore here assume that the Bridegroom, although he had called to the Bride to open to him, was not without the means of opening for himself; and that this manifestation of his energy, and, so far, of his person, was on his part entirely spontaneous, equally with his refraining from displaying himself further, and with his subsequent withdrawal. To this correspond, in the history of Christ, first, his various appearances, at different times, to his disciples, after his resurrection from the dead; and secondly, the various miracles, which, during the first preaching of the gospel, he enabled them to work. Both the one and the other were, so to speak, fragmentary. They sufficiently attested that he who had been dead was now alive, and that he could make known his presence when and how he would, but they amounted not to a renewal of the continuous outward earthly companionship which the disciples had held with him in time past. Of the appearances of the Lord Jesus after his resurrection from the dead there are two which in some degree recall even the imagery of the passage before us: those, namely, to his assembled apostles, first on the evening of the resurrection, and then again a week later. The doors were shut; the sorrowing Church had ensconced herself from the world without; but the returning Bridegroom was not thereby prevented from manifesting himself within. When we pass to the miracles wrought by the early believers, we find even here language used which offers some degree of coincidence with the imagery of the Song. The prayer of the apostles in Acts IV. 30 is that God would "stretch forth his hand" to heal, that so signs and wonders may be done by the name of his holy child Jesus; and of the disciples who went about preaching the word after the martyrdom of Stephen it is written, in Acts XI. 21, that "the hand of the Lord was with them," this being the phrase whereby is expressed the manifestation of the Lord's presence through visible tokens. It may be stated generally that the hand, or the finger, is in Scripture the symbol of power in operation: cf., in the Old Testament, Exod. III. 20, VIII. 19, &c.; and, in the New Testament, Luke XI. 20. And so the early interpreters took it[1]. *And my bowels were disquieted with yearning for him.* The partial manifestation thus vouchsafed quickens the desire of the Church to behold him altogether. Compare that passage in the address of Peter to the Jews after the healing of the lame-born man, in which he speaks of the "times of refreshing" that should "come from the presence of the Lord" when he should send unto them Jesus Christ, Acts III.

---

[1] Eusebius: Χεὶρ νοεῖται ἡ ἐνεργητικὴ αὐτοῦ δύναμις.

19, 20. The reading עָלָיו, "for him," which some have on mere Jewish and manuscript authority replaced by עָלַי, "for me," is upheld by all the ancient versions. *Up I arose*. Literally, "I arose." So too at the beginning of the next verse the literal rendering is simply "I opened." But in both places the use, contrary to Hebrew custom, of the pronoun אֲנִי, "I," is emphatic; and seems to indicate an alertness and forwardness which must in an English rendering be expressed in some other manner. *Myrrh*. The emblem, as elsewhere, of death: "that myrrh is the symbol of death," says Gregory of Nyssa, "no one versed in the sacred writings will doubt." It expresses here, first, the inward self-denial with which the Church, in striving after the holiness of her Lord, is continually mortifying the deeds of the flesh; and secondly, the "dying daily" of outward suffering, crowned in many instances by actual martyrdom, which has been the continual lot of the Church while treading in her Lord's footsteps[1]. *Liquid myrrh*. By this is denoted the myrrh which exudes naturally from the myrrh-tree, and which is choicer in quality than that which is artificially extracted. It is apparently the same with that designated in Exod. xxx. 23 by a name which our English Version translates "pure myrrh," but which others render "free" or "spontaneous myrrh." *Upon the handles of the bolt*. Where the Bridegroom's hands had been. Every memorial of Christ's presence, every outward thing connected with the records of his presence, becomes to the Church an

---

[1] Cyril: Τὰ στάζοντα σμύρναν λέγει τὰ ὁμολογοῦντα χείλη τὸν θάνατον.

incentive to that self-devotion whereby she becomes a partaker in the fellowship of his sufferings. Whether at times an excessive importance has not been attached to such outward memorials, it is not perhaps needful here to enquire. The forms which the career of self-denial inspired by them has assumed may not be in every case such as to obtain universal approval: the spirit of such career can hardly fail to be commended and admired. At a comparatively late period the most memorable display of it consisted in the sacrifices made by Christian Europe in the wars of the Crusades to recover the sepulchre of the Redeemer from the hands of the infidels. *My beloved had turned and was gone.* A testimony that the manifestations of Christ's presence in such appearances as that from heaven to the apostle Paul, or in the outward miracles wrought by the early believers, were not intended to be more than temporary. They were, at the first, proofs of his resurrection: after a time such proofs were no longer needed. There were those who were permitted to see that so they might believe; but it was at the same time declared, "Blessed are they that have not seen, and yet have believed." *For what he had spoken.* Our English Version has "when he spake." As a rendering of the Hebrew either is admissible. The Hebrew verb is in the infinitive; and when transferred into the indicative must be expressed in the present, the preterite-perfect, or the preterite-pluperfect, according to circumstances. Here the reference must be to the words uttered by the Bridegroom when he first presented himself at the door, ver. 2; for there is no record of his speaking subsequently. *I sought him, but I did not find him,* See back, III. 2. It is observed by Hengstenberg that there is an undeniable reference to these words in what is said by our Lord, Joh. VII. 33, 34: "Yet a little while am I with you, and then I go unto him that sent me. Ye shall seek me, and shall not find me: and where I am, thither ye cannot come"; and also in Joh. VIII. 21: "I go my way, and ye shall seek me, and shall die in your sins: whither I go, ye cannot come." The verbal reference cannot indeed be well gainsaid: it does not however necessarily lead to the two conclusions which have been partially based upon it, that the Bride of the Song is the Jewish nation, not the Church of God, and that her inability to find her Beloved is to be viewed as a judgment upon her for her previous sin and neglect. The former conclusion would, in identifying the Bride with the Jewish nation, tear asunder the Song of Songs from the whole of the rest of the Old Testament, the promises of which pertained to the Jews only so long as they remained the Church of God, and have now, since their rejection as a nation, passed to the Universal Church of Christ. The other corresponding conclusion, which would view the Bride as here punished for her previous sin by the withdrawal of her Beloved, is not in harmony with what had been said in the preceding verse of myrrh dropping from her hands. For if that imply, as it must imply, that she sought him with devout mortification and self-denial, it is certain, from all that Scripture tells us of God's dealings, that her prayers could not be refused, so far as the fulfilment of them did not interfere with God's higher purposes of love. The words "Seek and ye shall find" must ever hold good for all that seek devoutly: it is only the wild cry of remorse and despair, the cry of a conviction which implies no real conversion of heart, that fails to obtain mercy from the heavenly throne of grace. That the Jewish seeking of Christ after he had quitted this earth was not a godly seeking of him is shewn by our Saviour's own words, "Ye shall seek me, and shall die in your sins." For the true illustration of this passage of the Song we must look rather to our Lord's discourse of love to his disciples than to his controversy with his Jewish opponents. In Joh. XIII. 33 he says to his disciples: "Little children, yet a little while I am with you. Ye shall seek me: and as I said unto the Jews, Whither I go, ye cannot come; so now I say to you." It is sufficiently evident that though the actual announcement was in each case the same, it was nevertheless made in a different spirit. Our Lord departed from his disciples not because they had not received him while he was present with them, but because it was expedient for their highest interests that he should go away. It is of such a departure that the passage before us speaks. Nevertheless when we read of the Bride seeking but not finding her Beloved, calling him but gaining no answer, it may be fairly asked whether the Church may not at times have longed too impatiently after Christ's outward presence; whether the "Even so, come, Lord Jesus" of truest love may not occasionally, through the lack of perfect faith, have unduly overpowered her appreciation of her present career of earthly labour and waiting. Something of this kind the apostle Paul, ardently as he loved the Lord's appearing, had to check in his Thessalonian converts by the second epistle which he addressed to them. And the same spirit may be traced in the post-apostolic times in the millennarian expectations of the earlier Christian Fathers, Irenæus, Justin, &c.; which the Church gradually shook off, as she attained to that sounder understanding of Scripture, and that healthier view of the contest to be waged against the world, which we find in the writings of Augustine. *The watchmen, &c.* Cf. III. 3. The material and essential difference between that passage and the present is that the watchmen are here represented as persecuting the Bride in her search for her Beloved. They smite her, they wound her, they treat her with contumely. The watchmen in III. 3 were explained to be the prophets of the Old Testament Church. Those here must correspondingly represent the teachers in the Church of the New Testament, together with all who exercise authority within her, and to whom the phrase "the watchmen of the walls" seems in an especial manner to point. If this interpretation be correct, we must infer that the Church of the Gospel was to suffer bitterly from her own ministers and ecclesiastical rulers. Whether such has not been the case, whether at different periods many of her members, who have loved the Lord Jesus Christ most truly, have not, individually and aggregately, been persecuted, held up to public disgrace, unjustifiably excommunicated, and martyred, it must be the province of history to tell. *My covering mantle.* It seems to be generally agreed that the word רדיד, occurring here and at Isaiah III. 23, denotes a wide and thin garment such as Eastern ladies to the present day throw over all the rest of their dress. The Germans well translate it Schleierkleid, "veil-garment." *I adjure you, &c.* The adjuration is both different from and somewhat shorter than that which we had before. *O! declare ye to him.* Others translate, "What will ye tell him?" But the words are rather the expression of a very earnest entreaty.

THE PRESENCE.

v. 9—viii. 4.

But Thou hast made it sure
By Thy dear promise to Thy Church and Bride,
That Thou, on earth, would'st aye with her endure,
Till earth to heaven be purified.

KEBLE.

9 *Chorus.* What is thy beloved more than another beloved,
O fairest among women?
What is thy beloved more than another beloved,
That thou dost so adjure us?
10 *Bride.* My beloved is bright and ruddy,
Foremost among ten thousand.
11 His head is finest gold;
His locks flow flowingly, black as the raven;
12 His eyes are as doves upon brooks of water,
Bathed in milk, resting upon fulness;
13 His cheeks are as a bed of spices, with towering heights of perfume-herbs;
His lips are lilies, they drop with liquid myrrh;
14 His hands are folding-panels of gold, inlaid with chrysolites;
His chest is shining ivory, covered o'er with sapphires;
15 His legs are pillars of marble, fixed on pedestals of fine gold;
His appearance is as Lebanon, princely as the cedars:
16 His tongue is sweetest sweetness, and he is all loveliest loveliness,—
Such is my beloved, and such my friend, O daughters of Jerusalem.

VI. 1. *Chorus.* Whither is thy beloved gone,
O fairest among women?
Whither is thy beloved turned,
That we may seek him with thee?

2. *Bride.* My beloved is gone down into his garden,
To the beds of spices,
To feed his flock in the gardens, and to gather lilies.

3. I am my beloved's, and my beloved is mine,
He who feedeth his flock among the lilies.

4. *Beloved.* Beautiful art thou, my love, as Tirzah,
Comely as Jerusalem,
Dazzling as an army with banners.

5. Turn thou thine eyes against me,
For they swell my heart with pride!
Thy hair is like a flock of goats
Hanging down the slope of Gilead:

6. Thy teeth are like a flock of ewes
Coming up from the wash-pool,
All appearing in pairs,
And not a lone one amongst them:

7. Like a slice of pomegranate are thy temples
Behind thy plaits.

8. Sixty there are of queens, and fourscore of concubines,
And damsels without number:

9. But one is she, my dove, my own one,
An only one of her mother, her parent's sole darling is she:

The daughters saw her, and called her blessed;
The queens and the concubines, and praised her.

10 *Chorus.* Who is she that looketh forth as the morn,
Fair as the argent-orb, pure as the orb of day,
Dazzling as an army with banners?

11 *Bride.* I went down into the garden of nuts,
To inspect the green shoots of the valley,
To see whether the vine were sprouting,
Whether the pomegranates were budding:

12 Or ever I was aware, my soul had made me
The chariots of my people the Freewilling.

13 *Chorus.* Return, return, thou Peace-laden!
Return, return, that we may gaze upon thee!
Bride. On what will ye gaze in the Peace-laden?
Chorus. As it were the dance of the Twofold Camp.

VII. 1 *Beloved.* How beautiful are thy steps in the sandals,
O daughter of the Freewilling!
The mouldings of thy thighs are like jewels, the work
of the hands of a master:

2 Thy navel is a round goblet,—be not liquor wanting,—
Thy belly a heap of wheat, set about with lilies.

3 Thy two breasts are like two young twins, fawns of
a gazelle;

4 Thy neck is a tower of ivory;
Thine eyes as the pools in Heshbon, by the gate
whose name is Multitude;

Thy nose as the tower of Lebanon that looketh toward Damascus;
5 Thy head upon thee is like Carmel,
And the tresses of thine head like royal purple,
Enfixed amid the wainscottings.
6 How fair art thou, how delightfully lovely, O daughter of allurements!
7 *Chorus.* This thy stature is like a palm-tree,
And thy breasts like clusters of fruit;
8 And I say, Let me climb this palm-tree,
Let me take hold of its branches,
And be thy breasts now as clusters of the vine,
And the smell of thy breath as citrons,
9 And thy speech as goodly wine,
Which, going straight to my beloved,
Causeth the lips of the sleepers to speak.

10 *Bride.* I am my beloved's, and his desire is toward me.
11 Come, my beloved, let us go forth into the field,
Let us sojourn in the villages;
12 Let us start early to the vineyards,
Let us see whether the vine be sprouting,
Whether the blossoms open,
Whether the pomegranates bud:
There will I give thee my love.
13 The mandrakes yield forth a fragrance,
And at our doors are all precious fruits,

  Both new and old,
  Which I have treasured up, my beloved, for thee!

VIII. 1 O that thou wouldest appear as brother of mine,
  As one that had sucked the breasts of my mother!
  Should I find thee without, I would kiss thee,
  And eke they should not despise me.
 2 I would hasten thee away to my mother's house,
   that so thou mightest teach me;
  I would cause thee to drink of spiced wine, of the
   juice of my pomegranate:
 3 His left hand should be under my head,
  And his right hand should embrace me.
 4 I adjure you, O daughters of Jerusalem,
  O! that ye upstir not, and O! that ye disturb not
  The play of love till it will it!

  It has been already explained that the present section of the Song sets forth the permanent spiritual relation between Christ and his redeemed Church. Although outwardly linked on to what went before by the enquiries of the daughters of Jerusalem in v. 9, "What is thy beloved..... that thou dost so adjure us?" and in VI. 1, "Whither is thy beloved gone.... that we may seek him with thee?" it contains none of the complaint or lamentation by which the preceding section was distinguished. The periods of action over which the two sections extend are contemporaneous. The scenes displayed in them are opposite in character, but not therefore mutually inconsistent; for the spiritual presence of Christ is not inconsistent with his bodily absence. As the preceding section was the shortest in the Song, so this is the longest. It consists of thirty-eight verses, which fall, by a symmetrical arrangement, into five main subdivisions, pieces, or groups. The central piece is formed by the four verses VI. 10—13. From their condensed and enigmatical character they are, as is frequently the case with the central pieces or verses of Hebrew poetry, very difficult to construe; and their meaning, comparatively seldom understood, has been frequently wrested to senses utterly foreign to the true intent of the Song. Literalizing criticism has here, from the nature of the case, been especially at fault. The real theme of these verses is the grandeur and might which, through the abiding presence of Christ with her, the Church possesses. They are enclosed by two groups of nine verses each, VI. 1—9, VII. 1—9, both of which, though themselves admitting of further subdivision, are mainly occupied with Christ's praise of the comeliness of his Bride. The two outside groups, V. 9—16, VII. 10—VIII. 4, consist each of eight verses. The former records the testimony of the Church to the graces of Christ: the latter displays her joy in communing with him, and her desire for his second appearing.

V. 9—16. *What is thy beloved, &c.* That the dramatic form may be preserved, a question is here put by the Chorus of the Daughters of Jerusalem, in order to furnish occasion to the description which follows. *My beloved is bright and ruddy.* Our English Version, following in the wake of other versions, renders "white and ruddy;" and interpretations of somewhat fanciful character have been based on the assumed contrariety of the two epithets here employed. But in the absence of all further indication of their contrariety, it is more natural to suppose that they were intended to harmonize: in fact, had it been otherwise, the Hebrew word צח, "bright," "clear," would have been replaced by one which was more definitely restricted to the meaning "white." The bright glow of the Beloved's countenance well accords with what we read of the appearance of the Lord Jesus Christ in the Revelation, I. 16, "his countenance was as the sun shineth in his strength." It betokens his native strength and energy; not unlike to that of the sun, "which is as a bridegroom coming out of his chamber, and rejoiceth as a strong man to run a race." *Foremost among ten thousand.* Distinguished above all the meaner throng as being marked out by his native perfection of comeliness for their fitting leader. Cf. Rom. VIII. 29, "that he might be the firstborn among many brethren." *His head is finest gold.* His essential royalty and his sterling and incomparable preciousness are here expressed. *His locks flow flowingly* (we may thus imitate the reduplication with which the Hebrew word is formed), *black as the raven.* These again are suggestive of the fulness of manly vigour. The association of the hair with manly strength would be especially natural to those who were familiar with the history of Samson. It is moreover to be observed that the hair and the locks of which this verse speaks are the same which had previously, in v. 2, been described as filled with dew, with the drops of the night; from which it may be gathered that the perfection of royal might of the Beloved Bridegroom had been unimpaired by the career of mortal suffering through which it had been his lot to pass. *His eyes are as doves upon brooks of water*. It was the Bride's eyes which had been previously compared to doves, I. 15, IV. 1. The first point of comparison is here the unbesoiled purity of the two things compared. From this we are led on to the associations which they respectively love. The dove chooses for its abode the neighbourhood of a running stream, where the scene over which it flits tells of a purity corresponding to and harmonizing with its own. So is it on scenes of moral purity that he, who is himself free from everything that defileth, loves peacefully to gaze. His eyes are purer than to behold evil, and cannot look on iniquity, Hab. I. 13. *Bathed in milk, resting upon fulness*. These two phrases, which belong to the eyes, not to the doves, illustrate respectively the two points of the comparison in the previous line. In regard of that purity by reason of which they resemble doves, the eyes of the Beloved Bridegroom are as pure from all defilement as if they had been fresh bathed in milk: this relates to the appearance which they themselves present. The remainder relates to the objects on which they choose to gaze: they "rest upon fulness," even as the doves "upon brooks of water": the use of the same preposition, על, "upon," shews that the two phrases are mutually illustrative. And the fulness which the Bridegroom contemplates is that fulness of all that is good and lovely and holy which is to be seen in the church by reason of the outpouring of the fulness of his own graces upon it, Eph. I. 23. This Christ loves to behold: this he selects as an appropriate abode, because its purity is akin to his own, even as the outward purity of the stream to that of the dove. *His cheeks are as a bed of spices.* The cheeks are that part of the face in which its charms come most prominently into view: it is therefore the loveliness of the heavenly Bridegroom that is here set forth. It is remarked by Hengstenberg that the Hebrew word for cheeks has an etymological reference to their charms. *With towering heights of perfume-herbs.* The image is that of garden-beds raised in the centre, and therefore resembling cheeks in respect of their convex form. *His lips are lilies, they drop with liquid myrrh.* Lips come into view as the channel of speech. The thing here symbolized is therefore the holiness of Christ's teaching, and the self-denying devotion, even unto death, which he should inculcate. The opening portion of the Sermon on the Mount, and the "If any man will come after me, let him take up his cross and follow me," will illustrate these characteristics of his discourse. Respecting the liquid myrrh, see on v. 5. *His hands are folding panels of gold.* The word גליל is applied, as we learn from 1 Kings VI. 34, to the separate portions of a folding door: the doors to the holy of holies of the temple consisted of two leaves, each of which in its turn consisted of two halves or folds. There is no passage in which the word denotes a "ring;" nor would this meaning be here so appropriate. The image is that of a door, not necessarily a large door, constructed in four or five separate folds, corresponding to the appearance presented by the hand when the fingers, while kept in contact with each other, are stretched at full length. The hand, as has been noted on v. 4, is the symbol of power in operation: the divisions of the separate fingers indicate the manifoldness of that power: the gold, its kingliness. *Inlaid with chrysolites.* For the stone intended, see Dict. of the Bible, s.v. Beryl. They betoken the preciousness of Christ's working. *His chest is shining ivory.* The ordinary Hebrew term for "bowels" is in this passage alone applied to the exterior of the human frame. By whatever precise term we render it, we shall not go substantially wrong, provided we remember that, as one of the main and central portions of the body, it here, in a general way, represents the whole body; and so, the person of the Lord Jesus Christ incarnate. Purity and preciousness are here again the qualities insisted on. Ivory comes before us as the purest substance of its kind: the preciousness of Christ's person is expressed by the sapphires with which the ivory is overlaid. The sapphire is here selected, because, being of a blue or azure colour, it is the gem which harmonizes best with ivory in its appearance. *His legs are pillars of marble, fixed on pedestals of fine gold.* Again the same qualities symbolized. Marble stands for purity, gold for royal worth. The marble legs set forth at the same time Christ's immovable faithfulness: he is the Rock of ages, "Jesus Christ the same yesterday, and to day, and for ever." Observe also that the "fine gold" of the feet towards the close of the description corresponds to the "finest gold" of the head towards the beginning of it, ver. 11; "so that from crown to foot he shines entire with unmeasured glory and majesty" (J. H. Michaelis). *His appearance is as Lebanon, princely as the cedars.* The delineation of the details of his person having been now concluded, his general nobility and princeliness come again, as in ver. 10, into view. As Lebanon among mountains, as the cedars of Lebanon among trees, such is he among men, first and foremost, bearing in his whole appearance the stamp of native matchlessness. And thus then the Bride has answered the question of the Daughters of Jerusalem, "What is thy beloved more than another beloved?" But although her reply to them is complete, yet the very process of enumerating the graces of his person leads her, in the fulness of her appreciation of them, to desire spontaneously to proclaim them with all possible emphasis of language, and so there yet follows in ver. 16 one further testimony to his perfections. *His tongue is sweetest sweetness.* Literally, "His palate is sweetnesses." The palate is here mentioned merely as the organ of speech, and must therefore, if we would retain the substantial meaning, be replaced in an English translation by the tongue. The plural "sweetnesses" manifestly expresses the intensity of sweetness. From this and the following clause, "he is all loveliest loveliness," we gather that the two great themes of the Bride's encomiums on her Beloved are, first, his speech, and secondly, his whole person. Alike in the teaching of Christ, and in his whole life and work, must we recognize that holy purity and that majestic strength which commend him to us as precious, and which proclaim him the king of men.

VI. 1—9. *Whither is thy beloved gone, &c.* Another question from the Daughters of Jerusalem, suggested in the first instance by the section V. 2—8 and by the Bride's final charge therein, gives occasion to the Bride to declare whither her Beloved is really gone. It will be observed that there is no uncertainty in her answer; and this shews that his relation to her is contemplated in a different point of view from that in which it had in v. 2—8 been exhibited to us. Then further this relation, so expressly set forth by the Bride in verses 2, 3, is appropriately unfolded in the six verses that follow by an address from the Beloved himself to the Bride. If dramatic consistency were strictly adhered to, we should have to regard this passage, together with VII. 1—9, as a narrative by the Bride of the words which had been addressed to her. It may in fact be so treated; but at the same time the dramatic form into which the Song is cast is so loose, that it is very far from necessary, in perusing these passages, to perplex ourselves with the thought that the words of the Beloved come to us at second-hand. *My beloved is gone down into his garden.* The garden which had been described in IV. 12—V. 1. See especially V. 1, "I am come into my garden, &c." Note, in the Hebrew of this verse, not only the rhyme between בגנים and שושנים, but also the resemblance in sound between לערוגות and לרעות. *To the beds of spices.* See IV. 14. *To feed his flock in the gardens, and to gather lilies.* See on II. 16. Under the dispensation of the gospel, no less than under that of the older covenant, Christ nurtures his people in the purity of holiness. But he now not only feeds his flock among lilies, but also gathers lilies; gathers with joy and acceptance from his people those fruits of holiness which through the grace of his Spirit they are continually bringing forth. The "garden" refers to the Christian body in its unity, the "gardens" denotes its manifoldness: in the New Testament we read, as Theodoret remarks, alike of the church and of the churches. *I am my beloved's, &c.* Compare II. 16. *Beautiful art thou, my love, as Tirzah.* The city of Tirzah is mentioned by Joshua, XII. 24, and was evidently in the tribe either of Ephraim or Manasseh. After the separation of the kingdoms it became the residence of the earlier kings of Israel, till Omri built the new capital of Samaria. See 1 Kings XIV. 17; XV. 21, 33; XVI. 6, 8, 9, 15, 17, 23. Even in days long subsequent it still retained somewhat of its former importance, being the head-quarters whence Menahem commenced his successful struggle for the throne, 2 Kings XV. 14, 16. Robinson is disposed to identify it with the modern Tallûzah, to the east of Samaria, and the north-east of Shechem; being probably the same place with that mentioned by Brocardus as Thersa, and by Schwarz as Tarza. This village lies in a high and commanding position; looking out towards the west over the high table-land spreading north from Mount Ebal, and towards the east over an extensive fertile district drained by one of the streams that flows into the Jordan. It is surrounded by immense groves of olive-trees, planted on all the hills around (Later Bib. Res. pp. 302, 3). The comparison of the Bride to Tirzah was the more appropriate as the name Tirzah signifies Pleasant. *Comely as Jerusalem.* The correspondence with the preceding clause shews that the reference is mainly to the site of Jerusalem, especially as beheld from the south. This may still be best described in the words of Tacitus: "Duos colles, immensum editos, claudebant muri, per artem obliqui, aut introrsus sinuati." Of the two hills on which Jerusalem thus stood, the western was the hill of the Old or Upper City: the eastern, the hill of the Lower City, or Temple-mount. Both the comparison to Jerusalem and that to Tirzah bespeak something noble and commanding in the Bride's appearance. *Dazzling as an army with banners.* The comparison well sets forth the majesty of the Church in all her manifold array. But it also indirectly betokens that she has set out upon a career of victory. It was perhaps suggested by the account, in Num. II, of the order of the tribes of Israel, when marshalled in their encampment under their several standards. *Turn thou thine eyes against me, for they swell my heart with pride!* Some vindication of this rendering will here be necessary on account of the difference between it and the rendering of our English

Version. It is hardly possible that מִנֶּגְדִּי should here mean "from me." There are cases, no doubt, in which "from before" and "from" are convertible, and therefore nearly equivalent: e. g. Isaiah I. 16, Jer. XVI. 17. But would "Turn thine eyes from before me" be a natural mode of expression? For howsoever turned, her eyes would still be "before him;" not so dazzling, doubtless, as when they gazed full upon him, yet still unmoved in point of actual position, and unconcealed. We might indeed, interchanging the persons, declare that the eyes of the Beloved would be no longer before the Bride, when she should cease to gaze; but we should thus be introducing a meaning to which the Hebrew words, as we have them, could not lead. We must then take מִנֶּגֶד not as involving motion, but in its frequent and indeed most usual sense of "opposite," "over against," cf. Gen. XXI. 16; Num. II. 2; Deut. XXVIII. 66; 2 Kings II. 7, &c. The מִן answers to the Latin *ex* in the phrases "ex hac parte," &c.: we in English use instead the preposition *on*, of which the *a* in "against" (Ang.-Sax. "ongegen") is merely the contraction; though even in our language *on* and *of* are often vulgarly interchanged ("of this side," &c.: cf. the word "off"). The only motion implied in the passage before us is entirely expressed by the הָסֵבִּי "turn thou;" and the full meaning is, "Thou who art standing over against me, bend thou thine eyes so as directly to meet mine[1]." Having compared his Bride to an army

---

[1] It admits of some doubt how the LXX. intended to take this passage, when they rendered it ἀπόστρεψον ὀφθαλμούς σου ἀπεναντίον

with banners, the Beloved desires to gaze on the full splendour of her appearance, in which indeed he may legitimately exult, because it has all virtually proceeded from himself and from his own devoted love. As the Creator at the beginning saw every thing that he had made, and, behold, it was very good, so may the Redeemer in like manner see of the travail of his soul and be satisfied: the glorious church which, even by earthly anticipation, he presents unto himself, is that which he himself hath sanctified and cleansed. *Thy hair is like a flock of goats,* &c. See on IV. 1—3, whence, with one or two unimportant variations, two verses and a half of the present section are repeated. *Sixty there are of queens, and fourscore of concubines, and damsels without number: but one is she,* &c. It is almost unnecessary to observe that we have here an Old Testament representation, drawn from a state of things in which polygamy existed. That there may in such a representation be a genuine and wholesome spiritual significance, we see by St Paul's development, in Gal. IV, of the spiritual import of the history of Abraham, Sarah, and Hagar. But there is a limit to the extent to which such representations, if logically carried out and completed, would coincide with the doctrine of which they are made the

μου, ὅτι αὐτοὶ ἀνεπτέρωσάν με. The verb ἀποστρέφω occasionally means "to turn" rather than "to turn away:" see the Greek rendering of 1 Kings VIII. 14; 2 Kings XX. 2 (Vatican text: only two MSS. beside the Alexandrine there read ἔστρεψεν). As to ἀπεναντίον, it signifies simply "opposite." So that the meaning of the Greek may be, "Turn thine eyes opposite me, for they enkindle my expectations;" which would be correct so far as concerned the earlier words.

embodiment; and it is therefore important to remark that in the present passage the queens and concubines are brought before us with reference only to the relations in which they severally stand to the Bridegroom, not to the relations in which he stands to them. These last the poet in no wise contemplates: the only sentiments of the Bridegroom which he unfolds are those sentiments of pure and devoted love to his one chosen Bride in which we read the love of Christ to his redeemed Church. Whom then do the queens, concubines, and damsels here represent? The general answer to this question seems to be correctly given by Theodoret; whose judicious and discriminating use of the exegetical labours of his predecessors may be tested by a comparison of his commentary on this passage with the exposition of it in the Homilies of Gregory of Nyssa. They are men, or bodies of men, outwardly drawn to Christ by motives that fall short of genuine love. There are many communities, or even nations, that are attracted to Christ by outward splendour; or (as Theodoret takes it) there are souls that seek Christ merely with an eye to future reward. These are queens: queens, but not really brides or consorts; devoted to the king's rank and honours rather than to his person. Again there are others who (as Theodoret explains it) render a slavish obedience, being urged thereto by fear of hell rather than by any nobler motive; or who (as we may also add) obey through constraint rather than through free love. These are concubines; but not true partners. There are others again who as damsel-attendants (Theodoret's explanation is here not so good) look on approvingly at the approach of others to Christ, and even assist in that approach with their several ministrations, but apparently without a full personal interest in it. In contrast to all these stands the One Church Catholic who loves Christ for his own sake, with such love as a true servant of Christ, Francis Xavier, has delineated in the beautiful hymn, "O Deus ego amo te." She can be but One; because the very love wherewith she loves Christ displays itself in an active love to all who are Christ's, and thus practically unites all her members together. "By this shall all men know that ye are my disciples, if ye have love one to another." As regards the "sixty" and the "eighty," we have of course in each case a definite number for an indefinite. The choice of the particular numbers seems to have been mainly dictated by a studied avoidance of the number seventy, to which a certain sacredness and completeness would have attached. It is no harmonious covenant-relationship in which the queens and the concubines stand to Christ: all is with them imperfect, and wide of the mark. A directly opposite view is erroneously taken by Hengstenberg. *My dove, my own one.* See on v. 2. *An only one of her mother, her parent's sole darling.* For the same reason that תמתי, lit. "my perfect one," may be rendered "my own one," may ברה, lit. "pure one" (not as English Version, "choice one") be rendered "sole darling." The exact meaning of the adjective is this, that she is her parent's exclusive child, that she constitutes her mother's entire offspring, and absorbs her undivided affections. She is her parent's "mere one"; and this would in fact be the best rendering, had not the word "mere," in its original sense, become somewhat antiquated. The two phrases "an only one of her mother" and "her parent's sole darling," do not therefore differ substantially in meaning. And both are but little more than metaphorical expressions, intended to bring out the matchlessness of the Church of Christ. She has none to share her glories: as a church, she alone, in her ideal and ultimate purity, is the true child of the Jerusalem which is above, which is the mother of us all. *The daughters saw her, and called her blessed.* Hengstenberg justly observes that this passage rests on Gen. xxx. 13, "And Leah said, Happy am I, for the daughters will call me blessed." We may perhaps infer from this that the word "daughters" is here used generally for "women": at the same time, as the queens and the concubines are mentioned in the next line, there seems to be no valid objection against taking the "daughters" as identical with the damsels of the preceding verse.

vi. 10—13. The central verses of the section. Ver. 10 is uttered by the Chorus of the Daughters of Jerusalem; vv. 11, 12, by the Bride herself; and ver. 13, in the main, by the Chorus, the question "On what will ye gaze, &c." in the mouth of the Bride being merely subservient to their eulogy. Thus then two verses in which the Bride speaks are enclosed by two in which the Chorus speak. *Who is she that looketh forth as the morn.* Hopeful brightness is here the point of comparison; a brilliant morning being but the commencement of a brilliant day. Compare Isaiah LX. 1 seqq., where it is prophetically said to the Church, "Arise, shine; for thy light is come, and the glory of the LORD is risen upon thee......And the Gentiles shall come to thy light, and kings to the brightness of thy rising." *Fair as the argent-orb, pure as the orb of day.* An attempt has been made to translate poetically the unusual terms by which the sun and moon are here, and in Isaiah XXIV. 23, XXX. 26, poetically designated. The points of comparison are indicated by the epithets employed. It is noted by commentators that the comparisons which we have in this verse are frequently found in Eastern poetry, particularly in that of the Arabs and Persians. Something of the same kind we have in Ecclesiasticus L. 6, 7, in the description of the high-priest Simon, the son of Onias. *Dazzling as an army with banners.* See above, VI. 4. The reason of this is now about to be explained. The spiritual presence of Christ with his Church has equipped her for the conflict which she is to sustain against all the opposing powers of the world. *I went down into the garden of nuts.* Such is the rendering of the LXX, Syriac, and Jerome. It has been generally followed by other translators. They confirm it by observing that the word אֱגוֹז "nut," although not found elsewhere in the Bible, is frequently used in Rabbinic Hebrew; and that a corresponding word, divested of the initial א, exists in Syriac and in Persian. Yet there are objections to this rendering. The singular number of the word אֱגוֹז is, to say the least, somewhat awkward. And then it is not easy to see why the garden should, in this important passage, be specially spoken of as a garden of nuts, when nuts are not so much as mentioned thoughout the rest of the Song. The following is the explanation given by Hengstenberg: "The garden is called a nut-garden only *a potiori*. That its appellation should here be derived from its nuts, while in II. 13 the foreground is occupied by the fig-tree and vine, arises out of the endeavour to embrace in the picture the whole of the riches offered by the holy land in noble products of the vegetable kingdom. Parallel to this is the endeavour to introduce into the representation as many local scenes of the holy land as possible." This, the best explanation that has been given in vindication of the current rendering, is not thoroughly satisfactory. Tremellius and Junius would derive אגוז from the root גזז, and make it signify "pruning:" "ad hortos putatos (Heb. putationis) descenderam." This is hardly probable, as גזז denotes not "to prune" but "to shear." Meanwhile is it certain that the received Hebrew text is correct? The Targum on this passage (we quote it, for convenience' sake, in Walton's Latin Version) runs as follows: "Dixit dominator seculi: In domo sanctuarii secunda quæ ædificata est per manum Cyri, habitare feci majestatem meam." The garden is here interpreted of the divine sanctuary, as usual; but why should the building which was reared by Zerubbabel and Jeshua be here connected exclusively with the name of the heathen Cyrus? We are naturally led to suppose that the Targumist found a hint about the heathen in the Hebrew text. He may well for אֲגֻוָּה have read הֲגוֹי or לְגוֹי. And the bearing of his paraphrase upon the Hebrew text is to us all-important, however wide of the mark may be his view of its meaning. That a transcriber may have changed a י into a ו will be readily allowed, as the two letters probably resembled each other in the older Hebrew alphabet. It is less easy to shew how the אֲגֻוָּה of our present text should have illegitimately acquired its initial א: it might have arisen from the א of the אֶל, the transcriber's eye having passed by mistake from the final ת of גִנַּת to the final ת at the close of the preceding verse. The text at which we have thus conjecturally arrived would construe somewhat as follows: "I went down into the garden of the throng"; and on comparing this with the succeeding verse, the general import would be that those whom the Bride had once known as a mere heathen throng, גוֹי, had suddenly become to her a churchly people, עַם. The passage would thus proclaim, along with other truths, the organization of the Gentiles into the Church of God: cf. Hos. I. 10, "It shall come to pass, that in the place where it was said unto them, Ye are not my people, there it shall be said unto them, Ye are the sons of the living God." We should not be justified, with the difficulty of the א and the testimony of the older versions against us, in definitely adopting this emendation; but there is a fair probability of its correctness, and we cannot view the received text otherwise than with suspicion. Moreover even the older versions do not necessarily confirm the א: they might have read הגיא. *To inspect the green shoots of the valley.* The word אֵב "shoot" (not as E. V. "fruit") occurs but in one other place, Job VIII. 12, where our E.V. renders it "greenness." Of the corresponding Arabic root Schultens says "varias agnoscit notiones, quæ revocari possunt ad *micationem, emicationem.*" The word indicates therefore a state of growth, and consequent immaturity. As regards the "valley," the mention of it is peculiar to this passage of the Song; and the "I went down" of the preceding clause carries a manifest reference to the fact of the garden of which the Bride here speaks being situate in a valley. The features then of the description on which stress is here laid differ considerably from those to which attention had in other passages been directed. The picture, if we may venture to complete it, is that of a daughter of Israel descending from her abode on the hill, where in safe seclusion she had dwelt, to the nursery of young plants which surrounded her in the valley below, and which, although hitherto mainly occupied in labours on her own limited demesne, she feels that she must regard as also committed to her care. That daughter of Israel is the Church of God; the hill of her abode is the land of Canaan, where the descendants of Jacob have instructed successive generations of the children of their own race in that knowledge of God which they have received; and the valley around is the Gentile world, where God is also preparing for himself a spiritual garden, and whither Israelitish apostles and teachers must go forth to train up souls without number in true and holy faith. Yet it was difficult for the daughter of Israel to realize that these plantations in the valley were to become in God's good time a paradise no less glorious than the hill-enclosure which she had hitherto accounted peculiarly her own. *To see whether the vine were sprouting, whether the pomegranates were budding.* To see whether there might be discerned any tokens that heralded a yielding forth of the fruits of righteousness, cf. II. 13. The history of Cornelius sufficiently shews that even in the Gentile world such tokens existed. *Or ever I was aware.* The Church of ancient days knew not the grandeur that she should eventually attain. Even when, after their Lord's ascension, the apostles went forth from Jerusalem to preach to all nations the gospel which they had received, they hardly dreamed what an army of spiritual warriors, soldiers of Christ no less than themselves, should rapidly spring up from all regions of the earth, to join in the Christian conflict against the powers of darkness. It was contrarily to all his previous expectations that Peter found himself compelled to acknowledge of the Gentiles to whom he had himself become the first minister of the tidings of salvation, that "God, which knoweth the hearts, bare them witness, giving them the Holy Ghost, even as he did unto us; and put no difference between us and them, purifying their hearts by faith" (Acts xv. 8, 9). *My soul had made me the chariots of my people the Freewilling.* Let our first care be to explain the designation "the Freewilling," here assigned to the newborn people of God. For that it is a special designation, and is to be viewed in the light of a proper name and not of a mere epithet, is shewn by the adjective being used in Hebrew without the article, although after a noun made definite by a suffix. Now both the verb נדב and the adjective נדיב (*nadib*) are, in the earliest passages in which they occur, employed to denote willing liberality in a sacred cause, spontaneous readiness to make offerings in the service of God, Exod. xxv. 2; xxxv. 5, 21, 22, 29. The verb in the Hithpael conjugation thus appropriately signifies the making that noblest and truest of offerings, the offering of oneself; Judg. v. 2, 9; 2 Chron. xvii. 16; Neh. xi. 2. It is manifest that no offering whatever can be thoroughly genuine, where the heart of the offerer has not first offered itself; and thus the adjective נדיב must, in its highest sense, express this self-dedication. Such is its meaning here. The essential characteristic of the true people of God, more especially of his Christian people, on whom no bondage of outward constraint is imposed, is that they have dedicated themselves freely to his service. Most justly then is the description of them summed up in this one word, the Freewilling. And the present verse of the Song manifestly implied, although without directly asserting it, that God should eventually have such a people, to serve under his banner, and to shew forth his praise. Strongly illustrative of it, and indeed connected with it, is the passage in Psalm cx, where it is said to the Messiah, "Thy people shall be willing (lit. shall be free-will offerings) in the day of thy power, in the beauties of holiness." Next, what is meant by the Bride being made "the chariots" of the people? (All translations which introduce a preposition before "the chariots"—"on," "to," "among," "on account of," &c. are grammatically untenable.) Two passages in the Books of Kings will help us to the true interpretation. In 2 Kings II. 12 Elisha calls Elijah "the chariot and the horsemen of Israel." In 2 Kings XIII. 14 King Joash addresses Elisha by the same title. It is intended that Elijah and Elisha had, each in their turn, been the true strength of Israel: they had been to Israel what chariots are to a military host. So then here the meaning is that the Church had unconsciously and unexpectedly become the source and channel of victorious might to all the willing people of God. But "my soul," she says, had made me. Hengstenberg observes that the soul similarly appears as the seat of courage in Judg. v. 21, "O my soul, thou hast trodden down strength." The doctrine however here delivered is that as it is a man's own personal courage that nerves others to attend him in the conflict, so is it the unshrinking and devoted zeal with which the Church prosecutes the task set before her that makes her the rallying-point for all who would join in the service of her Lord. Not to attract them to herself, but simply to do Christ's will, is her own primary and immediate aim; and meanwhile it is in that direct obedience to Christ that the true magnet of her attraction to others lies. That she really attracts them is shewn by her speaking of them not as God's people, or as Christ's people, but as "my" people. Before quitting this verse, we may arrest any false or onesided inferences that might be drawn from it by observing that the strength which the Church communicates to others she derives herself from Christ, and that her influence depends not merely on her own unaided example, but on that presence of the Spirit of Christ of which she partakes. We may remark too how thoroughly the anticipations of the verse agree with those of Isaiah LX. 4 seqq. *Return, return, thou Peace-laden!* "Return," that is, "in peace from thy victorious conflict!" The Chorus of the Daughters of Jerusalem here prophetically celebrate the conquests which the Bride should achieve, and the blessings of divine peace with which, successfully issuing from all her struggles, she should return homeward to enrich her children. The phrase "to return in peace," meaning "to return triumphant from battle," is in the Bible of frequent occurrence: see Josh. x. 21; Judg. VIII. 9, XI. 31; 1 Kings XXII. 28. This obvious source of illustration Hengstenberg has either overlooked or neglected, through his desire to identify the return of the Bride with the future return of the Jewish nation in heart to God; an identification which has but little to recommend it, except that, being found in Cassiodorus, it is not destitute of ancient authority. As in the previous verse the Bride had bestowed a special designation on the people who should follow her, so here a like designation is bestowed upon herself, expressive of the triumph reserved for her: "The Shulamith," "The Peace-laden," lit. "the bepeaced."¹ The name is derived from the same root as "Solomon," and stands in partial correspondence with it. The two names differ however in import: "Solomon" is simply "peaceful," and the contests of war were over ere Solomon's reign began: "Shulamith" is "peace-laden," "peace-crowned," and expresses the triumphant return from an arduous conflict which it was needful, with heroic constancy, to maintain. The latter name implies therefore a period of struggle as well as a final victory: the chariots of war are the necessary prelude to the homeward return. And it is of course only through anticipation of the ultimate triumph that the Bride can be spoken of as the Peace-laden. Such an anticipation we evidently here have; and hence the occurrence of the name in this one passage only. The whole meaning is lost when "Shulamith" is treated as the simple and original name of the Bride, as is done by the literal interpreters. *That we may gaze upon thee.* All naturally desire to gaze upon a conqueror in the fulness of his triumph. *As it were the dance of the Twofold*

---

¹ The word שׁוּלַמִּית is a feminine verbal noun of a passive form, like the masculines גּוּפִין, יוּבָל, סוּנָּר, to which may perhaps be added the proper names אוּלָם, חוּרָם, חוּשָׁם. Such forms virtually agree with that of the Pual verb, if the long וּ be regarded as compensating for the general omission of the dagesh in the second radical; and, in fact, in the case of the word עֻנָּב, several MSS. give in one passage the equivalent form עֻנָב. In the name שׁוּלַמִּית the remembrance of the dagesh is additionally kept up by the actual introduction of it, against all rule, into the *third* radical.

Camp. The Hebrew term Mahanaim, "two camps," "two hosts," recalls the scene of Jacob's vision, when returning from Mesopotamia to Canaan. "Jacob went on his way, and the angels of God met him. And when Jacob saw them, he said, This is God's host: and he called the name of that place Mahanaim" (Gen. XXXII. 1, 2). Why Mahanaim, not Mahaneh? Why two hosts instead of one? Because the import of the vision was this, that Jacob's own visible host of followers was being succoured by God's host of ministering spirits, and so that his own natural weakness was being upheld by divine strength from on high. The two hosts were the earthly and the heavenly: the one, marching obediently along its appointed road, found itself in the succouring presence of the other. From the narrative in Genesis the name Mahanaim is accordingly transferred into the Song, to express the invisible aid by which the company of God's people are reinforced and upheld in the hour of conflict and of danger. The fact of its having (like Shulamith) the article prefixed shews that it is not to be taken as a mere local name, but is to be construed with reference to its etymological and historical significance. As to the dance, dancing was among the Hebrews an expression of joy, Psalm XXX. 11, and, not least, of the joy of victorious triumph. Miriam's companions danced to celebrate the triumph of the passage of the Red Sea (Exod. XV. 20): Jephthah's daughter would have danced to welcome back her father (Judg. XI. 34): with dances the women of Israel celebrated the return of David from his victory over Goliath

(1 Sam. XVIII. 6), and that of Judith from the slaughter of Holofernes and his forces (Judith XV. 12, 13). The substantial meaning then of the clause before us may be expressed in less enigmatical language as follows: "We shall behold the Church of God celebrating with appropriate rejoicings the victory which, through the presence of God's spiritual army with her army, through divine might uplifting her natural weakness, she has been enabled to achieve." Let us here not forget the parallel passage Psalm XXXIV. 7: "The angel of the LORD encampeth round about them that fear him, and delivereth them."

VII. 1—9. Through two-thirds, at least, of this passage, the Beloved speaks. It will be seen that the general theme of the eulogy is not so much the comeliness of the Church in her retirement, as the graceful dignity with which she goes forth to propagate the faith among men. It is therefore that the description begins from the feet. *How beautiful are thy steps in the sandals.* There are three passages in other parts of Scripture which have been generally and rightfully adduced in illustration of these words. Isaiah LII. 7: "How beautiful upon the mountains are the feet of him that bringeth good tidings, that publisheth peace, &c." Nahum I. 15: "Behold upon the mountains the feet of him that bringeth good tidings, that publisheth peace!" Eph. VI. 15: "Your feet shod with the preparation of the gospel of peace." It is the former two of these passages that bear most directly upon the meaning here. The "steps" indicate the activity of the Church in bearing forth the tidings of salvation: the "sandals" the due preparation which she makes, and the equipment with which she furnishes herself for this work. *Thou daughter of the Freewilling.* In the last verse but one of the preceding chapter, the title "the Freewilling" was applied to the people whom the Church gathered round her standard. Here she herself is described as the daughter of the Freewilling. There is thus a slight change made in the details of the representation. But the exact relationship is a matter of no great importance. The truth intended to be conveyed is that the Church is the very embodiment, as it were, of willingness. *The mouldings of thy thighs are like jewels, the work of the hands of a master.* The point of comparison is the beauty and fulness of shape: it is in the beauty of the form to which the jewel is wrought that the evidence of the skill of the artificer is seen. The word חמוק, which we have rendered "moulding," from a root signifying "to turn round," "to turn away," may be well taken as denoting a convex curvature, which, as we follow it, recedes from the eye. The particular eulogy in this clause corresponds appropriately, in respect of the parts of the body described, to the Bride's eulogy on her Beloved in v. 15. And as well-formed limbs contribute to gracefulness and ease of movement, we may read here an encomium on that organization of the Church which adapted her for carrying effectually forth the tidings of salvation. *Thy navel is a round goblet,—be not liquor wanting.* Note the homœophony in the Hebrew. The idea to be conveyed is that from the body of the Church flow copious draughts of refreshment. Cf. John VII. 38, 39: "He that believeth on me, as the scripture hath said, out of his belly shall flow rivers of living water. But this spake he of the Spirit, which they that believe on him should receive." What is thus true of each individual believer is true yet more directly of the Church at large. *Thy belly a heap of wheat, set about with lilies.* The explanations that have been offered of the origin of this imagery are but conjectural; such as that heaps of newly-threshed wheat were stuck round with thorns, in order to keep off the cattle, and that for the hedge of thorns the poet has here substituted a fence of lilies; or again, that such heaps were surrounded or covered with garlands of flowers, indicating the joy of the husbandman at the return of the harvest. And again the Jewish custom, adduced in illustration by Selden, of scattering grains upon a newly-married couple, in token of the wish that they might increase and multiply, is, it must be confessed, more likely to have sprung from this passage than to have been referred to in it. We must be content to let the figure rest in a certain degree of obscurity. Thus much however is easily seen, that the wheat points to the nourishment which should be found in the Church, the spiritual nourishment of the bread of life; and that the lilies indicate the lovely purity of such nourishment. Moreover it could not well fail to be noticed by Christian interpreters, familiar with the sacramental tokens of the Lord's Supper, that the wheat and the liquor, the bread and the wine, of this verse furnish the most obvious sources of strengthening and refreshment. In reference to the view which some commentators, setting the laws of language at defiance, have wished to take of this verse, as though it described not the person but the dress of the Bride, Dr Mason Good observes that in the literal sense of the original there is no indelicacy, and that the bard is merely assuming a liberty, and that in the chastest manner possible, which we are daily conceding in our own age to every painter and sculptor of eminence." But his own translation can hardly be admitted as accurate. *Thy two breasts, &c.* With reference to these, as the fountains of nourishment, see above, on IV. 5. *Thy neck is as a tower of ivory.* To wit, for majestic beauty. In IV. 4, "like the tower of David, &c." which see. It is hardly probable that the tower of David was even ornamented with ivory, as there is in Scripture no intimation to that effect. Ivory was however imported and used by Solomon (1 Kings x. 18, 22). At a later period Ahab constructed an ivory palace (1 Kings XXII. 39), in imitation, probably, of those of other southern climes, cf. Psalm XLV. 8; and this may well have suggested the imaginary tower of ivory to which the poet here compares the neck of the Bride. We thus obtain another clue to the true date of the Song. It is mentioned in Kitto's Cyclopædia, s. v. Ivory, that there exists in India an octagonal ivory hunting-tower, built by Akbar, twenty-four miles to the west of Agra. *Thine eyes as the pools in Heshbon.* Heshbon, the ancient capital of the Amorite Sihon, afterwards a

Levitical city of Israel (Numb. XXI. 26; Josh. XXI. 39, &c.) stood sixteen miles east of the point where the Jordan enters the Dead Sea. The ruins, situate on a low hill commanding a wide prospect, are extensive, though uninteresting in character: there are many cisterns among them, and one considerable reservoir, which some have thought to be one of the pools mentioned in the present passage, though Irby and Mangles deemed it too insignificant. The comparison here must be explained by recurring to that in v. 12. The eyes of the Beloved were there described as resembling doves upon brooks of water; as pure, and as resting upon a purity in harmony with their own. Now if the eyes of the Beloved rested upon the eyes of the Bride (cf. VI. 5), the latter would themselves be the brooks of water. They are here compared to the pools of Heshbon; pools, as we may well suppose, into which channels of water abundantly streamed, and in which the purity of the water was in great measure preserved; and which furthermore served for the supply of all that desired. Directed themselves to Christ, and gazing on his lustre, the eyes of the Church become the pools in which the image of Christ is reflected, and in which all the streams of pure doctrine are concentrated. There is moreover here, without much doubt, an etymological allusion to the meaning of the word Heshbon, "thought," "meditation," (Aquila, ἐπιλογισμόν). This allusion was early recognized, probably by Origen, and is referred to by Philo of Carpasia. What else, in its substance, is Christian doctrine, than contemplation of Christ, and meditation on his work? *By the gate whose name is Multitude.* Lit., "by the gate of Bath-rabbim, i.e. of the daughter of many." Whether this was really the name of any of the gates of Heshbon we have no means of knowing. The most probable supposition is that the poet had in view that gate of Heshbon which opened north-eastward, in the direction of Rabbah of Ammon, and that for the name Gate of Rabbah he substituted Gate of Bath-rabbim, in order to fix attention on the etymological meaning. But against this there is the objection that the one known reservoir of Heshbon, mentioned above, is on the south side of the city. For with reference to the meaning, it is sufficiently clear that the gate of which the poet speaks must be the gate of approach to the pools, the portal through which the multitude of the Gentile world presses to drink to the full of the clear and unruffled waters of Christian doctrine. *Thy nose is as the tower of Lebanon that looketh toward Damascus.* We read generally in 1 Kings IX. 19 of fortresses, &c. which Solomon erected in Lebanon. The remarkable feature about the tower here referred to would be its conspicuousness when beheld from the neighbourhood of Damascus. And thus through this image is set forth the spectacle of combined beauty and strength which the Church should present to the heathen world. At the time that the Song was written the Syrians were the most persistent and the most powerful of the enemies of Israel, and Damascus was therefore the most fitting representative of the world as opposed to the Church. And the poet, while he prophetically sets forth the attractions which the Church should possess for all who would approach to taste of her fulness, does not fail to proclaim also how she should stand erect in her majesty as a defenced city against all that should strive with her, so that they should gaze on her with admiration, and, fighting against her, should not prevail. *Thy head upon thee is like Carmel.* The words "upon thee" shew that the crown is here about to be placed on all the previous parts of the eulogy. Now the two main points of commendation which have run through this eulogy are, first, the Bride's graceful strength, and secondly, her inexhaustible richness in ministering to her children's needs. We should naturally expect to find these same points here insisted on together; nor are we disappointed. In Mount Carmel, the long ridge of which stretched from the interior of the Holy Land in a north-westerly direction to the headland on the south of the bay of Accho, in which it terminated, graceful elevation was combined with great natural fertility. Its height, by actual measurement, was not indeed great; but situate between two plains, and running out into the sea, it was seen to unusual advantage, and thus formed one of the most prominent features of the central portion of the territory of Israel. Its fertility was marked by its name: it was the "Park" or the "Garden" of the land, a fitting image of that Church of Christ which is the garden of the world. *And the tresses of thine head.* To the praise of the head that of the hair naturally succeeds. The Hebrew term is generally taken as denoting hair which hangs down, and this is, on the whole, the most appropriate meaning. *Like royal purple.* The latter part of this verse is, according to the ordinary syntax, so utterly obscure, that we may well follow one of the Greek translators, the Syriac, and Jerome in making ארגמן the construct noun before מלך (Anon. ὡς πορφύρα βασιλέως, Jer. "sicut purpura regis"), thus transferring the latter word from the following to the present clause. (Hence, probably, the "regis purpura" of the hymn "Vexilla regis prodeunt," see above, p. 152.) The introduction of purple in the comparison now before us has induced some to render the word כרמל (Carmel) in the preceding clause by "crimson," as if it were כרמיל, in order to make the parallelism more complete. Without assenting to this, we may well allow that the sound of the word Carmel brought up the remembrance of the colour of similar name, and that this partly suggested the "purple" of the present clause. The first and most obvious point of resemblance of the Bride's hair to purple lies in the preciousness of its beauty; and royal purple would of course be purple of the most precious kind. It is not easy however, in tracing out the full prospective meaning of the language employed, to deny all reference in the "royal purple" to the precious blood of Christ with which the Church has now been redeemed, the most truly royal dye of which it is possible for expositor to speak or for poet to sing. So Philo of Carpasia, &c. It must be further remembered, as was before remarked on IV. 1, that the hair of the Bride is of itself a testimony to the native richness of her person. *Enfixed amid the wainscottings.* The picture is that of a rich chamber on the walls of which carved wooden panels alternate with purple hangings. The former serve to relieve and to shew off the beauty of the latter, to which latter the well-ordered and well-fastened tresses of the Bride's hair are compared. The sense of the word רהטים, properly "troughs," is determined by that of the nearly identical word רחיטים, "boardings," in I. 17. Probably we must picture the wainscotting, with its breaks of purple hanging, as arranged in parallel vertical trough-like lines or panels. We can hardly fail to be struck with the contrast of the two images employed by the poet in this verse, borrowed the one from the richest scenes of natural beauty, the other from the richest scenes of artificial luxury. *O daughter of allurements.* We may follow the Syriac and Aquila in dividing the בתענגים of our Hebrew text into the two words בת ענגים. *This thy stature is like a palm-tree, &c.* It is a matter of considerable difficulty to determine into whose lips this and the succeeding two verses are put. That through all three verses it is the Bride who is addressed, would appear from the received punctuation of the suffix pronoun, which should always be respected, unless there be very good ground to the contrary. The distinction however between "thy," masculine, and "thy," feminine, disappears in a Greek no less than in an English translation; and Origen and Theodoret, while they allowed that the Bridegroom addressed the Bride in ver. 7, supposed that in ver. 8 the Bride in her turn expressed her desire to the Bridegroom, and that having been herself first compared to a palm-tree, she now applied the same simile to her Beloved. In favour of this view, it might be contended, was the occurrence of the expression "my beloved" in ver. 9; which, on the other hand, some of the most recent interpreters, as Delitzsch and Hengstenberg, explain by a sudden change of speakers, a sudden interruption of the Bride, in the middle of that verse. Neither the change of speakers which the Greek Fathers assume at the beginning of ver. 8, nor yet the change which the last-named interpreters introduce into the middle of ver. 9, has the aspect of being natural. It is more probable that there is a change of speakers at the beginning of ver. 7; and that as the encomium of the Beloved on the Bride had been sufficiently brought to a close at the end of ver. 6, so here the Chorus of the Daughters of Jerusalem take up the strain of his praises, describing the attraction which she possesses for them, and their desire to be associated with her. The word "this" at the beginning of ver. 7, involving a double reference both to the aspect of the Bride as beheld by them, and to the praises of the Bridegroom upon her, may, on the whole, not inappropriately serve to mark the commencement of their address; nor can the employment in ver. 8 of the 1st person singular be deemed any serious objection to the view that it is the Chorus that is speaking. And it is in favour of this view that the actual encomium of the Beloved on the Bride would then, like the similar encomium in the preceding chapter, be limited to six verses. In other words, VI. 10—13 being the centre-piece of the section, VII. 1—6 would correspond in position to VI. 4—9, and the supplementary VII. 7—9 to the introductory VI. 1—3. We may therefore, on the whole, adopt this view, as the most probable; without however asserting its correctness in terms of unbecoming confidence. It may be observed that many interpreters have put the entire passage VII. 1—9 into the mouth of the Chorus. But internal evidence is against this, not to speak of the evidence supplied by the structure of the Song. The recondite character of the similes in VII. 1—6 renders them more appropriate in the mouth of the Beloved than in that of the Chorus; and we can hardly separate VII. 3 from IV. 5, where the Beloved is undoubtedly the speaker. It is in favour of our view of a change of speakers at the commencement of ver. 7 that the imagery here assumes a simpler and (so to speak) more natural character. The Bride is compared by the Daughters of Jerusalem to a palm-tree in respect of her majestic beauty. The Bridegroom has expressed the same thing by means of other similes, ver. 4. *And thy breasts to clusters of fruit.* Are we to connect this with the preceding simile, and so understand clusters of dates? Or shall we, looking on to the next verse, suppose that clusters of grapes are intended? The latter is preferable. For it will be observed that then the division of the next verse will correspond to the division of this: its earlier half will unfold the simile of the palm-tree, in its latter half we shall pass to the simile of the fruit. Moreover the Hebrew word for clusters is so generally applied to clusters of grapes, that it naturally denotes them unless the contrary be expressed. Lusciousness is, in this simile, the point of comparison. *Let me climb this palm-tree, let me take hold of its branches.* It is probable that the word סנסנים (*sansinnim*), which only occurs here, specially denotes the peculiar boughs or branches of the palm-tree, for which we have in English no distinctive term. Interpreters generally assume that the wish here expressed of climbing the palm-tree originates in the desire of gathering the dates that grow upon it. It is more likely that the secret lies simply in the attraction of its majestic beauty; attraction of the same kind with that which the summit of a noble mountain has for the traveller whose eye is continually resting upon it. We desire—such is the feeling—to unite ourselves as closely as possible to the magnificence which we behold. *And be thy breasts now, &c.* The longing which the Daughters of Jerusalem here display to be associated with the Bride, and to taste of her richness, is well illustrated by Isaiah LXVI. 10, 11: "Rejoice ye with Jerusalem, and be glad with her, all ye that love her;...that ye may suck, and be satisfied with the breasts of her consolations; that ye may milk out, and be delighted with the abundance of her glory." *Thy speech.* Properly, Thy palate: see on v. 16. *Which, going straight to my beloved.* So completely do the Daughters of Jerusalem here view themselves as participating in the glories of the Bride, that they, as it were, identify themselves with her, and speak of the Bridegroom as My Beloved. The Church has absorbed all that is capable of generous feeling into herself: she and the Daughters of Jerusalem no longer stand apart; and this is the true crowning-point of her earthly glory. Thus the real significance of this expression, "my beloved," in the present verse is satisfactorily explained. Our observations above, on ver. 7, will have shewn that its presence here had occasioned much difficulty. Several critics had proposed to reject it altogether, as an interpolation that had erroneously crept in from ver. 10. But for this there was no authority; and had the Beloved been really speaking here, it would have been better to have translated thus, "Which, going straight to him whom thou callest My Beloved, &c.:" it might have been argued that the phrase "*my* beloved" sounded more affectionate than "*thy* beloved," and was therefore preferred out of a desire to retain in this passage all possible endearment of language; and this might have been illustrated by the parallel use of the expressive "within *my* heart" for "within *his* heart" in Psalm XXXVI. 1, if the received text of that verse be correct, which is, however, doubtful. But better than even this hypothetical explanation is the explanation at which we have actually arrived by viewing the Daughters of Jerusalem as the speakers. *Causeth the lips of the sleepers to speak*[1]. The whole

---

[1] In so difficult a passage some variations of text must be expected; and for שפתי ישנים, "the lips of the sleepers," the LXX, Syriac, and Aquila apparently concur in reading שפתי ושנים, "my lips and teeth;" to which reading the versions of Symmachus and Jerome also lend partial and indirect support. It has, however, the disadvantage of being ungrammatical, the true Hebrew for "my lips and teeth" being שפתי ושני. Moreover, the received text is decidedly upheld by the

verse exhibits the secret of the attraction which the Church possesses for the Daughters of Jerusalem, and of the influence which she exerts over the hearts of men. The palate, or speech, of the Bride, here compared to goodly wine, represents the prayers and praises which she offers to Christ; which proceed from her directly to him; and which, by so proceeding, induce even the listless to join in them. For the spiritually asleep are more easily drawn to echo the worship which they hear the Church pouring forth to her Lord, than to respond to the exhortations addressed immediately to themselves. How many slumbering hearts have been waked by the Psalms of David! Yet those psalms are in general the language of worship, not of admonition. It is by her own reverence and earnestness in worshipping that the Church excites the reverence and earnestness of others : the nearer and more direct her own communion with her Lord, the more surely will she entice others to commune with him also.

VII. 10—VIII. 4. The Bride speaks throughout; and describes, in the first four verses, her joy in the company of her Beloved. It is still the spiritual presence of Christ with the Church which is depicted. *I am my beloved's.* In this affectionate reiteration of what she had before expressed, cf. II. 16, VI. 3, the Bride reveals the whole depth of her love. It is her greatest joy to belong to him who on the mountain of myrrh has redeemed her unto himself. *And his desire is toward*

Targum, and yields a more appropriate meaning; we therefore adhere to it.

me. Cf. Psalm XLV. 11, "so shall the king greatly desire thy beauty:" also the last address of the Beloved, concluding with VII. 6. Ginsburg's rendering, "it is for me (as a duty) to desire him," although grammatically admissible, is less natural, and destroys the expression of mutual love which, according to the analogy of other passages in the Song, we should here expect. *Come, my beloved, let us go forth into the field, let us sojourn in the villages.* The clue to the interpretation of these words must be sought in those which follow. It will then appear that they speak not of the exercise of pure meditation (as a comparison of Gen. XXIV. 63 might suggest), but rather of patient labour. In the words of Origen, "The Bride puts in her entreaty in behalf of those that are in need; and quitting her more domestic associations in the abodes of wealth, she desires to go forth to take the charge over them. It is they who are to her field and villages, the vineyards and the pomegranates for which she cares." And doubtless in this very labour of love she will realize her own communion with her Lord; partly because she is expressly carrying out his will, and because whatever she does for others in his name she does for him; partly also because his presence and his blessing will accompany her in all her movements, and in all that she thus undertakes for him, she will feel that he is with her. Compare Acts VIII. 4, 25; XI. 19—21: "Therefore they that were scattered abroad went every where preaching the word......And they... preached the gospel in many villages of the Samaritans

......And the hand of the Lord was with them." *Let us start early.* And therefore be diligent in our work, cf. Psalm LXIII. 1, &c. *Let us see whether, &c.* Compare VI. 11. It was thus that the apostles, when they went down to Samaria, Acts VIII. 14, had the opportunity of discerning the results of their Master's previous teaching among the Samaritans, and of entering into his labours, as he himself had forewarned them, John IV. 35—38. *There will I give thee my love.* Wheresoever the labours of the Bride or of her Lord had prospered, wheresoever the fruits had appeared which she desired to behold, there, it must be remembered, all became incorporated into the person of the Bride herself. The newest and most distant converts to the Christian faith became, by their conversion, as truly members of the one Catholic and Apostolic Church, as those from whom the tidings of salvation had been by them received. So that whether it be a Paul or an Onesimus who is proving by his life the devotion of himself to the Lord Jesus Christ, whether it be the original Christian band in Jerusalem or the new-formed Christian band in Rome that is labouring for the conversion of fresh souls to him, it is equally the Bride that is yielding her love unto her Lord. Each new local habitation, each fresh centre of labour, in which, through previous loving labour, she establishes herself, will multiply the offerings which she, even "she" and none other, is bringing as proofs of her devotion to him. And thus each new territory which opens itself to her gaze, each new people of the very existence of which she for the first time hears, commends itself straightway to her as a new channel through which she may convey to her Beloved her love. In illustration of the stress which must thus necessarily be laid on the single word "there," cf. Hosea I. 10, Rom. IX. 26. It was in the true spirit of the Bride's words in this passage that holy Gregory, when he beheld the Anglo-Saxon youths at Rome, declared that they who were the subjects of King Ella must be made to sing Alleluia. *The mandrakes yield forth a fragrance.* The mandrake, Atropa mandragora, is a low herb, with dark green leaves resembling those of the Belladonna, and a root like that of a carrot. The flower is, according to some, purple: according to others, white and reddish: the fruit, when ripe, in the beginning of May, is of the size and colour of a small apple. The Hebrew name of this plant is held to signify love-plant; and certain peculiar properties are in the East popularly ascribed to it. (See, in Maundrell's Journey, the account of his interview with the Samaritan Priest: also other references in Kitto's Cyclopædia.) It is mentioned elsewhere in Scripture only in Gen. XXX. 14—16. The fruit, although, according to Maundrell, of an ill savour (Thomson speaks of it as insipid and sickly), is described by Mariti as of a most agreeable odour. *At our doors.* At the doors of our dwelling, cf. I. 17, and therefore immediately surrounding us. *All precious fruits.* Precious fruits of all kinds, cf. IV. 13. *Both new and old.* If the fruits represent holy virtues, and holy works, the meaning will be that the Church of the New Covenant will not only bring forth all such holy works as those by which the saints of olden time obtained a good report, but will also distinguish herself by the practice of duties which were in ancient times comparatively overlooked. It is certainly among the glories of the Christian dispensation to have developed a far stronger sense of the duty of brotherly love, and to have uprooted polygamy, and, in great measure, slavery. At the same time, the present passage distinctly implies that we cannot afford to throw away the burning examples of the deeds of faith of a more imperfect age. With it may be compared Matth. XIII. 52, in which the Lord Jesus Christ recognizes the excellence both of old and of new doctrine. But the reference which some have found here to Levit. XXVI. 10 is uncertain. *Which I have treasured up, my beloved, for thee.* Compare 2 Cor. v. 9: "We labour, that, whether present or absent, we may be accepted of him." While this clause sets forth the desire of the Church to consecrate her every work as a love-offering to Christ, it also serves as an introduction to that expression of desire for his more entire presence to which we now proceed. *O that thou wouldest appear as brother of mine.* At length the Song verges towards its conclusion. The Bride, the Church, although blest with the spiritual presence of her Beloved, cannot but long for his personal re-appearing. She desires his outward coming or παρουσία: she desires to behold him once more in the human body which he assumed when at his incarnation he became the brother of mankind. Why should she not? For indeed this desire, the desire of all them that love the Lord's appearing, is not inconsistent with an earnest cherishing of his spiritual presence during the season of his personal absence. *As one that had sucked the breasts of my mother.* It was as the seed of the woman, nurtured by her in infancy, and growing up under her fostering care to maturity, that Christ became, and still remains, our brother, and that as such he will hereafter again reveal himself. The mother, alike of the Bride and of the Beloved, was previously explained of the Jewish nation, and may here, since that restriction is now unnecessary, be taken more generally of the whole human race[1]. *Should I find thee without.* Or, "in the street"; in reference to the imagery of III. 2 seqq., V. 7. The case seems here to be purely hypothetical. Origen by "without" understands "without Jerusalem," where Jesus was crucified. This, unfolded by the aid of the New Testament, would lead to the meaning that the Church desires to behold that Lord who was once crucified for her, and who still bears the tokens of his Cross and Passion. But the language of the Song must not be pressed too far. The great desire of the Bride is to find her Beloved anyhow and anywhere. *I would kiss thee.* That is, would welcome thy closest presence. The prayer for the Beloved's first appearing was "Let him kiss me," I. 2. *And eke they should not despise me.* Having now found him whom she had so ardently desired, she should no more be despised and insulted as she had been when

---

[1] Cassiodorus writes: "Mater synagogæ in hoc loco ipsa humana natura intelligitur, de qua ipsa synagoga exorta est."

she sought for him through the streets in vain, v. 7. *I would hasten thee away to my mother's house.* See on III. 4. The substance of the meaning is that such is now her great desire, to gaze upon him in human form upon earth. The various blessings of Christ's final appearing are here one by one enumerated. *That so thou mightest teach me.* Cf. 1 Cor. XIII. 12: "Now we see through a glass darkly; but then face to face: now I know in part; but then shall I know even as also I am known." *I would cause thee to drink of spiced wine.* We saw, on IV. 16, that all the various products of the Bride's garden represented the various acts and affections of devotion of the Church to her Lord. Wine, in particular, symbolizes the joint participation of both host and guest in the joys of a feast, and therefore their mutual communion with each other. What the Church here offers to Christ, she has all along been drinking herself. As to the wine being spiced, it will portend, if we recall the symbolical significance of myrrh as the principal ingredient, that the death of Christ lies at the root of all the communion of the Church with him. And this is in fact exactly what is outwardly represented to us in the sacrament of the Lord's Supper. It is of a wine which may be figuratively described as spiced with death, a wine associated with the memory of all our Lord's mortal sufferings, that we there partake; and by it we shew forth the Lord's death till he come. All the genuine devotion which our several sacramental acts have represented he will then enable us to present to him in its most perfect form, himself then drinking of the fruit of the vine new with us in his Father's kingdom (Matt. XXVI. 29). *Of the juice of my pomegranate.* In other words, "of the richest potion that I can offer thee." The pomegranate seems to have been esteemed the choicest of the fruits from which drinks were made. It is more than once mentioned among the richest products of Canaan, Deut. VIII. 8; Joel I. 12; Haggai II. 19. Compare, moreover, in the Song, IV. 13; VI. 11; VII. 12. Representations of it were also introduced, but with what exact symbolism is not clear, on to the hem of the ephod and into the architecture of the temple. In IV. 3, VI. 7, the reference is to the beauty of its hues. *His left hand, &c.* See on II. 6. *I adjure you, &c.* The form of adjuration nearly corresponds to that in II. 7, III. 5, but is shorter. For the explanation of it, see on II. 7. *O! that ye upstir not, and O! that ye disturb not, &c.* The מה expresses a more urgent entreaty than the אם of the earlier passages. It is curious that it should be employed in v. 8 in a positive sense, "O!", here in a negative sense, "O! not." Such however seems to be plainly the case. Even in English, "O! will ye upstir" might be an entreaty either to upstir or not to upstir, according to the context.

LOVE'S TRIUMPH.
viii. 5—12.

WITH THE CONCLUSION.
viii. 13, 14.

Præparata, ut sponsata,
Copuletur Domino.

5 *Chorus.* Who is this that cometh up from the wilderness,
   Leaning upon her beloved?
   Bride. Under the citron-tree I raised thee up:
   There thy mother brought thee forth,
   There she brought thee forth that bare thee.
6 Set me as a seal upon thine heart,
   As a seal upon thine arm!
   For love is strong as death;
   Jealousy is stubborn as the grave:
   Its flashes are flashes of fire, flame of the Eternal.
7 Floods avail not to quench love,
   Streams cannot sweep it away:
   Though a man should for love offer all the wealth of his house,
   He would be met with utter scorn.
8 We have a little sister,
   And she hath no breasts:
   What shall we do for our sister
   In the day that she be demanded as a bride?
9 *Beloved.* Be she wall, we will build for her an enclosure of silver;
   Or be she door, we will fasten together for her boards of cedar.

10 *Bride.* I am a wall, and my breasts are as towers:
   Therefore am I become in his eyes as one that
       findeth the favour of peace.
11 A vineyard owneth Solomon in Baal-hamon:
   He hath let out the vineyard unto keepers,
   That every one should bring for the fruit thereof
       a thousand pieces of silver.
12 My vineyard, that which is mine own, is before me:
   Thine be the thousand, O Solomon,
   And two hundred be there for those that keep the
       fruit.

The sixth section of the Song depicts the final union of the Bride and her Beloved. It consists of eight verses, VIII. 5—12.

Vv. 5—7. *Who is this that cometh up from the wilderness.* Compare on III. 6. That passage described the termination of her first, this the termination of her second long period of waiting. *Leaning upon her beloved.* Neither the root רפק nor any derivative from it occurs elsewhere in the Bible; but the meaning "to lean" is established by the rendering of the Greek and Syriac translators and of Jerome, and by the corresponding meanings of the root in Arabic. Ginsburg also adduces the Talmudic word מרפק, "an arm," on which one leans[1]. It is by the supporting, though in-

---

[1] It is probable that some transcriber, not understanding the word מתרפקה, suggested, in the margin, מתפנקת; and that from the

visible, power of her Beloved that the Bride has been carried through all the trials of her desert-pilgrimage, and therefore it is on him that she is now at the last, in her hour of reward, appropriately represented as leaning. *Under the citron-tree I raised thee up.* This and the remainder of the verse are addressed, as the gender of the Hebrew suffix-pronouns shews, by the Bride to the Beloved. Commentators who could not read the Song in the original Hebrew have not, of course, always known this. And indeed of recent scholars, some, as Delitzsch and Renan, have wished, by altering the vowel-points, to change the gender of the suffixes. Now the mention of the citron-tree carries us back to II. 3. It there represented that spiritual presence of Christ which the Church of the Old Testament by anticipation enjoyed before his actual coming in the flesh. The import of the imagery is not seriously altered when the shadow of the citron-tree is made to stand generally for the spiritual influence from on high which rested on the Church of God. Under the power of this spiritual influence then, the Church of the Old Testament in due time raised up her divine Redeemer. In the language of the apocalyptic vision, she, the " woman clothed with the sun, and the moon under her feet, and upon her

margin this crept into the text, either superseding מתרפקת, as in the Chaldee paraphrase (ומתפנקין על רחמי מרהא); or obliterating the previous מן־המדבר, as in the copy used by the LXX. (Τίς αὕτη ἡ ἀναβαίνουσα λελευκανθισμένη); or else, as in Jerome's copy, finding room for itself without displacing its neighbour (de deserto, deliciis affluens, innixa super, &c.). The uncorrupted text has been happily preserved to us in our Masoretic MSS. and by the Syriac version.

head a crown of twelve stars," "being with child cried, travailing in birth, and pained to be delivered;" and at length, in her appointed time, "brought forth a man child, who was to rule all nations with a rod of iron" (Rev. xii. 1—5). Is it asked how the working of the Divine Spirit, here symbolized by the citron-tree, had directly contributed to this wondrous birth? It is readily answered, that to the Spirit of God must be traced all that system of laws by which the Church of Israel was gradually trained to holiness, and of the true spirit of which, and of the holiness implied in the observance of them, Christ was the crowning and most perfect representative; again, that to the Spirit of God must be traced all that wondrous typical ceremonial which eventually found in Christ its completion and fulfilment; again, that it was the Spirit of God that rested in an especial manner on those several lines of Israelitish kings and priests and prophets that all culminated in the person of the One Great Anointed; and again, that it was the working of the Spirit that caused so many passages in the earlier history of the Church of Israel to foreshadow the history of him whose way was being thus gradually prepared before him. In all these several ways was the Church of Israel made by the Spirit the means of raising up the long-expected Christ; who in his turn, by his dutiful and consistent submission to all the ordinances of the Church of Israel, testified that it was from her that he had sprung. *There thy mother brought thee forth, there she brought thee forth that bare thee.* The previous clause set forth the ecclesiastical, these declare the physical descent of the Saviour of mankind. His mother is here, as in III. 11, the Nation of Israel, as distinguished from the Church of Israel, symbolized by the Bride. It was the Bride, the Church, that raised him up: it was the Mother, the Nation, that brought him forth. And this too, no less than the other, was through the wondrous operation of the Spirit of God. By the Holy Ghost was Christ conceived in the Virgin Mary. It moreover seems probable that in the words in which the angel Gabriel announced to the Virgin what should come to pass, there was a reference to the imagery of the shadow of the citron-tree in the passage of the Song before us: "The Holy Ghost shall come upon thee, and the power of the Highest shall *overshadow* thee: therefore also that holy thing which shall be born of thee shall be called the Son of God" (Luke I. 35). Why else should the angel have made use of this remarkable expression, "overshadow"? But we must pass from this to another question which may here suggest itself. Be it, some will say, that under the citron-tree the Bride had originally raised up her Beloved, be it that under the citron-tree his Mother had born him; why nevertheless should the Bride here dwell upon this, now that she is united with him to be parted never more? Clearly, in order to shew how intimately connected with her he was; and how it was as one thus intimately connected with her that he was now finally manifested to her. In other words, he is come for the second time, even as he came at the first, in the flesh; the glorified, but still the very Son of Man. He appears to the Bride, according to her prayer, as her brother, as one that has sucked the breasts of her mother. He is to her both brother and bridegroom: as such he had previously declared himself (IV. 9), and as such she now, at his re-appearing, welcomes him. Thus all is explained. *Set me as a seal upon thine heart, as a seal upon thine arm.* The Hebrew word for "seal" "denotes either an impression or a signet-ring. That the latter is here intended is shewn by the parallel passages in Haggai and Jeremiah. The force of the comparison rests upon the inseparableness of a signet-ring from the person, and on the diligent care with which it is guarded. Cf. Jer. XXII. 24: 'Though Coniah the son of Jehoiakim king of Judah were the signet upon my right hand, &c.:' also Haggai II. 23, where there is perhaps an allusion to our present passage. Signet-rings were worn either, suspended by a string, on the breast (Gen. XXXVIII. 18), or else on the hand; to which customs regard is here had. Instead, however, of the hand, the arm is mentioned, as being the symbol of the active display of succouring might, cf. Psalm LXXXIX. 10, LXXVII. 15. The heart here comes under review as the source of love, the arm as the outward manifestation of it" (Hengstenberg)[1]. *For love is strong as death.* Is it of her love to her Beloved, or of her Beloved's to her, that the Bride is here speaking? We may prepare the way for a reply to this enquiry by observing that a

---

[1] So, nearly, Theodoret: καρδίαν μὲν τὸ θεωρητικὸν τῆς ψυχῆς ὠνομάσας, βραχίονα δὲ τὸ πρακτικόν.

corresponding question may be asked in reference to a simpler portion of Holy Scripture, Rom. VIII. 35. Is the love of Christ in that passage our love to him, or his to us? The former is the general view of the ancient, the latter of the modern interpreters. But, in fact, both are in a measure right; and neither his love to us nor ours to him can be excluded. For while fully acknowledging that his love to us takes precedence of ours to him, and that we thus love him because he first loved us, we must yet remember that it is love's greatest glory and reward to draw forth a corresponding affection from him towards whom it is directed, and to propagate itself by enworking its own echo wheresoever it strikes. We may call that the perfection of love, when two hearts beat in such entire unison the one with the other as to reciprocate in all fulness each other's attachment. And in such a case either of the two parties, in speaking of the love that reigns between them, does not define, for there can be no object in defining, whether it be his own or the other's love that he intends: the two have practically become as one. So is it in the striking and beautiful description before us. By love being as strong as death is primarily meant that love will not more easily part with its object than death with its victim. More than this is not here directly asserted. But in proportion as it was felt that there was a power which was mightier than death, while it made no war upon love, (and the death and resurrection of Christ were the manifestation of the existence of such a power,) so was it also necessarily recognized that in the universe

Love reigns supreme. *Jealousy is stubborn as the grave*, lit. "as hades." By jealousy is here denoted that resolute and devoted attachment which will not suffer its object to be torn from its grasp. Such attachment is as unyielding, as relentlessly tenacious, as is hades in respect of its prey. Our English Version here gives "jealousy is cruel as the grave;" and since the relentlessness of the latter constitutes its cruelty, the term "cruel" may perhaps be metaphorically allowed to express also, with quaint force, the relentlessness of the former. There is, in the Hebrew, an elegant alliteration between the three words of this clause. *Its flashes are flashes of fire.* For "flashes," our English Version gives "coals." But the Hebrew term is used also of the sudden springings of the arrow from the bowstring, Psalm LXXVI. 3, and of the strokes of pestilential disease, Deut. XXXII. 24; and the force of the present clause is lost if the word be rendered in English by a particular instead of by a general term. The likeness of love to fire is here asserted, not assumed. That likeness consists, first, in its impetuous energy, and secondly, and still more importantly, in its uncontrollable power. *Flame of the Eternal.* In Hebrew, *Shalhebethjah*, שלהבתיה, a compound word, formed, no doubt, by the poet for the occasion. It is well known that in the eleventh century the Palestinian and Babylonian editors of the Hebrew Bible, Ben Asher and Ben Naphtali, the other discrepancies of whose respective copies related solely to the Hebrew vowels and accents, were at issue in reference to this one word, as to whether its two parts should be kept together or should be separated by a hyphen. Doubtless they should be kept as closely as possible together, the word following the analogy of מַאְפֵּלְיָה in Jer. II. 31. No parallelism is gained by dividing the word into two, for "Jah," the most sacred name of God, would hardly be used as parallel to "fire": much force is at the same time lost by destroying the unusual appearance which the word, undivided, presents[1]. What now is its true meaning? That the earlier element in it, though of disputed etymology, signifies "flames," is by all admitted. As to the latter element, "Jah," it seems clear that the phrase "of God" is constantly used in Hebrew to distinguish that which is excellent of its kind: thus Psalm XXXVI. 6, "mountains of God," i.e. "great mountains;" LXXX. 10, "cedars of God," i.e. "goodly cedars;" Jonah III. 3, "a great city to God," i.e. "an exceedingly great city:" cf. also Acts VII. 20, ἀστεῖος τῷ Θεῷ, "fair to God," i.e. "exceeding fair." And in Gen. XIII. 10, "the garden of the LORD," even the name Jehovah seems to be similarly employed. We can hardly altogether separate the interpretation of the term before us from the interpretation of such phrases as these; though on the other hand, as Jah is the concentrated and most emphatic form of the sacred name Jehovah, it may well be that the "flames of Jah" will bear a somewhat higher meaning than "flames of God."

[1] To the genuineness of the word, and also to its unity, testimony not open to suspicion is borne by the LXX, who render it φλόγες αὐτῆς, incorrectly treating the last letter as the suffix. Jerome and the Syriac seem somehow to have dropped the last two letters altogether.

The adjunct "of God" would imply that a thing was exalted above all things of its kind, even as God is exalted above the universe: the adjunct "of Jah" will correspondingly involve the assertion of that eternal character which we ascribe to God in the name Jah, or Jehovah. The term before us imports then not, as some have taken it, that love emanates from the Eternal, however true that doctrine be; but that the principle of love is itself eternal. And the consolation to be derived from the eternity of love is the consolation of knowing that death and hell (hades) must bend, as indeed they have bent, to its power. *Floods avail not to quench love, &c.* Floods and streams stand occasionally as representing severe trials and persecutions; sometimes as representing death itself. Cf. Rev. XII. 15; Isaiah XLIII. 2; Psalm CXXIV. 4, 5, &c. The Christian employment of a stream as the image of death is mainly connected with the passage of the Israelites across the Jordan. In the verse before us however it must not be supposed that the words bear any definite allegorical meaning: rather, imagery is here exerting all its resources to set forth the victorious might of love. *Though a man should for love offer all the wealth of his house, &c.* Not all the outward wealth that a man could tender would induce love to forgo its object: the proffered bribe would be indignantly rejected. On the other hand, the New Testament has told us of One who surrendered everything, even life itself, for the sake of the Church whom he loved, and has taught us how she is summoned to render to her Saviour a corresponding affection.

We must not part from this noble passage without again referring to Romans VIII. 35—39 as the place in the New Testament where it finds its fullest parallel: "Who shall separate us from the love of Christ? shall tribulation, or distress, or persecution, or famine, or nakedness, or peril, or sword?...Nay, in all these things we are more than conquerors through him that loved us. For I am persuaded, that neither death, nor life, nor angels, nor principalities, nor powers, nor things present, nor things to come, nor height, nor depth, nor any other creature, shall be able to separate us from the love of God which is in Christ Jesus our Lord."

Vv. 8, 9. *We have a little sister, and she hath no breasts.* Hitherto it has scarcely come into consideration throughout the Song, who are the persons, whether Israelites or Gentiles, of whom the Church consists. The prospects of the Church, as a Church, have indeed been unfolded to the very end of time; but she has been viewed in her continuity, a continuity unaffected by the catholic character which she was, in point of fact, to assume after the day of her espousal to her Lord. Only in VI. 11, and in VII. 11, 12, did we have intimation of the nurturing labours which the Church should undertake beyond the limits of her original demesne, and of the extended powers of fruitfulness which should thereby accrue to her. In the passage now before us the Church, while taking her stand, in reference to her Beloved, on that full communion of intercourse with him to which the Song in its progress had gradually conducted us (hence the "we" of this and the verse following) reverts, nevertheless, in reference to her own constitution, to that position which she occupied, as the Church of Israel, towards the Gentile world, at the time that the Song was written. That Gentile world, with all its yet undeveloped germs of faith towards God, the world to which the Hirams of Tyre, and the Queens of Sheba, and, above all, the Naamans of Syria belonged, she personifies as her little sister, who had as yet not reached to womanhood. It cannot surprise us that the ancient Church should be encouraged to look upon the Gentile world as a sister, when we find punishment denounced upon Edom for not treating Israel as a brother (Obad. 10—12). This image could however only hold good for the period anterior to Christ's coming, for the period during which the sister was little and not yet ripe for marriage: when she entered into marriage she would be no longer distinct from her elder sister, but would be incorporated with her, so that the Bride should still be but one. In the "we," the Bride, taking counsel respecting her sister, associates her Beloved along with herself. Similarly in the ensuing verse, the Beloved, replying, refuses, by the use of the "we," to separate himself from his Bride. And thus in fact it is seen that all God's earlier dealings in adjusting the relation between his chosen people and the Gentiles must be regarded and explained from the point of view of the fulfilment of his ultimate purpose, that of uniting the whole universal Church in the closest communion to his Son Jesus Christ our Saviour. *What shall we do for our sister in the day that she be demanded as a bride?*

The Church, foreseeing the call which the Gentile world will receive, looks with some degree of apprehension on its present immaturity, and asks how it may be fitted to enter into the covenant-relationship, or how assisted to bear aright the expected dignity. *Be she wall, &c.; or be she door, &c.* The substance of the answer is this: We will build her up, and that in full glory. The image of building is one of very frequent occurrence in Hebrew. See for example Jer. I. 10, XVIII. 9, XXIV. 6, XXXI. 4, XXXIII. 7, XLII. 10; Psalm XXVIII. 5, LXXXIX. 4; Gen. II. 22. It underlies even the etymology of the language, the words for "son" and "build" being etymologically connected, because the family is viewed as built up of children. And from the Hebrew idiom it has passed through the Greek οἰκοδομέω and the Latin-English "edify" into ecclesiastical use (see Acts IX. 31, and the New Testament passim), the Christian Church thus perpetuating the hallowed language of Canaan. Such then being the image which the poet has here chosen to employ, the walls and the doors come into view as two of the most obvious features of every edifice. (In like manner in the New Jerusalem, Rev. XXI., the "bride adorned for her husband," it is the walls and the gates which the seer selects for special description.) "We will build up our Gentile sister," is the assurance of the Beloved to the Bride, "in full proportions, and with all that is needful for her; and every part of her framework shall be of the costliest. As for her wall of enclosure, we will fence her around with silver: as for her doors, of cedar alone, and of no inferior wood, shall they be constructed. Thus, tender and unfurnished though she now appear, she shall not in her bridal-day be found wanting, but shall, through divine grace, display, in all richness, the glories that are meet for the spouse of Christ." The word טירה, from the root טור "to surround," is here used in its original sense, as denoting any sort of wall, fence, enclosure, or external fortification. The phrase "Be she wall," or "door," signifies "So far as she be a wall," or "door," or, as we should express it, "As for wall for her," "As for door for her." The two aspects in which she is viewed are mutually supplementary: cf., for the syntax, 2 Cor. v. 13. "Upon her" is the meaning usually assigned to עליה; but it will bear also the meaning "for her," "on her account," and this is more appropriate. The mass of modern interpreters, more especially of the literalists, give a very different turn to this verse. They take "wall" and "door" as figurative expressions for "impregnable" and "open to seduction;" and explain thus, that if the sister should resist all assaults upon her virtue, she should be rewarded with decorations; whereas if she yielded, she should be punished by being barricaded or locked up. But it may be hoped that this has now been lastingly set aside by the just criticism of Renan: "Cette interprétation," he says, "donne lieu à de graves difficultés. Je n'insiste pas sur ce qu'elle a de fade et de languissant. Admettons, contre toute vraisemblance, que les créneaux d'argent dont parlent les frères [?] puissent désigner une sorte de parure qui soit la récompense de la vertu de la jeune fille, il restera encore un trait dont la signification est une énigme. Si les frères veulent punir leur sœur dans le cas où elle commettrait quelque faute, pourquoi la menaçent-ils de panneaux de cèdre? Il est évident que cette circonstance implique une idée de richesse et de luxe. *Créneaux d'argent, panneaux de cèdre* se répondent. Ni l'une ni l'autre de ces deux alternatives ne renferme une idée de punition ou de récompense." To this it may be added that the phrases "we will build an enclosure of silver," "we will fasten together boards of cedar," cannot be legitimately treated as alternatives which exclude each other. The very presence of them in Holy Scripture at all implies that both alike must in some way be eventually fulfilled. The same thing is evident from their position at the close of the Song, when the dramatic interest is at an end. No dramatist would be at the pains, in his concluding scene, of troubling his audience with an elaborate balancing of hypothetical eventualities. It must in fairness be here remarked that Renan's own interpretation of the verse is not less improbable than that which he rejects.

Vv. 10—12. The Bride describes the unalloyed happiness which she at last has reached. *I am a wall, and my breasts are as towers.* She takes up in her own behalf the imagery of the preceding verse. Her little sister disappears from view: if we would remember her at all, we must think of the two as incorporated together. For in fact Christ "hath made both one," having "broken down the middle wall of partition" between them (Eph. II. 14). But it is better not to press or to extend the imagery where it cannot fully apply. Whether the Gentiles have been incorporated or not, the Bride is the Church, and the Church can be but one. Her words may be thus paraphrased: "I am now, through divine goodness, in the enjoyment of everything needful: safely secured against all assault from without, and strong in the possession of those graces which attest my meetness for communion with my Lord, and my ability to nurture up my children for him." Compare much of the description in Isaiah LX. *Therefore am I become in his eyes as one that findeth the favour of peace*, lit. "as one that findeth peace." By a compressed phraseology, the Bride declares both that she has found favour in the eyes of her Lord (a phrase of continual occurrence, Gen. VI. 8, &c.), and also that through this favour she has emerged triumphant from all her pilgrimage and conflict, and has become in very truth the Shulamith or Peace-laden (cf. VI. 13). The tense of the verb is the preterite-present: "I am become," not "I was." Observe also that the "in his eyes" is placed before "as one that findeth, &c.," in order that it may be seen that the comparison is not with others who have found favour in the eyes of that same Beloved, but rather with all who have found favour in the eyes of their own bridegrooms, associates, or sovereigns. *A vineyard owneth Solomon in Baal-hamon*. The verb, as before, is the preterite-present. The Beloved is now once more described by his typical name, Solomon, The Peaceful; and appropriately so; for peace has now fallen to the lot of the Bride, and of that peace he is the author. The name Baal-hamon calls for a somewhat longer explanation. It signifies etymologically, Place of the Multitude: it plainly stands therefore as a designation of the tumultuous world throughout which the vineyard of the heavenly Solomon, in other words the Church of Christ, is now established. This is all that we directly require to know for the due interpretation of this passage of the Song, though we should feel a natural interest in discovering whence the name was borrowed. The actual spot which the poet had in view was probably the same with that of which we have mention in Judith VIII. 3 as Βελαμὼν or Βαλαμὼν, Syr. Baalmon, E. V. Balamo. It was near to Dothaim, or Dothan; and accordingly about five miles north of the present Tell Dothân, and on the slope which forms the southern boundary of the plain of Jezreel, we find a village, Yâmôn, or el-Yâmôn, which may well be the representative of the ancient Baal-hamon. Such a corruption as that of Hamon into Yâmôn, by the change of ה into י, is partially paralleled in the corruption, by the change of ה into י, of Hukkok into Yâkûk. The village stands about four miles north-west of Jenin or En-gannim, and is distant some fifteen miles northward from Samaria, Shechem, and Tirzah. With the scenery of this part of the land of Israel the author of the Song seems to have been familiar. The slope on which el-Yâmôn stands is probably well adapted for vines; but it is not necessary to suppose that the historical Solomon had a vineyard in Baal-hamon, and whether he had or not must remain entirely uncertain. *He hath let out the vineyard unto keepers.* The vineyard represents the Church in her organization: the keepers of the vineyard are, first, the various officers and ministers in the Church[1], and secondly, all the members of the Church, so far as any responsibility, in respect either of themselves or their brethren, rests upon them. *That every one should bring for the fruit thereof a thousand pieces of silver.* In our Saviour's parable of the wicked husbandmen the keepers have to render not a sum of money, but the fruits themselves, Matth. XXI. 34. The one is however the equivalent of the other; and the two representations are therefore substantially identical. The meaning is that it is the part of the keepers in the Church to see that its several members yield forth their fruits to Christ. Cf. Phil. IV. 17: "I desire fruit that may abound to your account." *My vineyard, that which is mine own, is before me.* The troubles by which the Bride had been overwhelmed are at an end. In the beginning of the Song, I. 6, she appeared as having lost her own vineyard wherein she would fain have laboured. In other words, she had been compelled to do the Lord's work in indirect ways of her own devising, instead of in the way divinely assigned her. Her vineyard is now, through the mercy of Christ, restored to her: the Church has everywhere her own proper work, which she may carry out in the very way which Christ commanded. *Thine be the thousand, O*

---

[1] So Theodoret: τοὺς τῇ ἱερωσύνῃ τετιμημένους.

Solomon, and two hundred be there for those that keep the fruit. Amid all her work the Church must diligently remember that Christ will look for the fruits that belong to him. But meanwhile she may also know that, for keeping the fruit of the vineyard, the ministers that labour in it will not go unrewarded, but will all receive their due recompense. It is this which the two hundred pieces of silver here represent. Cf. 1 Cor. III. 8: "Every man shall receive his own reward according to his own labour." Also 1 Cor. III. 14: "If any man's work abide ... he shall receive a reward." Also 2 Tim. II. 6, of which the true meaning is this: "Of husbandmen, he that laboureth must be the first to partake of the fruits:" in other words, "He that laboureth must be the first to receive the husbandman's share of the fruits:" a proof that there is a share for the husbandman, and that it is designed as the reward of labour. It has not been made to appear that there is any symbolism in the exact ratio which two hundred bears to a thousand. Probably the meaning is simply that the keepers shall receive that which is right. In the parable of the unmerciful servant the ratio of the one debt to the other is as 1,250,000 to 1 · this can merely denote that the ratio is enormously, nay, infinitely, large.

13 *Beloved.* O thou that dwellest in the gardens,
  The companions are listening for thy voice: let me hear it.
14 *Bride.* Haste thee, my beloved, like a gazelle or young hart
  Upon the mountains of spices.

The Song is terminated by an Epilogue of two verses. Of these, the one is uttered by the Beloved: the other by the Bride. Both speak from the point of view of the period at which the Song was written: they have not yet outwardly met. Both desire the advent of the blessedness which the Song has depicted. Their words are strictly of the nature of an epilogue, and form no part of the drama.

Ver. 13. *O thou that dwellest in the gardens.* The gardens, more than one in number, are here substantially identical with the vineyards of I. 6, in which, after having been thrust out from her own vineyard, the Bride was labouring. See on I. 6. Even in these less authorized and less welcome scenes of labour the lilies of true holiness might yet be found: even they therefore may be described by the pleasant name of gardens, used elsewhere, in VI. 2, of the heritage of the Church of the New Covenant. The Beloved's words to the ancient Church in her abasement are thus words of encouragement. *The companions.* These were mentioned before only in I. 7. It will be remembered that they represented the false shepherds of Israel, of whose contumelies the Church stood in perpetual fear, while, with unsatisfied longings, she pursued her humble but patient labours. *Are listening for thy voice.* Among those who outwardly seemed to treat the Church but with scorn, there were many who, in their better moods, took a secret delight in listening to her teaching. So, doubtless, is it still; and it is in the thought of this that the Church feels encouraged to persevere with diligence in even the most openly uninvited and outwardly unrequited of her labours. We lament over the discovery of the deafness of many who appear to be listening; but O! let us not forget how many may be privily listening of those that appear to be rudely and immoveably deaf! *Let me hear it.* An invitation, not to say a bidding, from Christ himself, that the Church should lift up her voice with faithful courage; whether in the accents of instruction and exhortation to all that come within reach of her utterance, or whether in those of supplication and praise, mounting up directly to him. Cf. also II. 14.

Ver. 14. *Haste thee, my beloved, like a gazelle or young hart.* The Church of Israel prays for the coming of him whom, though promised to her, it has not yet been her privilege to behold. Compare on II. 8, 9; 17. *Upon the mountains of spices.* To wit, the "mountain of myrrh," and the "hill of frankincense," of IV. 6: the mountains of Christ's passion, by his visit to which his espousal with the Church was to be accomplished. The prayer is necessarily an Old Testament prayer: the Song would not otherwise be an Old Testament Song. But as the Church of ancient days prayed for the advent of her Redeemer, so will the Church of these more blessed times pray not less ardently for the advent of her final Deliverer, from whom, after that he shall again appear, she shall no more be parted. "Amen. Even so, come, Lord Jesus."

THE END.

I.

INTRODUCTION TO THE STUDY AND USE OF THE PSALMS.

2 Vols. 8vo. 21s.

Mr Thrupp's learned, sound and sensible work fills a gap hitherto unfilled by any of its predecessors. The book deserves to be strongly recommended to all students—not the learned only but all educated persons—who desire to understand soundly the literal, and so to be able to realize intelligently the typical or prophetical meanings of the Psalter. It is the work of a painstaking and careful Hebrew scholar, of a sound English divine, and of an interpreter singularly fair and straightforward. We heartily commend the book to all intelligent students of a portion of the Bible, more often read but very commonly less understood than others, and which in private reading is much more frequently than it should be the subject of an unintelligible devotion.—GUARDIAN.

II.

ANTIENT JERUSALEM.

A new Investigation into the History, Topography and Plan of the City, Environs and Temple. Designed principally to Illustrate the Records and Prophecies of Scripture. With Map, Plans and other Illustrations. 8vo. cloth, 15s.

A well directed and able endeavour to throw additional light upon the history and topography of the Holy City, by observing, more care-

[MR THRUPP'S ANTIENT JERUSALEM, *continued*.]

fully than preceding writers have done, the notices on such points afforded by Scripture, and thus making the Bible itself its own interpreter......The object of the volume throughout is not merely historical or antiquarian, but it is to illustrate Scripture: and those who read it with this view will find reason to be grateful to the Author for the assistance it affords towards obtaining more clear and definite ideas of the various localities, with the names of which they are familiar, and which from so many sacred associations and their spiritual and typical use, are invested with perpetual and universal interest.—LITERARY CHURCHMAN.

III.

PSALMS AND HYMNS

FOR PUBLIC WORSHIP.

Selected and Edited by the REV. J. F. THRUPP.

Second Edition, cloth, 2s.; or £7. 10s. per 100 copies. Limp cloth, second paper, 1s. 4d.; £5 per 100 copies.

IV.

THE CHRISTIAN INFERENCE
From Leviticus xviii. 16,

Sufficient Ground for Holding that according to the Word of God Marriage with a Deceased Wife's Sister is unlawful. A Letter to the Rev. Dr McCaul. 8vo. 1s.

WORKS BY C. J. VAUGHAN, D.D.
VICAR OF DONCASTER.

1. Expository Sermons on St Paul's Epistle to the Philippians. 7s. 6d.
2. Lessons of Life and Godliness. Sermons preached at Doncaster. Second Edition. 4s. 6d.
3. St Paul's Epistle to the Romans. With English Notes. Second Edition. 5s.
4. Memorials of Harrow Sundays. Third Edition. 10s. 6d.
5. Epiphany, Lent and Easter: Expository Sermons. Second Edition. 10s. 6d.
6. Notes for Lectures on Confirmation. With Prayers. Fourth Edition. 1s. 6d.
7. Revision of the Liturgy. Second Edition. 4s. 6d.
8. The New Educational Code dispassionately Considered. Third Edition. 1s.

WORKS BY R. C. TRENCH, D.D.
DEAN OF WESTMINSTER.

1. Synonyms of the New Testament. Fourth Edition. Fcap. 8vo. cloth, 5s.
2. Hulsean Lectures for 1845—46.
   CONTENTS. 1. The Fitness of Holy Scripture for unfolding the Spiritual Life of Man. 2. Christ the Desire of all Nations; or the Unconscious Prophecies of Heathendom. Fourth Edition. Fcap. 8vo. cloth, 5s.
3. Sermons preached before the University of Cambridge. Fcap. 8vo. cloth, 2s. 6d.

WORKS BY THE LATE ARCHDEACON HARDWICK.

1. Christ and other Masters. A Historical Inquiry into some of the chief Parallelisms and Contrasts between Christianity and the Religious Systems of the Ancient World. With special reference to prevailing Difficulties and Objections. Second Edition, with the Author's latest corrections and Prefatory Memoir by the Rev. Francis Procter. 2 vols. crown 8vo.
2. A History of the Christian Church, during the Middle Ages and the Reformation. (A.D. 590-1600.) 2 vols. crown 8vo. cloth, 21s.
   Vol. I. History from Gregory the Great to the Excommunication of Luther. Second Edition. Edited by Francis Procter, M.A. Vicar of Witton, Norfolk. With Maps.
   Vol. II. History of the Reformation.

WORKS BY THE LATE PROFESSOR ARCHER BUTLER.

1. Sermons, Doctrinal and Practical. Edited, with a Memoir of the Author's Life, by the Very Rev. Thomas Woodward, M.A. Dean of Down. With Portrait. Fifth Edition. 8vo. cloth, 12s.
2. A Second Series of Sermons. Edited by J. A. Jeremie, D.D. Regius Professor of Divinity in the University of Cambridge. Third Edition. 8vo. cloth, 10s. 6d.
3. History of Ancient Philosophy. A Series of Lectures. Edited by William Hepworth Thompson, M.A. Regius Professor of Greek in the University of Cambridge. 2 vols. 8vo. cloth, £1. 5s.
4. Letters on Romanism, in Reply to Mr Newman's Essay on Development. Edited by the Very Rev. T. Woodward, Dean of Down. Second Edition, revised by the Ven. Archdeacon Hardwick. 8vo. cloth, 10s. 6d.

WORKS BY THE LATE ARCHDEACON HARE.

Charges delivered during the Years 1840 to 1854. With Notes on the Principal Events affecting the Church during that period. Also an Introduction, explanatory of Archdeacon Hare's position in the Church with reference to the parties which divide it. 3 vols. 8vo. cloth, £1. 11s. 6d.

Miscellaneous Pamphlets on some of the Leading Questions agitated in the Church during the Years 1845—51. 8vo. cloth, 12s.

The Victory of Faith. Second Edition. 8vo. cloth, 5s.

The Mission of the Comforter. Second Edition. With Notes. 8vo. cloth, 12s.

Vindication of Luther from his English Assailants. Second Edition. 8vo. cloth, 7s.

Parish Sermons. Second Series. 8vo. cloth, 12s.

Sermons preacht on Particular Occasions. 8vo. cloth, 12s.

⁎ The two following Books are included in the Three Volumes of Charges, and may still be had separately.

The Contest with Rome. With Notes, especially in answer to Dr Newman's Lecture on Present Position of Catholics. Second Edition. 8vo. cloth, 10s. 6d.

Charges delivered in the Years 1843, 1845, 1846. Never before published. With an Introduction, explanatory of his position in the Church with reference to the parties which divide it. 6s. 6d.

MACMILLAN & CO.'S

LIST OF

NEW AND POPULAR WORKS.

SECOND EDITION.
RAVENSHOE.
BY HENRY KINGSLEY, Author of 'Geoffry Hamlyn.'

3 Vols. crown 8vo. cloth, £1 11s. 6d.

'Admirable descriptions, which place "Ravenshoe" almost in the first rank of novels. Of the story itself it would really be difficult to speak too highly. The author seems to possess every essential for a writer of fiction.'—LONDON REVIEW.

SECOND EDITION.
RECOLLECTIONS OF GEOFFRY HAMLYN.
BY HENRY KINGSLEY. Crown 8vo. cloth, 6s.

'Mr. Henry Kingsley has written a work that keeps up its interest from the first page to the last—it is full of vigorous stirring life. The descriptions of Australian life in the early colonial days are marked by an unmistakable touch of reality and personal experience. A book which the public will be more inclined to read than to criticise, and we commend them to each other.'—ATHENÆUM.

SECOND EDITION.
TOM BROWN AT OXFORD.
3 Vols. £1 11s. 6d.

'A book that will live. In no other work that we can call to mind are the finer qualities of the English gentleman more happily portrayed.'—DAILY NEWS.

'The extracts we have given can give no adequate expression to the literary vividness and noble ethical atmosphere which pervade the whole book.'—SPECTATOR.

TWENTY-EIGHTH THOUSAND.
TOM BROWN'S SCHOOL DAYS.
BY AN OLD BOY. Fcp. 8vo. 5s.

'A book which every father might well wish to see in the hands of his son.'—TIMES.

EIGHTH THOUSAND.
SCOURING OF THE WHITE HORSE.
By the author of 'Tom's Brown's School Days.'

With numerous Illustrations by Richard Doyle. Imperial 16mo. Printed on toned paper, gilt leaves, 8s. 6d.

'The execution is excellent..... Like "Tom Brown's School Days," the "White Horse" gives the reader a feeling of gratitude and personal esteem towards the author. The author could not have a better style, nor a better temper, nor a more excellent artist than Mr. Doyle to adorn his book.'—SATURDAY REVIEW.

WORKS BY THE REV. CHARLES KINGSLEY.

CHAPLAIN IN ORDINARY TO THE QUEEN, RECTOR OF EVERSLEY,
AND PROFESSOR OF MODERN HISTORY IN THE UNIVERSITY OF CAMBRIDGE.

WESTWARD HO!

NEW AND CHEAPER EDITION. Crown 8vo. cloth, 6s.

'Mr. Kingsley has selected a good subject, and has written a good novel to an excellent purpose.'—TIMES.
'We thank Mr. Kingsley heartily for almost the best historical novel, to our mind, of the day.'
— FRASER'S MAGAZINE.

TWO YEARS AGO.

NEW AND CHEAPER EDITION. Crown 8vo. cloth, 6s.

'In "Two Years Ago," Mr. Kingsley is, as always, genial, large-hearted, and humorous; with a quick eye and a keen relish alike for what is beautiful in nature and for what is genuine, strong, and earnest in man.'—GUARDIAN.

ALTON LOCKE, TAILOR AND POET.

NEW EDITION. Crown 8vo. cloth, 4s. 6d. With New Preface.

☞ This Edition is printed in crown 8vo. uniform with 'Westward Ho!' &c., and contains a New Preface.

THE HEROES.

GREEK FAIRY TALES FOR THE YOUNG.

SECOND EDITION, with Illustrations. Royal 16mo. cloth, 5s.

'A charming book, adapted in style and manner, as a man of genius only could have adapted it, to the believing imagination, susceptible spirit of youths.'— BRITISH QUARTERLY REVIEW.
'Rarely have these heroes of Greek tradition been celebrated in a bolder or more stirring strain.'—SATURDAY REVIEW.

ALEXANDRIA AND HER SCHOOLS.

Crown 8vo. cloth, 5s.

THE LIMITS OF EXACT SCIENCE

AS APPLIED TO HISTORY.

INAUGURAL LECTURE AT CAMBRIDGE. Crown 8vo. 2s.

PHAETHON:

LOOSE THOUGHTS FOR LOOSE THINKERS.

THIRD EDITION. Crown 8vo. 2s.

NEW AND CHEAPER EDITION (FIFTH THOUSAND).

Handsomely printed on toned paper and bound in extra cloth. With Vignette and Frontispiece from Designs by the author. Engraved on Steel by C. H. Jeens. 4s. 6d.

THE LADY OF LA GARAYE.

By the Hon. Mrs. NORTON. Dedicated to the Marquis of Lansdowne.

'The poem is a pure, tender, touching tale of pain, sorrow, love, duty, piety, and death.'—EDINBURGH REVIEW.

'A true poem, noble in subject and aim, natural in flow, worthy in expression, with the common soul of humanity throbbing in every page through wholesome words.'—EXAMINER.

GOBLIN MARKET AND OTHER POEMS.

By CHRISTINA G. ROSSETTI. With Two Illustrations from Designs by D. G. Rossetti. Fcp. 8vo. cloth, 5s.

'As faultless in expression, as picturesque in effect, and as high in purity of tone, as any modern poem that can be named.'—SATURDAY REVIEW.

THE LUGGIE AND OTHER POEMS.

By DAVID GRAY. With a Preface by R. MONCKTON MILNES, M.P. Fcp. 8vo. cloth, 5s.

'Full of the purest and simplest poetry.'—SPECTATOR.

SECOND EDITION.
EDWIN OF DEIRA.

By ALEXANDER SMITH. Fcp. 8vo. cloth, 5s.

'The poem bears in every page evidence of genius controlled, purified, and disciplined, but ever present.'—STANDARD.

'A felicitous and noble composition.'—NONCONFORMIST.

BY THE SAME AUTHOR.
A LIFE DRAMA AND OTHER POEMS.

4th Edition, 2s. 6d.

CITY POEMS.
5s.

BLANCHE LISLE AND OTHER POEMS.

By CECIL HOME. Fcp. 8vo. cloth, 4s. 6d.

'The writer has music and meaning in his lines and stanzas, which, in the selection of diction and gracefulness of cadence, have seldom been excelled.'—LEADER.

'Full of a true poet's imagination.'—JOHN BULL.

THE POEMS OF ARTHUR HUGH CLOUGH,

SOMETIME FELLOW OF ORIEL COLLEGE, OXFORD.

With a Memoir by F. T. PALGRAVE. Fcp. 8vo. cloth, 6s.

'Few, if any, literary men of larger, deeper, and more massive mind have lived in this generation than the author of these few poems, and of this the volume before us bears ample evidence...... There is nothing in it that is not in some sense rich either in thought or beauty or both.'—SPECTATOR.

Uniform with 'WESTWARD HO!' 'GEOFFRY HAMLYN,' &c.

THE MOOR COTTAGE:
A TALE OF HOME LIFE.

By MAY BEVERLEY, author of 'Little Estella, and other Fairy Tales for the Young.' Crown 8vo. cloth, price 6s.

'This charming tale is told with such excellent art, that it reads like an episode from real life.'—ATLAS.

'The whole plot of the story is conceived and executed in an admirable manner: a work which, when once taken up, it is difficult to put down.'—JOHN BULL.

Uniform with 'WESTWARD HO!' 'GEOFFRY HAMLYN,' &c.

ARTIST AND CRAFTSMAN.

Crown 8vo. cloth, price 6s.

'Its power is unquestionable, its felicity of expression great, its plot fresh, and its characters very natural... Wherever read, it will be enthusiastically admired and cherished.'
— MORNING HERALD.

Uniform with 'WESTWARD HO!' 'GEOFFRY HAMLYN,' &c.

A LADY IN HER OWN RIGHT.

By WESTLAND MARSTON. Crown 8vo. cloth, price 6s.

'Since "The Mill on the Floss" was noticed, we have read no work of fiction which we can so heartily recommend to our readers as "A Lady in her Own Right:" the plot, incidents, and characters are all good: the style is simple and graceful: it abounds in thoughts judiciously introduced and well expressed, and throughout a kind, liberal, and gentle spirit.'
— CHURCH OF ENGLAND MONTHLY REVIEW.

THE BROKEN TROTH:
A TALE OF TUSCAN LIFE FROM THE ITALIAN.

By PHILIP IRETON. 2 vols. fcp. 8vo. cloth, 12s.

'The style is so easy and natural... The story is well told from beginning to end.'—PRESS.

'A genuine Italian tale—a true picture of the Tuscan peasant population, with all their virtues, faults, weaknesses, follies, and even vices... The best Italian tale that has been published since the appearance of the 'Promessi Sposi' of Manzoni... The 'Broken Troth' is one of those that cannot be read but with pleasure.'— LONDON REVIEW.

FOOTNOTES FROM THE PAGE OF NATURE:

OR, FIRST FORMS OF VEGETATION.

A popular work on Algæ, Fungi, Mosses, and Lichens.

By the Rev. HUGH MACMILLAN, F.R.S.E. With numerous Illustrations and a Coloured Frontispiece. Fcp. 8vo. 5s.

'Admirably adapted to serve as an introduction to the study of more scientific botanic works, and to throw a new interest over country rambles by bringing into notice the simple forms of vegetation everywhere to be met with.'—SATURDAY REVIEW.

REDUCED IN PRICE TO FIVE SHILLINGS.

GLAUCUS;

OR, WONDERS OF THE SEA SHORE.

By CHARLES KINGSLEY, M.A. Rector of Eversley, and Chaplain in Ordinary to the Queen. Containing beautifully Coloured Illustrations of the Objects mentioned in the work. Royal 16mo. elegantly bound in cloth, gilt leaves, 5s.

'One of the most charming works on Natural History . . . written in such a style, and adorned with such a variety of illustration, that we question whether the most unconcerned reader can peruse it without deriving both pleasure and profit.'—ANNALS OF NATURAL HISTORY.

STRAY NOTES ON FISHING AND NATURAL HISTORY.

By CORNWALL SIMEON. With Illustrations, 7s. 6d.

'If this remarkably agreeable work does not rival in popularity the celebrated "White's Selborne," it will not be because it does not deserve it . . . the mind is almost satiated with a repletion of strange facts and good things.'—FIELD.

THE

HUMAN HAND AND THE HUMAN FOOT.

By G. M. HUMPHRY, M.D. F.R.S., Lecturer on Surgery and Anatomy in the University of Cambridge.

With numerous Illustrations. Fcp. 8vo. cloth, 4s. 6d.

'The marvels of creative wisdom are herein set forth plainly and simply, and yet withal scientifically and correctly . . . every explanation is given which can by any chance be needed to render the subject perfectly clear and intelligible, whilst most carefully executed engravings are profusely scattered through the text. In this little volume there is stored up such an amount of valuable information written in an entertaining form as deserves to gain for it admission into the library of every one.'—ENGLISH CHURCHMAN.

LIFE ON THE EARTH;
ITS ORIGIN AND SUCCESSION.
By JOHN PHILLIPS, M.A., LL.D., F.R.S., Professor of Geology in the University of Oxford. Crown 8vo. 6s. 6d.

'It is not without gratitude as well as pleasure that one receives at such a time a careful and condensed summary of the present unquestionable results of scientific research, proceeding from one who has great clearness and soundness of intellect, and the richest and completest knowledge.'—NONCONFORMIST.

THE STORY OF A BOULDER;
OR, GLEANINGS BY A FIELD GEOLOGIST.
By ARCHIBALD GEIKIE. Illustrated. Fcp. 8vo. cloth, 5s.

'We do not know a more readable book on a scientific subject, and it will be invaluable to young people, as well as interesting to those who are already acquainted with the subject it treats of.'—CLERICAL JOURNAL.

LIFE AND CORRESPONDENCE OF M. DE TOCQUEVILLE.

Translated from the French. By the Translator of 'Napoleon Correspondence with King Joseph.' With numerous additions. 2 vols. crown 8vo. 21s.

'The appearance of this work will be welcomed by every politician and every Englishman capable of appreciating exhaustive and solid thought.'—SPECTATOR.

'Few men of the nineteenth century have attained a more remarkable influence. . . . Charming as specimens of style, they are of infinitely greater value as showing the inner life of a man who was as simple as a child, and yet as gifted as any of the many learned writers and scholars whom France has produced.'—BELL'S MESSENGER.

PICTURES OF OLD ENGLAND.
By Dr. REINHOLD PAULI. Translated, with the author's revision, by E. C. OTTÉ. With a Map of London in the Thirteenth Century.
Crown 8vo. extra cloth, 8s. 6d.

CONTENTS:
I. CANTERBURY AND THE WORSHIP OF ST. THOMAS À BECKET.
II. MONKS AND MENDICANT FRIARS.
III. PARLIAMENT IN THE FOURTEENTH CENTURY.
IV. ENGLAND'S EARLIEST RELATIONS TO AUSTRIA AND PRUSSIA.
V. THE EMPEROR LOUIS IV. AND KING EDWARD III.
VI. THE HANSEATIC STEEL YARD IN LONDON.
VII. TWO POETS, GOWER AND CHAUCER.
VIII. JOHN WICLIF.

'There are some books so admirable, that merely general criticism subsides into "*Read, it will satisfy you.*" Dr. Pauli's work is of this kind.'—NONCONFORMIST.

GARIBALDI AT CAPRERA.

By COLONEL VECCHJ. With Preface by Mrs. Gaskell, and a View of Caprera
Fcp. 8vo. cloth. 3s. 6d.

'After all has been told, there was something wanting to the full and true impression of the Patriot's character and mode of life; as every one who reads this artless and enthusiastic narration will certainly admit. Mrs. GASKELL says she knows that "every particular" of this full and minute account may be relied upon; and it has an air of truth that commends it even when it is most extravagant in its admiration.'—NONCONFORMIST.

ROME IN 1860.

By EDWARD DICEY, author of 'Life of Cavour.' Crown 8vo. cloth. 6s. 6d.

'So striking and apparently so faithful a portrait. It is the Rome of real life he has depicted.'—SPECTATOR.

THE ITALIAN WAR OF 1848-9,

And the last Italian Poet. By the late HENRY LUSHINGTON, Chief Secretary to the Government of Malta. With a Biographical Preface by G. STOVIN VENABLES. Crown 8vo. cloth, 6s. 6d.

'Perhaps the most difficult of all literary tasks—the task of giving historical unity, dignity, and interest to events so recent as to be still encumbered with all the details with which newspapers invest them—has never been more successfully discharged. . . Mr. Lushington, in a very short compass, shows the true nature and sequence of the event, and gives to the whole story of the struggle and defeat of Italy a degree of unity and dramatic interest which not one newspaper reader in ten thousand ever supposed it to possess.'—SATURDAY REVIEW.

EARLY EGYPTIAN HISTORY.

FOR THE YOUNG.

WITH DESCRIPTIONS OF THE TOMBS AND MONUMENTS.

By the Author of 'Sidney Grey,' &c. and her Sister. Fcp. 8vo. cloth, 5s.

'Full of information without being dull, and full of humour without being frivolous; stating in the most popular form the main results of modern research. . . We have said enough to take our readers to the book itself, where they will learn more of Ancient Egypt than in any other popular work on the subject.'—LONDON REVIEW.

DAYS OF OLD;

OR, STORIES FROM OLD ENGLISH HISTORY.

FOR THE YOUNG.

By the Author of 'Ruth and Her Friends.' With a Frontispiece by W. HOLMAN HUNT. Royal 16mo, beautifully printed on toned paper and bound in extra cloth, 5s.

'A delightful little book, full of interest and instruction. . . fine feeling, dramatic weight, and descriptive power in the stories. . . They are valuable as throwing a good deal of light upon English history, bringing rapidly out the manners and customs, the social and political conditions of our British and Anglo-Saxon ancestors, and the moral always of a pure and noble kind.'—LITERARY GAZETTE.

HOW TO WIN OUR WORKERS.

A Short Account of the Leeds Sewing School for Factory Girls. By Mrs. HYDE. Dedicated by permission to the EARL of CARLISLE. Fcp. 8vo. limp cloth, 1s. 6d.

This work is intended to exhibit the successful working of an Institution for bringing the Working-girls of a large town into communication and sympathy with those who are separated from them by social position.

'A little book brimful of good sense and good feeling.'—GLOBE.

OUR YEAR.

Child's Book in Prose and Rhyme. By the author of 'John Halifax.' With numerous Illustrations by CLARENCE DOBELL. Royal 16mo. cloth, gilt leaves, 5s.

'Just the book we could wish to see in the hands of every child.'—ENGLISH CHURCHMAN.

LITTLE ESTELLA,
AND OTHER FAIRY TALES.

By MAY BEVERLEY. With Frontispiece. Royal 16mo. cloth, gilt leaves, 5s.

'Very pretty, pure in conception, and simply, gracefully related . . . genuine story-telling.'—DAILY NEWS.

MY FIRST JOURNAL.

A Book for Children. By GEORGIANA M. CRAIK, author of 'Lost and Won.' With Frontispiece. Royal 16mo. cloth, gilt leaves, 4s. 6d.

'True to Nature and to a fine kind of nature. . . . The style is simple and graceful a work of Art, clever and healthy-toned.'—GLOBE.

AGNES HOPETOUN'S SCHOOLS AND HOLIDAYS.

By Mrs. OLIPHANT, author of 'Margaret Maitland.' With Frontispiece Royal 16mo. cloth, gilt leaves, 5s.

'Described with exquisite reality . . . teaching the young pure and good lessons.'—JOHN BULL.

DAYS OF OLD:
STORIES FROM OLD ENGLISH HISTORY.

By the author of 'Ruth and Her Friends.' With Frontispiece. Royal 16mo cloth, gilt leaves, 5s.

'A delightful little book, full of interest and instruction . . fine feeling, dramatic weight, and descriptive power in the stories.'—LITERARY GAZETTE.

DAVID, KING OF ISRAEL.

A History for the Young. By JOSIAH WRIGHT, Head Master of Sutton Coldfield Grammar School. With Illustrations. Royal 16mo. cloth, gilt leaves, 5s.

'An excellent book . . well conceived, and well worked out.'—LITERARY CHURCHMAN.

RUTH AND HER FRIENDS.

A Story for Girls. With Frontispiece. Third Edition. Royal 16mo. cloth, gilt leaves, 5s.

'A book which girls will read with avidity, and cannot fail to profit by.'
—LITERARY CHURCHMAN.

SECOND EDITION.
GEORGE BRIMLEY'S ESSAYS.

Edited by WILLIAM GEORGE CLARK, M.A. Public Orator in the University of Cambridge. With Portrait. Crown 8vo. cloth, 5s.

CONTENTS:

I. TENNYSON'S POEMS.
II. WORDSWORTH'S POEMS.
III. POETRY AND CRITICISM.
IV. ANGEL IN THE HOUSE.
V. CARLYLE'S LIFE OF STERLING.
VI. ESMOND.
VII. MY NOVEL.
VIII. BLEAK HOUSE.
IX. WESTWARD HO!
X. WILSON'S NOCTES.
XI COMTE'S POSITIVE PHILOSOPHY.

'One of the most delightful and precious volumes of criticism that has appeared in these days. . . To every cultivated reader they will disclose the wonderful clearness of perception, the delicacy of feeling, the pure taste, and the remarkably firm and decisive judgment which are the characteristics of all Mr. Brimley's writings on subjects that really penetrated and fully possessed his nature.'—NONCONFORMIST.

MEMOIR OF THE
LIFE OF THE REV. ROBERT STORY
LATE MINISTER OF ROSNEATH, DUMBARTONSHIRE.

By ROBERT HERBERT STORY, Minister of Rosneath. Crown 8vo. cloth, with Portrait, 7s. 6d.

*** This volume includes several important passages of Scottish Religious and Ecclesiastical History during the Second Quarter of the present Century. Among others, the ROW CONTROVERSY, the RISE of the IRVINGITE MOVEMENT, the EARLY HISTORY of the FREE CHURCH, &c. &c.

THE PRISON CHAPLAIN:
A MEMOIR OF THE REV. JOHN CLAY,
LATE CHAPLAIN OF PRESTON GAOL.

With selections from his Correspondence and a Sketch of Prison Discipline in England. By his SON. With Portrait, 8vo. cloth, 15s.

'It presents a vigorous account of the Penal system in England in past times, and in our own. . . It exhibits in detail the career of one of our latest prison reformers; alleged, we believe with truth, to have been one of the most successful, and certainly in his judgments and opinions one of the most cautious and reasonable, as well as one of the most ardent.'
SATURDAY REVIEW.

MEMOIR OF GEORGE WAGNER
LATE INCUMBENT OF ST. STEPHEN'S, BRIGHTON.

By JOHN NASSAU SIMPKINSON, M.A. Rector of Brington, Northampton.

Third and cheaper Edition. Fcp. 8vo. 5s.

'A more edifying biography we have rarely met with . . If any parish priest, discouraged by what he may consider an unpromising aspect of the time, should be losing heart we recommend him to procure this edifying memoir, to study it well, to set the example of the holy man who is the subject of it before him in all its length and breadth, and then he will appreciate what can be done even by one earnest man; and gathering fresh inspiration, he will chide himself for all previous discontent, and address himself with stronger purpose than ever to the lowly works and lofty aims of the ministry entrusted to his charge.'
LITERARY CHURCHMAN.

FAMILY PRAYERS.

By the Rev. GEORGE BUTLER, M.A. Vice-Principal of Cheltenham College and late Fellow of Exeter College, Oxford. Crown 8vo. cloth, 5s.

CAMBRIDGE CLASS BOOKS
FOR COLLEGES AND SCHOOLS
PUBLISHED BY
MACMILLAN & CO.

A set of Macmillan & Co.'s Class Books will be found in the Educational Department (Class 29) of the International Exhibition, and for which a Medal has been awarded.

Arithmetic. For the use of Schools. By BARNARD SMITH, M.A., Fellow of St. Peter's College, Cambridge. New Edition. Crown 8vo. cloth, 4s. 6d.

A Key to the Arithmetic for Schools. By BARNARD SMITH, M.A., Fellow of St. Peter's College, Cambridge. Second Edition. Crown 8vo. cloth, 8s. 6d.

Arithmetic and Algebra, in their Principles and Application: with numerous systematically arranged Examples, taken from the Cambridge Examination Papers. By BARNARD SMITH, M.A. Fellow of St. Peter's College, Cambridge. Eighth Edition. Crown 8vo. cloth, 10s. 6d.

Exercises in Arithmetic. By BARNARD SMITH. With Answers. Crown 8vo. limp cloth. 2s. 6d. Or sold separately, as follows:— Part I. 1s. Part II. 1s. Answers 6d.

An Elementary Treatise on the Theory of Equations, with a Collection of Examples. By I. TODHUNTER, M.A. Fellow and Mathematical Lecturer of St. John's College, Cambridge. Crown 8vo. cloth, 7s. 6d.

Euclid. For Colleges and Schools. By I. TODHUNTER, M.A., Fellow and Principal Mathematical Lecturer of St. John's College, Cambridge. Pot 8vo. [In the Press.

Algebra. For the use of Colleges and Schools. By I. TODHUNTER, M.A. Fellow of St. John's College, Cambridge. Second Edition. Crown 8vo. cloth, 7s. 6d.

Plane Trigonometry. For Colleges and Schools. By I. TODHUNTER, M.A. Fellow of St. John's College, Cambridge. Second Edition. Crown 8vo. cloth, 5s.

A Treatise on Spherical Trigonometry. For the use of Colleges and Schools. By I. TODHUNTER, M.A. Fellow of St. John's College, Cambridge. Crown 8vo. cloth, 4s. 6d.

Examples of Analytical Geometry of Three Dimensions. By I. TODHUNTER, M.A. Fellow of St. John's College, Cambridge. Crown 8vo. cloth, 4s.

A Treatise on the Differential Calculus. With numerous Examples. By I. TODHUNTER, M.A. Fellow and Assistant Tutor of St. John's College, Cambridge. Third Edition. Crown 8vo. cloth, 10s. 6d.

A Treatise on the Integral Calculus. With numerous
Examples. By I. TODHUNTER, M.A. Fellow and Assistant Tutor of St.
John's College, Cambridge. Second Edition. Crown 8vo. cloth, 10s. 6d.

A Treatise on Analytical Statics. With numerous
Examples. By I. TODHUNTER, M.A. Fellow of St. John's College, Cambridge.
Second Edition. Crown 8vo. cloth, 10s. 6d.

First Book of Algebra. For Schools. By J. C. W. ELLIS,
M.A., and P. M. CLARK, M.A. Sidney Sussex College, Cambridge.
[Preparing.

Arithmetic in Theory and Practice. For Advanced
Pupils. By J. BROOK SMITH, M.A. Part First. 164 pp. (1860). Crown
8vo. 3s. 6d.

A Short Manual of Arithmetic. By C. W. UNDERWOOD,
M.A. 96 pp. (1860). Fcp. 8vo. 2s. 6d.

Introduction to Plane Trigonometry. For the use of
Schools. By J. C. SNOWBALL, M.A. Second Edition (1847). 8vo. 5s.

Plane and Spherical Trigonometry. With the Construction and Use of Tables of Logarithms. By J. C. SNOWBALL, M.A.
Ninth Edition, 240 pp. (1857). Crown 8vo. 7s. 6d.

Plane Trigonometry. With a numerous Collection of
Examples. By R. D. BEASLEY, M.A. 106 pp. (1858). Crown 8vo. 3s. 6d.

Elementary Treatise on Mechanics. With a Collection
of Examples. By S. PARKINSON, B.D. Second Edition, 345 pp. (1860).
Crown 8vo. 9s. 6d.

A Treatise on Optics. By S. PARKINSON, B.D. 304
pp. (1859). Crown 8vo. 10s. 6d.

Elementary Hydrostatics. With numerous Examples
and Solutions. By J. B. PHEAR, M.A. Second Edition. 156 pp. (1857).
Crown 8vo. 5s. 6d.

Dynamics of a Particle. With numerous Examples.
By P. G. TAIT, M.A. and W. J. STEELE, M.A. 304 pp. (1856). Crown 8vo.
10s. 6d.

A Treatise on Dynamics. By W. P. WILSON, M.A.
176 pp. (1850). 8vo. 9s. 6d.

Dynamics of a System of Rigid Bodies. With numerous Examples. By E. J. ROUTH, M.A. 336 pp. (1860). Crown 8vo. 10s. 6d.

Geometrical Treatise on Conic Sections. With a Collection of Examples. By W. H. DREW, M.A. 121 pp. (Second Edition, 1862). 4s. 6d.

Solutions to Problems contained in a Geometrical Treatise on Conic Sections. By W. H. DREW, M.A. (1862). 4s. 6d.

Elementary Treatise on Conic Sections and Algebraic Geometry. By G. H. PUCKLE, M.A. Second Edition. 264 pp. (1856). Crown 8vo. 7s. 6d.

Elementary Treatise on Trilinear Co-ordinates. By N. M. FERRERS, M.A. 154 pp. (1861). Crown 8vo. 6s. 6d.

A Treatise on Solid Geometry. By P. FROST, M.A. and J. WOLSTENHOLME, M.A. 8vo. [In the Press.

A Treatise on the Calculus of Finite Differences. By GEORGE BOOLE, D.C.L. 248 pp. (1840). Crown 8vo. 10s. 6d.

The Algebraical and Numerical Theory of Errors of Observations and the Combination of Observations. By the Astronomer Royal, G. B. AIRY, M.A. Pp. 103 (1861). 6s. 6d.

The Construction of Wrought Iron Bridges, embracing the Practical Application of the Principles of Mechanics to Wrought Iron Girder Work. By J. H. LATHAM, M.A. C.E. With numerous plates. Pp. 282 (1858). 15s.

Mathematical Tracts. On the Lunar and Planetary Theories, the Figure of the Earth, Precession and Nutation, the Calculus of Variations, and the Undulatory Theory of Optics. By the Astronomer-Royal, G. B. AIRY, M.A. Fourth Edition (1858), pp. 490. 15s.

An Elementary Treatise on the Planetary Theory. By C. H. H CHEYNE, B.A. Scholar of St. John's College, Cambridge. [Preparing.

A Treatise on Attractions, Laplace's Functions, and the Figure of the Earth. By J. H. PRATT, M.A. Second Edition. Crown 8vo. 126 pp. (1861). 6s. 6d.

An Elementary Treatise on Quaternions. By P. G. TAIT, M.A., Professor of Natural Philosophy in the University of Edinburgh. [Preparing.

Singular Properties of the Ellipsoid, and Associated Surfaces of the Ninth Degree. By the Rev. G. F. CHILDE, M.A. Mathematical Professor in the South African College. 8vo. 10s. 6d.

Collection of Mathematical Problems and Examples With Answers. By H. A. MORGAN, M.A. Pp. 190 (1858). Crown 8vo. 6s. 6d.

Senate-House Mathematical Problems. With Solutions
  1848-51. By FERRERS and JACKSON. 8vo. 15s. 6d.
  1848-51. (Riders.) By JAMESON. 8vo. 7s. 6d.
  1854. By WALTON and MACKENZIE. 8vo. 10s. 6d.
  1857. By CAMPION and WALTON. 8vo. 8s. 6d.
  1860. By ROUTH and WATSON. Crown 8vo. 7s. 6d.

Hellenica: a First Greek Reading-Book. Being a History of Greece, taken from Diodorus and Thucydides. By JOSIAH WRIGHT, M.A. Second Edition. Pp. 150 (1857). Fcp. 8vo. 3s. 6d.

Demosthenes on the Crown. With English Notes. By B. DRAKE, M.A. Second Edition, to which is prefixed Æschines against Ctesiphon. With English Notes. (1860.) Fcp. 8vo. 5s.

Juvenal. For Schools. With English Notes and an Index. By JOHN E. MAYOR, M.A. Pp. 464 (1853). Crown 8vo. 10s. 6d.

Cicero's Second Philippic. With English Notes. By JOHN E. B. MAYOR. Pp. 168 (1861). 5s.

Help to Latin Grammar; or, the Form and Use of Words in Latin. With Progressive Exercises. By JOSIAH WRIGHT, M.A. Pp. 175 (1855). Crown 8vo. 4s. 6d.

The Seven Kings of Rome. A First Latin Reading-Book. By JOSIAH WRIGHT, M.A. Second Edit. Pp. 138 (1857). Fcp. 8vo. 3s.

Vocabulary and Exercises on 'The Seven Kings.' By JOSIAH WRIGHT, M.A. Pp. 94 (1857). Fcp. 8vo. 2s. 6d.

First Latin Construing Book. By E. THRING, M.A. Pp. 104 (1855). Fcp. 8vo. 2s. 6d.

Sallust.—Catilina et Jugurtha. With English Notes. For Schools. By CHARLES MERIVALE, B.D. Second Edition. Pp. 172 (1858). Fcp. 8vo. 4s. 6d. Catilina and Jugurtha may be had separately, price 2s. 6d. each.

Æschylus.—The Eumenides. With English Notes and Translation. By B. DRAKE, M.A. Pp. 144 (1853). 8vo. 7s. 6d.

St. Paul's Epistle to the Romans. With Notes. By CHARLES JOHN VAUGHAN, D.D. (1861). Crown 8vo. 5s.

The Child's English Grammar. By E. THRING, M.A. Demy 18mo. New Edition (1857). 1s.

Elements of Grammar taught in English. By E. THRING, M.A. Third Edition. Pp. 136 (1860). Demy 18mo. 2s.

www.ingramcontent.com/pod-product-compliance
Lightning Source LLC
Chambersburg PA
CBHW021954220426
43663CB00007B/808